Invest to Win

Earn and Keep Profits in Bull and Bear Markets with the GainsMaster Approach

TONI TURNER AND
GORDON SCOTT, CMT

Mc
Graw
Hill

New York   Chicago   San Francisco   Lisbon   London   Madrid   Mexico City
Milan   New Delhi   San Juan   Seoul   Singapore   Sydney   Toronto

1 2 3 4 5 6 7 8 9 0 DOC/DOC 1 8 7 6 5 4 3 2

ISBN: 978-0-07-179838-9
MHID: 0-07-179838-2

e-ISBN: 978-0-07-179839-6
e-MHID: 0-07-179839-0

This publication is designed to provide accurate and authoritative information in regard to the subject matter covered. It is sold with the understanding that neither the author nor the publisher is engaged in rendering legal, accounting, or other professional service. If legal advice or other expert assistance is required, the services of a competent professional person should be sought.
—*From a Declaration of Principles Jointly Adopted by a Committee of the American Bar Association and a Committee of Publishers and Associations*

McGraw-Hill books are available at special quantity discounts to use as premiums and sales promotions, or for use in corporate training programs. To contact a representative, please e-mail us at bulksales@mcgraw-hill.com.

This book is printed on acid-free paper.

I dedicate this book to my husband, Mike.

You provide a bottomless well of patience and encouragement.

You are, indeed, the wind beneath my wings.

—Toni Turner

■

I dedicate this book to my sweetheart and wife, Karole.

Your encouragement and support on this project

made it not only possible but worth all the toil.

—Gordon Scott

Contents

ACKNOWLEDGMENTS   xi

INTRODUCTION   1

CHAPTER ONE

And Away We Go!   7

You Hold the Power ✦ News in a New York Minute ✦ The Global Financial
Markets—A Community Affair ✦ What's in It for You? The Benefits of
Investing in the U.S Stock Market ✦ Bubbles and Belly Punches: The
Challenges and Risks of Investing in the Stock Market ✦ What We Bring
to the Party ✦ What Role Do "Personal Gains" Play? ✦ **Personal Gains:**
Commitment: The Foundation of Success

CHAPTER TWO

Unlocking Your Investment Potential   21

What I Learned from Working with 1000 Individuals ✦ What I Learned from
Two People … ✦ Four Keys of the GainsMaster Approach ✦ Turning the
Four Keys ✦ **Personal Gains: Success Comes with Single-Purpose Focus**

CHAPTER THREE

The Market in Motion: 40
How the Stock Market Travels Through Time

Analyze Your Opportunities—The Ever-Changing View from Above ✦ The
Natures of the Beasts ✦ Dueling Market Rulers—Who They Are, How They
Move Markets ✦ Emotion in Motion: Demand and Supply ✦ How We
Measure the Markets— The Major Indexes ✦ **Personal Gains:** *Personal
Beliefs Dictate the Direction of Our Lives*

CHAPTER FOUR

Reading the Market's Mood   56

Turning Key 2: Evaluating Market Conditions by Reading the Market's
Mood ✦ When the Market Shows GO and STOP Signs ✦ Indicator 1: The
Twelve-Month Moving Average ✦ Indicator 2: Volatility ✦ Indicator 3:
Safety-Seeking Behavior ✦ Recognizing the GO and STOP Signs
✦ Combining the Indicators ✦ **Personal Gains:** *Build on Your Strengths*

CHAPTER FIVE

Your Investing Edge: The Art of the Chart   82

Price: The Master of the Universe ✦ How We Plot Simple Line Charts
✦ A Quick Reference to Bar Charts ✦ How Candlesticks Shine Light on
Our Charts ✦ How Candles Are Structured ✦ Your Best Money-Making
Friend—The Trend ✦ Moving Averages: Simple Lines That Say a Lot
✦ Your Moving Average Toolbox ✦ Moving Averages as Decision-Support
Tools ✦ **Personal Gains:** *Resiliency—Your Essential Skill for Success*

CHAPTER SIX

Analyzing Company Performance: 118
Fundamental Research for Investors

The Tasks of Fundamental Research ✦ Look for the Green—Recognizing Signs of Growth ✦ Watching for Blue Skies—Recognizing Evidence of Opportunity ✦ The Forward P/E Ratio ✦ Insider Trading: Bad for Martha, Good for Investors ✦ Institutions: Investors with Commitment ✦ Get a Jump Start on Fundamental Research—Stocks to Consider in a GO-Sign Market ✦ Screen Your Calls: Picking Stocks by Appointment Only ✦ Identify What to Buy When the Market Is in STOP Mood ✦ **Personal Gains:** *Gratitude: A Powerful Tool for Prosperity*

CHAPTER SEVEN

Mind Your Own Business: 141
What You Need to Succeed

Choosing Your Investment Broker ✦ Selecting Your Account Category ✦ Getting Familiar with the T+3 SEC Rule ✦ Evaluating Broker Recommendations ✦ Turning into the Financial Networks ✦ Let's Mine the Web ✦ Read All about It—Financial Newspapers ✦ **Personal Gains:** *Create and Sustain a Vibrant Self-Image*

CHAPTER EIGHT

Exploring the World of Exchange Traded Funds   158

ETFs: What They Are ✦ ETFs: How You Can Benefit ✦ ETFs: What Are You Getting Into? ✦ ETFs: Where to Find Them ✦ ETFs: Consider the Weighting Categories ✦ Understanding Net Asset Value (NAV) ✦ A Quick Look at Exchange Traded Notes (ETNs) ✦ Let's Sample ETF Sectors ✦ Asset Allocation Strategies Using ETFs ✦ **Personal Gains:** *What's Your Emotional IQ?*

CHAPTER NINE

Two Simple Strategies for Investing to Win   183

Switching between Opportunity and Safety ✦ Strategy One: Keep it in the Fridge ✦ Strategy Two: Making Some Dough ✦ **Personal Gains:** *How Emotions Influence Investing*

CHAPTER TEN

Customized Investing: 208
Finding a Strategy That Suits You

The Way of the Sculptor: Charlie's Strategy for Small but Consistent Gains ✦ The Way of the Gardener: Rita's Strategy for a Big Harvest ✦ **Personal Gains:** *Think Less, Decide Better!*

CHAPTER ELEVEN

What's Your Style . . . Growth or Value?   241

Investing in Growth Stocks—Earnings, Earnings, Earnings ✦ Meet the Masters of Growth Investing—Phillip Fisher and William O'Neil ✦ Takeaway Points from Phillip Fisher and William O'Neil ✦ Where to Find High-Potential Growth Stocks ✦ Risk Management for Growth Stocks and ETFs—The Best Insurance for Your Profits ✦ Investing in Value Stocks—Bargains and Dividends ✦ Meet the Masters of Value Investing— Benjamin Graham, Warren Buffett, and Peter Lynch ✦ Takeaway Points from Graham, Buffett, and Lynch ✦ Where to Find High-Potential Value Stocks ✦ Size Matters ✦ What You Need to Know about Dividends ✦ Risk Management for Value Stocks ✦ The Best of Both Worlds ✦ **Personal Gains:** *Overwhelmed? Delegate It!*

CHAPTER TWELVE

Anticipating Market Opportunities: 272
How Investors Can Make Gains from Sector Rotation

Where Does It Come From? Identifying the Inputs of the Investment Mechanism ➔ What Is It Doing Here? Recognizing the Operating Rules of Institutional Investors ➔ Where Is It Going? Identifying Opportunities by Seeing the Outputs of Investor Decisions ➔ **Personal Gains:** *Make Your Circle Bigger*

CHAPTER THIRTEEN

Invest with a Winning Mindset 291

Personal Gains: *Look Forward . . . to Your Compelling Future*

INDEX   302

Acknowledgments

Toni → Writing a book is a journey like no other… it is a labor of love, hard work, indeed a labor of stretching one's very soul. Those wonderful people who share this journey with us deserve a large portion of credit for the book's completion.

First, I would like to offer my appreciation to Gordon Scott, who is a fantastic writing partner.

Next, a big "thank you" goes to my husband Mike. Once again (fourth book!) he's endured cold dinners, vague answers, and dead houseplants.

Thanks go to my daughter, Adrienne, who is an ever-present support system of wisdom, joy, and serenity. I also want to thank my family members, Chuck, Gail, Tammy, Missy, Jenny, John, and Mishelle, and all our grandchildren for their hugs and encouragement.

Both Gordon and I send much appreciation to Jennifer Ashkenazy, senior acquisitions editor at McGraw-Hill, for her consideration, patience, and efficiency at propelling this book through the multimonth publishing process. We also thank publisher Mary Glenn for her support and enthusiasm for this project.

Our gratitude also goes to our agent, Deidre Knight, of The Knight Agency, who is truly a mega-agent and the best business ally and friend an author could have.

Special thanks to our team at ToniTurner.com, Director of Operations Tina Hoesli, Content Coordinator Kathleen Kelley, and Market Research Technician Annette Helsper. Thanks also to Beverly Pickens, Cydney Creech, and David Barely. Finally we very much appreciate the support from Jeff Gibby and everyone at MetaStock, who kindly provided the charting software we used for this book.

Gordon ➔ First and foremost, I acknowledge my loving family members. Perhaps now that this book is done, I will be better at relaying phone messages.

I acknowledge the work, professional courtesy, and friendship of others that I have drawn from in crafting the insights of this book. Toni's expert tutelage and partnership should be mentioned first, but other experts deserve mention, including William Chin of e3m Investments, Van Tharp of Van Tharp International, Jake Freifeld of Chilmark Hill Capital LLC, Dave Keller CMT of Fidelity Mutual, and a uniquely special thank you to Chuck LeBeau—you are never forgotten.

Introduction

INVESTING IS easy. Anyone with a qualified brokerage account can do it. The tricky part is making—and keeping—profits. That's where we come in. Whether you are a novice investor or a skilled financial professional, *Invest to Win* will show you simple, step-by-step methods for finding, managing, and profiting from investing opportunities. We'll explain how you can gain the knowledge and skills you need in order to formulate and customize your portfolio so it meets your investing objectives.

In the chapters that follow, we are going to show you when, where, and how to find winning stocks and exchange-traded funds in the U.S. stock market. We will also explain how to manage your market positions during different market climates, using our GainsMaster approach, so that you can keep your losses small, while maximizing your gains.

"Hold it," you say. "I already have a financial advisor. I let him guide me through the stock market."

No problem. You may want to consider reading this book so you can ask your advisor informed questions and refine your investing goals. That can add nicely to your bottom line.

This Book Is for You

If you've ever earned swell profits in the stock market... and then ridden them down to devastating losses, this book is for you.

If you've ever wondered which sectors do well in bull (trending higher) markets and where you can find safety in bear (trending lower) markets, this book is for you.

If you've ever wondered which stock to buy, when to buy it, or when to sell it, then this book is for you.

Finally, if you've wished for a book that would "take you by the hand" and steer you through the financial-markets maze in a simple and friendly manner, this book is for you.

Gordon Scott CMT (Chartered Market Technician) and I (Toni Turner) have taught thousands of traders and investors how to maneuver in the market and emerge victorious, profits in hand.

Does our path require a chunk of time and commitment from you? You bet! *Any worthwhile endeavor requires time and personal commitment to achieve results.*

Are you smart enough to learn our techniques and apply them to your investing portfolio? Absolutely! *You don't need a master's degree in economics to understand our approach to the market. You* do *need the time and desire to apply our suggestions appropriately.*

Do you need a large amount of money to invest? *No, you can start small, with $1,000, or even a bit less, and add to your capital as you go.*

How *Invest to Win* Can Help You Achieve Your Investing Goals

Investors have long been handcuffed to the "buy-and-hold" method of investing. During the 2001 and 2008 bear markets, investors lost trillions of dollars, because this time-honored, yet sometimes ineffectual, method left investors unprepared to respond.

We are convinced now, more than ever, that self-directed investors—including those with advisors who know how (or are willing to learn)—need to discover a simple, straightforward process that maximizes profits while minimizing risk, both in the current market environment and in the markets we are likely to experience in the future.

Why "more than ever"? Because conducting research and finding the data necessary for sound investing has never been easier, while at the same time, financial markets are experiencing turmoil not seen in decades.

Today's global economy is vastly more interconnected than ever before. As you've surely noticed, events in a single region of the world can dramatically affect financial markets the world over. These events can easily touch you, the individual investor, and subject your portfolio to forces you don't recognize or understand.

During the inevitable period when a bull market tops out and rolls into a nose dive, instead of remaining chained to the antiquated "buy-and-hold" approach and mutely enduring the agony of watching your hard-earned funds evaporate, you—as a self-directed investor—can be proactive. You can take profits on certain portfolio assets and apply rigorous risk-management techniques to those remaining. When the bulls show signs of returning, you can be ready with your watch list of new opportunities and be set to enter at the right time.

Simply put, to win in today's markets, you need to build the knowledge and skill set you need to protect your account from risk and know how to take advantage of profit-making opportunities when they arise.

Why We Wrote This Book

It was a crisp, but sunny, spring morning. As I glanced out of the window of my office, I noticed the trees were just beginning to sprout new green shoots.

The phone on my desk buzzed; our receptionist informed me Gordon Scott was calling. I'd met Gordon a few months before, and since then, had worked on several business projects with him. I'd grown to appreciate his integrity, his wide range of knowledge of the financial markets, and the way he genuinely cared about the success of his trading and investing students.

"Good morning, Toni."

"Hey, Gordon, what's up?"

"I . . . well, I have a new project idea I'd like to run by you."

Although he paused, I could sense excitement in his voice.

"Sounds good," I replied. "Let's hear it."

"It's... it's a book idea," he started slowly. "You and I would co-author it."

"Hmm." I drew in a deep breath and let it out slowly. I knew from experience that writing a book demands tremendous commitment in both time and energy.

Gordon continued, his words tumbling out. He described a book that would give investors a step-by-step, easy-to-use method for investing that would combine the best of the fundamental and chart-analysis worlds. It would answer the questions that investors have had for decades as to how to earn profits and then keep them intact. We would also inspire our readers to achieve success by experiencing minimal losses and maximum gains.

As I listened to his explanation, I bit my lip, trying not to laugh out loud. Not because I thought his idea unworkable—quite the opposite. For even though I was well aware of the large amount of effort involved in writing a book, the very brainchild Gordon was describing to me had wandered around in my psyche for the past year. Now, it appeared, Gordon had read my mind. Further, he was speaking our combined thoughts.

Finally, he took a breath. "What do you think?"

"I think it sounds like a lot of work," I replied, testing his resolve and, admittedly, probing my own.

His voice quieted. "Yes. Yes, it will be."

"Plus, writing a book takes a terrific amount of planning."

"I'm sure it does."

"And the actual writing adds hours to your workload each day."

"I understand."

I continued with my long litany of reasons why writing a book demands a huge draw of time and energy from its author. I listened for any sound of hesitance in his replies, but there were none.

Invest to Win was born on that bright spring morning. The finished copy you hold in your hand represents the result of our combined ideas, knowledge, and research.

How This Book Is Organized

The first four chapters in *Invest to Win* provide you with a foundation from which you can build your investing goals. First, we'll look at how you can identify your personal risk parameters. Then we'll discuss the basics of market machinations and simple techniques evaluating overall market conditions.

In Chapters Five through Eight, we'll show you how to read price charts in an easy-to-understand format. Then we'll move to time-friendly ways to check company fundamentals, and show you where and how to find the information you need. You'll discover how to create a customized list of stocks that could be potential winners, with just a few mouse clicks. Chapter Eight is dedicated to the popular and versatile asset class known as exchange traded funds, and how to include them in your portfolio at the most opportune times.

Chapters Nine through Thirteen are all about simple techniques, strategies, and tactics that smooth the icing on your investing cake. We will discuss risk management fully, so you will know how to keep the profits you earn, and not give them back in a cranky bear market.

Most important, woven throughout each chapter is our comprehensive and straightforward approach to the market, the "Gains-Master" approach. This unique and valuable method will give you stepping stones for creating a personal investing strategy and then implementing it with success.

Toward the end of each chapter, you will find a bulleted section, "Key Points to Remember." These points summarize the chapter's content and act as a quick review.

After "Key Points to Remember," you will discover a segment titled "Personal Gains." Each Personal Gain focuses on a motivational concept that can help you keep a sense of balance in today's hectic markets.

As the authors of *Invest to Win*, Gordon and I are dedicated to bringing you—the individual investor—timely, compelling, and actionable information you can use to succeed in both bull and bear markets—for years to come. Now let's get started!

CHAPTER ONE

And Away We Go!

— Toni —

CHANCES ARE you're a reasonably bright person, possibly between the ages of 25 and 80. You've probably worked at one job or another for most of your life. And, through good sense or good fortune, you have gathered enough money to fund an investment account.

You may have a stockbroker you like and trust, but you want to understand how the stock market maneuvers, for your own peace of mind. Or, maybe you have been investing on your own for a few years, but would like to take a more hands-on approach and drive your capital gains to a higher level. Finally, perhaps you are brand new to the stock market, a bit overwhelmed by the size of it all, and want a guiding hand to help lead you on the world's most exciting street, Wall Street.

So... where do you start? How do you choose the right stocks, in the right sectors, at the right time? When do you buy? How do you manage the position so you don't lose your shirt or blouse? More important, how do you know when to sell, either to protect your capital or to take profits off the table?

That, of course, is what this entire book is about. Gordon and I have been engineering our way through this challenge for years now. Separately and as a team, we've taught thousands of stock market traders and investors how to take profits from the market.

First, we've noted that the technology advances of the last two decades have empowered individual investors like never before. In the "old days," let's say before the early 1990s, information about publicly-held companies that issued common shares to their stock holders, was held (it seemed) in sacred vaults by stiffly-suited vault keepers known as stockbrokers. These bespectacled men and women sat in their mahogany offices and pushed thick reports with shiny covers across their desks to us—their clients.

"Take this quarterly report home and read it," the broker would say, peering at us down his nose through his bifocals. "If you like the numbers, we'll purchase three hundred (or three thousand, depending on our account size) shares for your account."

"Very impressive," we murmur, staring at the shiny cover and leafing through the binder.

Once home, we open the report and scan through the first two pages. *Sleek.* The pictures of the company's stalwart headquarters and dignified CEO look reassuring. After that, though, the printed paragraphs morph into convoluted financial jargon, punctuated with long rows of mind-numbing numbers. *Good grief. Good cure for insomnia*, we think. We slap the binder closed and place it on our desk, making a mental note to read it thoroughly . . . *soon*.

A few days later, our broker calls. "How about that company we talked about? Riveting quarterly report, wasn't it? What do you say? Shall we add three hundred shares to your portfolio?"

"Uh, looks like a great company," we agree lamely, eyeing the unread report on our desk. "Sure. OK. Let's go for it."

A couple of days later, the stock-purchase confirmation arrives in the mail. We note with some satisfaction that we own three-hundred shares of the shiny stock. Then our gaze drifts to the commission—$252.00. *Geez.* That comes to about two percent of the purchase price! We file the statement in a desk drawer, blow out a breath, and walk away. *The doggoned stock better move higher.*

Those days are over. Freed from the once-hallowed halls of doughty stock brokerage firms and their hefty commissions, investors have been liberated by computers and the ever-present, content-rich Internet. We are the "vault keepers" now, and we have quarterly reports (should we ever *really* want to read them) as close as our keyboards.

Since by law, stock transactions have to be executed through a registered broker, we can't ignore stockbrokers completely. (The truth is, most of them are knowledgeable professionals who give good advice.) But by now, most of us have opened investing accounts at an online discount broker.

Many of you make your own investing decisions. You rely on your own research, and your own opinions. And, you hold the power to buy and sell stocks via computer or wireless device, with a keystroke, at your convenience, and often paying only single-digit commissions.

You Hold the Power

Say you've got a particular stock you want to research. Go online to your broker's website—or one of any number of other financial sites—and you can journey through the company's fundamentals, such as P/E (price-to-earnings) ratio, earnings per share, graphs of quarterly earnings growth, annual dividend (if paid), and fundamental comparisons to competing companies. (If those terms make you scratch your head, don't worry. They're simpler than they sound, and you'll soon understand them.)

You can also spend a few moments scanning information on the sector where your stock resides. Along with the information provided in later chapters, you can decide if this is—or is not—a good time to enter that arena.

Best of all, once online, you can access historical price charts of your target stock. In the same way that "If you know where a person's been, you can tell where he or she is going," price charts show, at a single glance, the past performance of the stock as relates to price. And, that performance, past and present, can broadcast signals as to the stock's price strength.

News in a New York Minute

Of course, whether we're active investors or not, the most prominent material we receive via satellite *every single minute of every day* is the news. The evolution of wireless networks and social media has accelerated news delivery to near-lightning speed. On a global basis, news arrives *as* happens, or seconds afterwards. We are instantly informed about uprisings and wars, storms, geopolitical events, and financial troubles the world over. To a greater or lesser degree, all of these events can affect the prices of stocks.

> **HOT TIP**
>
> As a savvy investor, your number one rule is to protect your capital at all times.

Does that mean we panic and dump all our portfolio's positions the same day a chunk of disruptive news blindsides us? *Absolutely not.* But as wise investors, we can learn and apply techniques that guide us to take prudent actions. *Then,* we know which news to let pass... and which news to investigate. We know when to hold our positions... and when to take action.

The Global Financial Markets: A Community Affair

From Sydney to Shanghai, from Berlin, to London, to New York, each weekday the sun rises and sets on our global community of financial markets.

Every trading day, the world over, traders and investors partake of the sumptuous buffet offered by the global markets. Indeed, we could say the smorgasbords of stocks, bonds, and other financial assets on display offer the most appealing—and exciting—goods in the world.

Why are they so attractive? Because it is in these settings that you can trade your dollars for shares (units of ownership) of the largest, most dynamic companies on earth. As these companies expand their businesses and become worth more, your shares of ownership increase in worth.

Want to sell your shares? If your stock has risen in value since you first purchased it, you will receive a higher price than you paid, and thus pocket a sweet profit.

Or, would you rather hold on to your shares on the chance that during the next five years or so, your share value will double, triple, or even multiply ten-fold? (We call that a "ten-bagger.") That scenario *can* become a reality, as long as you assess your risk and manage it appropriately.

By now you are thinking, "Hey, stock prices go down, too. The stock market isn't all ice cream and apple pie."

You're absolutely right. If you've participated in the equities market for any length of time, you've experienced price retracements and corrections, some of which have been devastating to investors. Falling prices are the risk that we take for the chance of potential reward.

Recessions and depressions mean less spending by companies *and* consumers, so demand for goods (produced by companies) shrinks. Shrunken demand results in decreasing company earnings. Lower earnings usually result in lower stock prices. A severe turndown can also cause what we call a "bear" market, which can last from several months to roughly two years.

In those situations, we agree with Ben Graham, famed economist and co-author of the legendary book *Security Analysis*, who said, "The investor should have a definite selling policy for all his common stock commitments, corresponding to his buying techniques" (Benjamin Graham and David Dodd, *Security Analysis*, New York: McGraw-Hill, 1996). We will show you such a "selling policy" in the chapters to follow.

On the "silver lining" side, please know that markets have an upside bias. Growth is more prevalent than contraction, and economic expansion dominates most of the time. That means stocks of stalwart companies increase in value more than they fall. We call rising stock prices throughout the majority of sectors for a protracted period of time a "bull" market. And here's more good news: on average, bull markets last longer than bear markets.

First and foremost, Gordon and I believe that your investment account should *always* be an asset—not a liability. To accomplish that objective, we will show you how to manage your account on a risk and time-friendly schedule that you will personalize to fit your objectives.

HOT TIP

A "position" identifies shares of a single stock (or other asset class). For example, if you purchase shares of Intel Inc. (INTC), you can say you own a "position" in Intel.

Strategy-wise, we'll push into a "full court press," when the bull is roaring. But when the bear emerges from his cave, growling and ready to fight, we confirm our position's protective stops, and perhaps even head to the sidelines. Our strategy is to earn—and keep—our profits. We have no intention of handing them over to a bad-tempered bear.

What's in It for You? The Benefits of Investing in the U.S. Stock Market

The following list offers some of the advantages of investing in the stock market.

▪ **Voted the "Most Likely to Succeed"**—For the past seven decades, stocks have returned about 10.5%. Corporate bonds returned 4.5%, U.S. Treasuries averaged 3.3%, and inflation grew 3+%. When Treasuries' return equals inflation, your return on Treasuries is zero. Figure in taxes, and you lose money on that deal. Over time, stocks offer capital appreciation *and* many pay an annual yield that exceeds that of Treasuries.

▪ **Convenience**—Imagine you see a home, or an office building, or piece of property you'd love to purchase. If the current owner is unwilling to sell it to you, you can't have it. *Period.* Or, say you already own a home, office building, or piece of property. You want to sell it. If no one offers to buy it, then you have to keep it until a buyer shows up. In other words, just because you *want to buy*, or *want to sell*, doesn't mean you can. Stocks and exchange traded funds (ETFs) are different. If you see a publicly traded company that looks attractive and fits into your investing objectives and risk management criteria—and you like the price—you can go to your broker's website, log into your account, and purchase shares of that company in a heartbeat. When you want to sell those shares, make a quick visit to your online broker and complete the sale.

▪ **Liquidity**—We say publicly traded stocks are "liquid." That means there are ample shares available during the trading day to buy and sell. So, if you see an attractive stock and want to purchase shares in it, assuming you have enough purchasing power in your investing account, you can own it in a nanosecond. As well, if you own a stock and want to sell it, someone at the stock exchange is always there to buy it. That means your stock portfolio is always "liquid."

▪ **You, the Business Owner, Minus the Headaches**—When you invest in stocks and their colleagues, ETFs, this offers you the advantages of owning a chunk of the world's most successful companies. Even better, you own them without the headaches of having to get up every weekday morning, put on a tie or high heels, and go to the office.

▪ **Timeliness**—During different economic environments, certain sectors (sector examples are: energy, technology, health care; we'll discuss these in detail later) thrive, while others tend to dive. Investing in the stocks and ETFs gives you the benefit of seeding your account with the right sectors at the right time, and then "harvesting" the gains given by those sectors at an opportune time.

■ **Double Your Pleasure**—Occasionally, stock prices not only rise in value, the shares, themselves, can multiply. If a company wants to make its shares more attractive and affordable to a wider audience of investors, the company's board of directors will authorize a "stock split" to create more shares, selling at a lower price.

If the company authorizes a 2-for-1 stock split, it doubles the number of outstanding shares and halves the current price. For example, if you own 100 shares of a stock selling at $50 a share, for a total value of $5,000, and the company authorizes a 2-for-1 split, you would own 200 shares priced at $25, with the same total value of $5,000.

> **HOT TIP**
>
> An exchange traded fund (ETF) represents a basket of stocks (or other assets) and targets a theme, for example, a sector, country, fixed income, or commodity.

Many stocks of U.S. industrial icons, such as the thirty stocks listed in the Dow Jones Industrial Average, have split ten times or more since they were first offered. McDonald's (MCD) went public (first issued stock certificates in a public offering) in 1965; subsequently, the stock has split eleven times. Imagine you bought 100 shares in 1965, for the offering price of $22.50 per share. As of this writing, forty-seven years later, you would now own 37,180 shares of the hamburger king, worth more than $3.6 million. *Very nice.*

> **HOT TIP**
>
> When we trade our dollars for shares of stock, Wall Street calls it a "trade." Just so, when we buy and sell stocks or ETFs, we are "trading" in the stock market.

Bubbles and Belly Punches: The Challenges and Risks of Investing in the Stock Market

Let's pretend we know an investor named Pamela. Pamela has a seven-year time horizon before she retires. She has put aside savings and intends to put that money into stocks to build a nest egg for her retirement. Pamela doesn't know, and no one tells her, that the market has moved up for the last four years. The uptrend, as we say, is "mature," and the major indexes are losing steam. Technology stock prices, especially, are considered to be forming a "bubble." Stock prices of market leaders such as Apple, Inc. (AAPL), and Google Inc. (GOOG) have flown to extremely high prices of late. Now, to most market pros, they appear overblown and subjects for profit-taking.

Pamela opens a brokerage account. Just as the market begins to scream south in a dive, she unwittingly plunks much of her hard-earned savings into technology stocks. Result? She loses a hefty percentage of her portfolio's value, and her retirement is delayed until the market recovers.

This story *could* have ended on a happy note. Had Pamela known that it is unwise to buy stocks without perusing the company's "fundamentals" and "technicals" as you will learn in the pages that follow, she would have known to wait for the market to pause and then show signs of strength before she purchased. She could have retired on time, and her savings would have grown nicely.

HOT TIP

Stock market "bubbles" form when prices—usually in a particular sector—have expanded too high, too fast. Just like real bubbles, when price bubbles "pop," the "air," or value, can collapse quickly. (In the pages that follow, we will show you how to avoid that scenario.)

Billionaire and mega-investor Warren Buffett says it perfectly. "In this game, the market has to keep pitching, but you don't have to swing. You can stand there with the bat on your shoulder for six months, until you get a pitch."

Whether we are teaching live seminars at financial forums or teaching online webinars, the question Gordon and I are asked most often is, "If I decide to buy shares of a certain stock, how do I know the right time to get in?"

In this book, using the GainsMaster approach, we are going to show you how to choose stocks and ETFs, and opportune entry methods, using simple, yet extremely effective measuring tools.

Please know, however, that while investing wisely in stocks and ETFs represents a terrific technique for growing your money, participating in the potential rewards of the financial markets also involves risk. When you purchase shares of stocks or ETFs, or any other asset class—no matter how carefully you evaluate the underlying companies, sector, or timeliness—there is always a chance your position can decrease in value.

After all, the financial markets don't stand still. And if they become agitated enough, they can act downright cranky. Every day, markets around the globe react to rising or falling interest rates, geopolitical events, economic and earnings reports, wars, weather, and seasonal forces. To that extent, risk is inherent to the stock market. It's baked in. It's part of the game and always present.

As a savvy investor, you will want to purchase equities in a market that has enough upside room to grow in an uptrend—as opposed to buying stocks in a market that appears to be toppy and overbought, as our investor, Pamela, did earlier. (We'll explain in upcoming chapters how to spot an overbought market.)

If you follow the guidelines we offer to you in this book, your losses should be minimal. Your profits will far exceed them. Before you invest money in stocks, however, consider your personal risk tolerance. If the thought of losing *any* amount of money in an equity position gives you hives, then you may want to avoid the financial markets and invest your money in more conservative vehicles, such as money-market funds or certificates of deposit.

What We Bring to the Party...

Some of you already know me from my earlier books, as the author of *A Beginner's Guide to Day Trading Online,* Second Edition, *A Beginner's Guide to Short-Term Trading,* Second Edition, and *Short-Term Trading in the New Stock Market.*

"Wow," you might say. "That's a lot of trading stuff. I'm not interested in buying and selling all day. I just want to buy good stocks, sit back, and make money. Do you know anything about investing?"

Sure do. I started investing in the stock market in 1991; I am both an investor and a trader to this day. Learning—and eventually teaching—faster-paced trading techniques added immensely to my knowledge of the stock market. The knowledge also enhanced my ability to earn profits.

Let me tell you something. I *love* the stock market. I fell passionately in love with this crazy arena from the first day I entered it, and the honeymoon is still on. Confession: I'm a bit of an adrenaline junkie. So perhaps my passion for the markets comes from being part of one of the most exciting show grounds on planet Earth. Whatever the reason, I am happy to learn new lessons from the market each day. My job is to pass those lessons—and what you can *earn* from them—on to you.

Gordon is also passionate about the stock market. As I mentioned in the Introduction, he is an active investor and trader, as well as a financial-markets coach. His credentials are impressive, as is his concern for his students; you will see both reflected in this book's content.

Going forward, let's talk about structure. Gordon and I are going to alternate chapters, more or less. That way, you get the best of both of us. Between us, we're going to provide you with a cornucopia of information dedicated to successful investing. And we'll have fun. So, let's go!

Key Points to Remember

➦ As an investor, your number one rule is to *protect your capital at all times.*

➦ All of the information you need to know about publicly traded companies is at your fingertips via the Internet.

➦ News arrives faster than ever before in history; that news can affect the financial markets to a greater or lesser degree.

➦ Financial markets of industrialized nations expand and contract.

➦ These expansions and contractions form cycles known as "bull" and "bear" markets.

➦ Your investment account should be an asset—not a liability.

➦ Investing appropriately in stocks and ETFs holds many benefits: capital appreciation, convenience, liquidity, owning a part of the world's most successful companies, timeliness, and stock splits that can garner big rewards over time.

➦ Risk is inherent to owning stocks and ETFs. Examine your personal risk tolerance before you invest.

What Role Do "Personal Gains" Play?

When we immerse ourselves in the stock market, it's easy to get caught up in the dizzying pace of this fast-moving environment. Added to that, the continuous information bombardment from newscasters, countries, companies, CEOs, policy makers, and earnings and economic reports can cause feelings of "overwhelm" to descend on even the most stalwart of market participants.

When I was new to the markets, I experienced stretches of time when I felt stymied and overwhelmed, even panicky. Only my knowledge of—and beliefs in—certain thought models kept me in the game.

Through the years, these thought models have encouraged me to keep reaching for my goals, both financial and non-financial. I believe that as we make gains financially, we enjoy them more if we also make gains in the other parts of our lives, such as health, career, and relationships.

At the conclusion of each chapter, I will briefly share these concepts with you as "Personal Gains." I trust they will inspire you to move ahead on the road to greater levels of success.

PERSONAL GAINS

— Toni —

Commitment: The Foundation of Success

Thomas Edison dreamed of a lamp that could be operated by electricity, began where he stood to put his dream into action, and despite more than ten thousand failures, he stood by that dream until he made it a physical reality. Practical dreamers do not quit.

—NAPOLEON HILL

When you step out on the road to a new goal or endeavor, three immediate steps must be taken. First, you have to believe in that goal. You have to know it is achievable, will benefit all who are involved, and that it will affect your life in a positive way. Second, you need to envision at least a shape of the desired result. And third, and perhaps most important, you must commit to that goal. Without commitment, few goals are reached.

When you form a new goal, take the time to envision the shape of the desired result and then commit to the process of achieving it, the commitment combined with the vision automatically brings new thoughts to the forefront to help form your "dream into action." Suddenly, you may find undiscovered or unused abilities you were unaware you had. New opportunities appear. In other words, good things start happening.

If Thomas Edison had not committed to his dream of creating the first light bulb, and held tightly to that commitment throughout ten thousand failures, our world would not have experienced indoor lighting as we know it today.

The next time you create a worthwhile new goal or objective, picture the outcome you want to achieve. Then, firmly *commit* to that outcome. Write down your commitment and refer to it often. Promise yourself—and better yet, a supportive friend—that you will take the necessary steps to see it through.

Your commitment acts as a focus of positive energy. Keep your energy focused on the outcome you want to attain, and as Thomas Edison did, you will soon see your goal as a "physical reality."

CHAPTER TWO

Unlocking Your Investment Potential

Gordon

MOST PEOPLE do not realize their own potential when it comes to investing. Did you know that, as a modern day investor, you can do things today that you couldn't do just two years ago? I'm not talking about leveraging your money in stock options or the Forex (currency) markets or taking wild risks with your money that was carefully saved over the years. I'm talking about making sensible choices that allow you to outperform many, if not most, of the professional portfolio managers out there.

In this book, Toni and I set out to help individuals unlock their investing potential by realizing just how much an advantage modern investors have over their predecessors. You won't hear about such things on major network television, because they are too busy reporting on tragedy and corruption in the financial world of one kind or another. While there is certainly no shortage of those stories, there is a quiet reality that has taken shape in the investing world over the past ten years. It is this: investing has gotten easier, less expensive, and better for the individual—a lot better!

The individual investor has gained advantages in three areas: improved technology, decreased costs, and greater access to investment choices. In this chapter I will explain these advantages. To do so I hope to tell you a little about myself and a typical conversation I often have with individuals who ask me for help in understanding more about the markets. Toni and I agree strongly that key details about the modern markets are not well understood by investors—people who cannot afford to be without that knowledge. Investors need to know the power they have available to them. They need a roadmap for how to put that power to work for them. That roadmap is what Toni and I call the GainsMaster approach.

The GainsMaster approach can be described in this oversimplified statement: start with yourself, then work outwards and manage your risk along the way. The approach has four parts to it:

1. Define your individual investing objectives.
2. Recognize what is going on in the markets.
3. Learn to discover and select investing opportunities.
4. Work to manage the risk that comes with investing.

Before diving into the approach, I'd like to describe what helped Toni and me to decide that we needed to articulate this approach. It comes from our work in teaching and training individuals to become better investors all over the world. One thing we both agreed was true from our own observations is that if you take the individual out of the equation, the equation no longer serves the individual. Investing strategies need to be built from the inside out.

What I Learned from Working with 1000 Individuals

I have worked for years as a coach of traders and investors. During those years I have worked one-on-one with over one thousand people. Throughout these interactions, I have constantly sought for better methods of investing that can be quickly learned and easily applied. Two themes have emerged consistently as I have both taught and learned from these individuals: Every investor is different, and each of them faces a complex, personal challenge to apply investing strategies. This challenge comes from the fact that no two investors get exactly the same results, even if they invest in the same thing. (See Van K. Tharp, D. R. Barton, Steve Sjuggerud, *Safe Strategies for Financial Freedom,* New York: McGraw-Hill, 2004, p. 229. My experience leads me to believe that investment success has more to do with the investor than with the investment.

Investing is an individual activity, and to do it effectively you need to factor yourself into the equation. The simplest technique for doing so has two steps: first, clearly identify your goals for investing; second, identify your personal tolerance for risk.

Once investors understand their unique characteristics, they can then simplify their investing strategies into activities that are congruent with their goals and their personality. The modern markets offer many useful tools which can be crafted into simple strategies. There is no shortage of good ideas or effective tools for investing in the markets. The big disconnect comes about when an individual investor tries to implement a strategy that doesn't really fit with his or her expectations or personal goals.

The simplest example of this is the concept of diversified, buy-and-hold investing in the stock market. A commonly expressed notion of investing is the idea that you should invest your money in a wide variety of stocks and then step back and let them grow. If one is weak, another will be strong and average out your returns.

That strategy has a weakness: the fluctuation of overall market prices. Between the years 2000 and 2010 prices fell by 40 percent or more from their highs on two separate occasions. In both cases the price action prompted many investors to move their money into cash, thus missing some or all of the upward moves that followed in the subsequent three years.

The notion that these same people could or should have held on and not sold out of the markets creates two problems. The first is that a fall in the stock market occurs to coincide with when the national economy is bad, jobs are being lost, and people are in financial distress. During those times some investors need to withdraw their savings or simply can't stomach the fluctuation in prices. They might prefer to buy and hold, but they cannot do so, because they need the money to address life's circumstances. Or they might know in their heads that they *should* hold on, but don't hold on when prices move too low for their tolerance of risk. They sell out of their investments merely to ease the pain they feel.

The second problem is even more profound. If an investor does not face an imminent need to withdraw funds and somehow manages to outlast his fears about the market's prices, he ultimately faces an uncomfortable reality: the lackluster gains over the past decade. Over the past 120 years, the market has shown a pattern of sorts. It seems to trend higher for about 17 years and then it seems merely to move up and down within a limited range, as it has done since the highest prices in the year 2000. Diversified buy-and-hold might seem like a great idea during the upward-trending years, but a prolonged range-bound market could create a tremendous amount of lost opportunity for someone saving for retirement.

Both of these problems show that a straightforward buy-and-hold strategy is fraught with unexpected difficulty for the investor, because the strategy itself is based on the idea that no response will ever be needed. As humans, we are not accustomed to sit idly by when things are moving in front of us. Our flight-or-fight instincts kick in, and we naturally want to respond—we want to do something when the market moves too quickly against us.

Far too many investors have not learned about the advantages the modern market offers. However, all investors today have a pressing need to find out about them. Their accounts won't manage themselves. Ever since 1987, people have experienced a chronic and growing need for good information about investing. When laws began to encourage corporations to offer the kinds of savings plans that require people to manage their own investments, investors found that educating themself on the topic was no longer optional.

Toni and I have worked for years to help individuals and groups learn successful methods for trading and investing. We feel that the main characteristics of a good investing system should be twofold: first, it should be simple; second, it should be powerful enough to help you meet your objectives. We likewise feel it is important to help you learn about the advantages available to investors today and how to use them in a strategy that is simple and powerful, but also quite flexible, so that it can be adjusted for a wide variety of goals.

The investing strategies presented in this book have been developed from a myriad of conversations with many individuals. Those conversations have common questions and answers that Toni and I have heard and evaluated over the years. What we have learned from them has prepared us to write this book from a unique perspective. We want to give you some ideas for investing that will help you win what you want from life by helping you better understand what you have to work with—both in yourself and in the markets.

People have a hard time changing old habits. Old habits are based on deep beliefs, and those beliefs were put in place for a reason—whatever reason that might be. It is much harder to question, evaluate, or change those beliefs than people might expect. This single fact explains why it is so very hard for some people to make deep changes in their behavior. Working to change your habits can be laborious, unpleasant, and all too frequently unproductive.

People don't like to change beliefs, but if you change your beliefs, you find that the change in your behavior follows much more rapidly. That was the experience I had with my most successful students. Those who could change their unproductive beliefs about themselves and about investing in general to something more constructive would often naturally find ways to be more successful investors—not to mention happier people.

I hope that what you learn in this book will help you bring about a positive change in your beliefs about investing and about yourself. To help this process along, I want to share a conversation with you. This conversation is between me and two other people. It is a fictional conversation based on actual conversations I've had with many people over the years. I hope that these two characters will accurately portray some concerns and questions that you may have about investing, and that in so doing this dialogue will help unfold the idea I've put forward in this chapter—that individual investors have significant advantages available to them today.

What I Learned from Two People...

Their names were Charlie and Rita, a father and daughter-in-law team who had invited me to lunch to help them with their investing. They sat across the table from me waiting for my answer to the question they had posed. It was a question I hear a lot, but I paused a moment to think about how best to respond. Then I took off my glasses and held them up as a prop.

"It's like this," I explained. "When you ask me what investing strategy will make you the most money, I have to help you see the answer through a proper lens. Some people might claim that investing should be done according to a strict formula, so that all you have to do is follow the right formula for allocating your money and, presto, you make money from investing. It sounds good in theory, but the reality of life rarely works out like that. The problem is not limited to the reality that the markets might have periodic crashes. The bigger part of the problem is that life happens to everyone. You can never tell when you might need to get out of the markets altogether for a while."

Charlie raised his chin, Rita tilted her head slightly. They looked skeptical, but interested.

"Investing is different for everyone," I continued. "What might work for me won't necessarily work for someone else. If you asked me how to improve your vision and I offered you my prescription glasses, you would think me simple minded for suggesting such a thing. Yet investors are all too often willing to take investing advice without bothering to check whether it suits their own objectives. You need to do that first. But once you do, then you have an advantage in the markets. You can see clearly how to react, regardless of what happens."

"Just knowing my own objectives is an advantage?" Charles asked.

"It is," I replied. "Too many investors jump from one idea to another with high expectations, only to have disappointing results."

"Been there; lost that money," Rita mumbled while running a finger along the edge of her napkin.

"On the other hand, if you know your objectives, it makes it easier to know how to stick with your game plan. Over time, that is a major advantage" (Joel Greenblatt, *The Big Secret for the Small Investor: A New Route to Long-Term Investment Success,* New York: Random House, 2011, pp. 145–146).

Charlie was in his sixties and a widower. He had done well for himself in building up savings from a fairly successful career as a manager in the telecommunications industry. In 2007 his retirement savings had been worth close to a million dollars, and he was eyeing an early retirement in just two more years. But 2008 had come along and reset the value of his account, and with it, his retirement timetable. I could see him considering my words, but at the same time, he idly clasped his hands behind the back of his white-haired head. He had brought Rita along to join our conversation because she was good with computers and had agreed to help him get set up so he could better manage his own account.

"I lost about half of my savings two years ago," he reiterated. "My objective was to retire early. Knowing my objective back then doesn't seem like it gave me any advantage."

"Don't confuse a life goal with your investing performance objective. We all have things we want in life, but to accomplish them we need to understand what we are willing to risk, or even sacrifice, to make them happen. Your investing objective isn't what you want to do with your money once you have it, it's the boundaries within which you are going to operate with your money. You need to decide how much you are willing to risk, and how much you are trying to target in return."

Charlie though about that for a moment, then leaned forward.

"So what I think you're saying is that I need to know how much I don't want to lose," he said.

"That's exactly right," I said. "If you don't have that spelled out in your objectives, then you don't know when to react. You get paralyzed by fear when the market goes bad."

"I guess that's what happened to me," he continued. "I heard the news about a financial crisis, but I didn't know what to do. I just held on and hoped for the best."

"But what can you do?" Rita waved in the air for emphasis. "The market goes up and down. We don't have control." Rita had her own reasons for being part of this discussion. She worked as a marketing consultant for large firms. Though she was in her early thirties, she was very good at what she did, and after a winding path between entrepreneurism and the business world, she was now highly compensated. Her retirement funds were finally starting to grow significantly, but she simply didn't have time to learn about investing. Hearing that her father in law knew somebody who offered a simple investing method, she was eager to join in the conversation.

"You are right. You do not have control over the market," I said, "but you do have control over your choices. And today the individual investor has better choices than ever."

"What kind of choices?" Rita replied.

"You can choose to move your money into places that are either more conducive to safety or better positioned for opportunity," I said. "People have always been able to choose one stock or another, but up until a few years ago, there weren't so many excellent choices for how to invest your money strategically. Now it is quite simple."

"So you're saying, if I know when to react, based on my own game plan, I can move my money to safety, as long as I know some safe places to put it?" Charlie considered for a moment before continuing. "How much will it take to learn how to spot those safe places? Do I have to take business-school classes? I'm too old to go back to school."

"Oh, boy." Rita rolled her eyes and sighed. "Manage my own money? I don't know. Fitting one more thing into my jam-packed schedule will be a challenge. And what with Joe, and the kids, and their schedules…" She shook her head and glanced at her smartphone.

Rita's life is crazy busy. I knew I'd have to keep this as simple as possible for her to have a hope of doing it.

"Besides," added Charlie, "the market's stopped going down now. Maybe I should just keep doing what I'm doing. My account is building back up. It's still not back up to where it was, but..."

I bit my lip.

"Well, heck, I can't keep doing what I'm doing," he conceded. "I have to protect what I have *now* so that a catastrophic year like 2008 doesn't hurt me again."

"Right! I don't want to lose any more either," Rita chimed in. "But I want my money to grow. I have to invest in *something*, don't I? I can't just let it sit in cash." Then, she added, "Speaking of cash, I keep hearing about the Fed doing their—" she searched for the words.

"Quantitative easing?" Charlie offered.

"Quantitative easing!" she agreed. "I read online that the more they keep doing that, the more it means horrendous inflation will surely soon follow. I mean... do I have to worry about that?"

"That's the good part," I told them excitedly. "Nowadays you don't have to be afraid of facing a situation like that. In fact, the answer to all of your concerns is that there is something you can do about the fluctuations in the market. The market offers easy access to almost any financial investment choice you could want, domestic stocks, international stocks, government bonds, corporate bonds, municipal bonds, commodities, real estate, foreign currencies, all of it!"

They both looked at me with blank stares.

"So how does that help us?" asked Rita.

I wanted to tell them that they could incorporate alternative choices into their game plan for any market condition. I wanted to explain the possible investment choices they could make, and how some of these investment choices could help them prepare for the doom and gloom scenarios. But the reality is, those topics aren't the right place to start.

Because of my experience over the years, I knew that first I had to help these two understand something more important. I needed to help them begin by understanding their personal investing profiles, and then build investment plans from there. I explained to Charlie and Rita that I wanted to help them implement what I called the GainsMaster approach.

"The GainsMaster approach requires that you turn four keys to unlock your investing potential." I said. "These keys will open the door to your winning investment strategy."

"The keys are personal attributes that describe who you are as an investor," I went on. "This identity will change over time. Identifying each of these keys helps you, as an investor, see what it is that you need to do with your portfolio. When you know who you are as an investor and what the market is doing in general, you will know whether you need to be seeking opportunities or simply seek safety for your money.

"These keys enable you to incorporate the advantages of improved technology, decreased costs, and greater access to investment choices. In turn, the keys will allow you to follow a strategy adapted to fit your busy lifestyle. Last, but not least, the keys will give you the power to recognize and respond to the changing conditions of the marketplace."

Four Keys of the GainsMaster Approach

"When you identify the four key elements of your investor profile, you will be able to choose an investing strategy that will likely help

HOT TIP

Inflation-resistant investment choices do exist. The easiest invest-ment choice to use to protect yourself against inflation is a thing called "inflation-protected treasury funds." You don't even have to know much about it to use it. You simply buy into this fund like a stock. Toni will explain more about exchange-traded funds, but the general idea is that this fund (which has the ticker symbol "TIP" as it happens), will invest in bonds for dedicated income, but also protect you against inflation and a weakening U.S. dollar.

you make use of the innovations that keep coming along to help investors," I continued. "Among all the instruments available to investors today, you will likely always be able to find a place where your money can either seek safety or opportunity. But to take advantage of these, you'll need to know what you are looking for and how to apply it once you find it. The four keys will help you put that information to work."

Rita picked up a pen and slid a notepad in front of her. I felt certain she wouldn't be disappointed if she could learn and apply what I was about to explain to her. Charlie leaned in as I continued.

Key 1: Define your objectives. "First you need to identify your performance objectives. These will change as you enter different phases of life. Specifically, you will want to choose how much account fluctuation you can tolerate over time. It may be helpful to think of fluctuation as loss. Your hope is that this loss is temporary, but when things are at their worst it will feel like loss, not merely fluctuation, so it is probably best to plan from that point of view.

"To identify your objectives, simply ask yourself two questions: first, how much loss do I want to avoid, and next, how long before I have the need to draw on my savings and stop contributing to them? If you answer these questions, you can classify yourself as having a low, medium, or high risk tolerance."

Key 2: Evaluate market conditions. "Second, you need to be able to recognize how the conditions of the market change. Though the market seems to shift its mood like the changing of the wind, that doesn't mean you can't anticipate changes in conditions." I paused a moment for that idea to sink in with Charlie and Rita.

"Let's carry on with the weather analogy. It doesn't take much to know that you can anticipate changes in temperature or precipitation if you simply track the seasons of the year. If you get familiar with cloud patterns, you can even anticipate when a storm is coming. Similarly, if you learn a little about how the market works, you can anticipate when conditions are likely to change.

This will tell you when investor moods make the market shift from seeking opportunity to seeking safety, prompting you to respond accordingly."

"This is actually a big advantage the small investor can gain," I explained. "If you can learn to read market conditions, you can make changes in your portfolio rather quickly if necessary."

Rita held up her hand. "Read market conditions? Are you serious?"

"I know that might sound complicated," I said. "However, don't worry. I can show you how to read the markets quickly and easily. You'll be surprised how fast you catch on."

Key 3: Choose your opportunities. "Third, you need to identify what opportunities are suitable for you, given your risk tolerance and the current market conditions. It is important to recognize that what might be an opportunity for one investor might not be an opportunity for another."

Charlie looked over to Rita. "So what Rita and I choose might be different. I'm at the end of my career, while she and Joe are in the middle of theirs."

"That's right," I said. "As we work through this approach together, I'll help you identify where you might find opportunities that are best suited for you, but those are likely to be quite different from Rita's choices. No matter what either of you chooses, you will both need to turn the fourth key to this approach."

Key 4: Manage your risk. "Finally, you will need to have a clear picture of how you plan to manage your risk. The markets are simply too volatile to wait out."

"So you think the doomsayers could be right?" Rita looked concerned. "You think we could somehow see the whole banking system collapse?"

"Dow 1000." Charlie added. "I've heard that."

"I don't claim to know what the future will bring," I said. "Personally, I think that serious financial catastrophe is less likely than many investors fear right now, but at the same time I don't think the next few years are going to be rosy for investors. And we don't have any guarantee that we won't face something worse than the last two bear markets we've seen.

"But no matter what the future brings, you can prepare yourself by simply managing your risk," I explained. "All you have to do is understand the maximum amount of money you could lose on any single investment and limit that amount with each investment you make. For example if you have $500,000 in your investing account, risking only $5,000 means that, no matter what happens, you could lose no more than one percent of your account—but I'll discuss that with you in greater detail later on."

After my explanation, Charlie and Rita looked at the list with worried expressions. I assured them that each of the four keys was easy to learn about and work with. I even had some suggestions to help them identify the things they needed to identify with each task. As the conversation wore on, I helped them identify how they might accomplish each task.

As I explained these things, Charlie and Rita looked visibly more relaxed. They told me they no longer felt so intimidated by the endeavor that lay before them. They felt confident that they would develop plans that would suit each of them—strategies for investing to win.

Turning the Four Keys

In the remainder of this chapter I will describe the information an investor would need to identify his or her objectives and thus turn Key 1. Chapters Three and Four will help you understand how to turn Key 2 by choosing a method to read the markets. Toni has some excellent information in Chapter Three about market cycles that you need to hear, and I'll show you a very simple way to identify major changes in market conditions when we get to Chapter Four.

The information for turning Key 3 will require that you learn a bit about analyzing companies and the movement of their stock prices. But don't worry; you don't have to enroll at the Wharton School of

Business to accomplish this. Internet-available resources are a major advantage to the modern investor, and these resources keep getting better over time.

In Chapters Five through Seven, Toni and I will help you understand the resources and methods you can use to identify opportunity. Investing opportunity can be found when individual investors are able to identify the performance of a company and the performance of its stock. A well-run company whose stock is flagging represents a longer-term opportunity.

Toni will explain how you can use technical analysis to identify prices that are on the rise relative to where they have been, and I will show you how you can use fundamental analysis to identify when a company's performance signals that its stock value should increase.

In Chapter Eight, Toni will give you some insight on how to identify potential investments. This information will help you choose from among many powerful exchange-traded funds that can help enhance your investing returns.

After that, in Chapters Nine and Ten, I will suggest GainsMaster-approach strategies that will enable you to address your own investing objectives and incorporate the advantages available to the individual investor. In Chapters Eleven through Thirteen, Toni and I will show you ways to further enhance those strategies and show you how to be prepared for the future, no matter what comes your way.

We know you'll find this an interesting excursion, but all journeys begin with a first step, and that step is to identify your own investing objectives. Let me return to the conversation and share with you what I told Charlie and Rita as I helped them turn Key 1. This was the first step towards developing an investing strategy completely customized to each of them.

Turning Key 1: How to Identify Your Objectives. "Charlie, Rita," I said, "your best place to start is to simply answer one question as carefully as you can. How much loss do you want to avoid?"

"I don't want to lose a penny," Charlie said without hesitation.

"I understand what you mean," I assured him, "but we all know that's not how investing works. Prices go up and down and you have to be patient and tolerate some fluctuation."

"I know it, but I don't like it," Charlie joked. "But go on, I do know what you mean."

"Here is what I have observed working with investors," I said. "Most people are not comfortable with their results if they see their account drop by more than twenty percent. A few panic and move to cash, but most are simply paralyzed. They don't know what to do. One investor I know simply stopped looking at his investing account altogether. He told me couldn't bear to open the monthly statements that came in the mail."

"Oh, yeah. I... uh... had a friend who did that too," Rita said with a wry grin, ducking her head sheepishly.

"Don't feel bad," I said, pulling out a notepad of my own. "That's the kind of thing that happens when you don't know what to do about the market's bad-mood years. But you can fashion a strategy to help you respond, if you identify how much risk you can tolerate. The main point is to make certain that you don't reach that point of panic, or paralysis, in your investments." I began to sketch on the pad. "Let me draw out this table to explain how you can identify where you are on a scale of risk tolerance."

I drew up a table that looked like Table 2.1, shown here.

"Now these are just general guidelines to get you thinking," I explained. Keep in mind that the normal risk tolerance for most people is about twenty percent. If you come up with a higher number than that, you'll want to carefully think about whether you've assessed your risk tolerance correctly."

"By these numbers I would come up with 12 percent," said Charlie. "So that means I won't lose more than 12 percent?"

"That means you'll make the choice to respond if your accounts lose more than 12 percent," I said. "What about you, Rita?"

"I've got 35, but that seems kind of high to me," she said.

"What is more important to you in your investments, whether it grows or whether it doesn't fluctuate very much?" I asked.

Personal Sensitivity	Percentage of Fluctuation to Allow
Time to Retirement Less than 5 Years	
Low	5
Medium	12
High	20
Time to Retirement 5 to 15 Years	
Low	10
Medium	20
High	30
Time to Retirement More than 15 Years	
Low	20
Medium	35
High	50

TABLE 2.1 Suggested levels of risk tolerance.

"That it grows," she said emphatically. "It's far too small to be of much use to me right now."

"Is there any likelihood that you will need the money within the next five to ten years?" I asked to double-check her initial assessment.

"Not that I know of, but even if something came up, I would say it is unlikely we'd need to dip into that money, because Joe's got a separate pension that he is building up as well," Rita offered.

"Sounds good," I said. "In that case, it might be that 35 percent is the right number for you. But don't be afraid to adjust it lower if that makes you feel more comfortable. No one loses money faster than a nervous investor, so it is important that you choose a low enough number to keep your from deviating from the rest of your investing plan."

"OK," said Charlie, "I can see how this would be helpful to know, but how does this help me understand how much gain I am targeting?"

"That's the easy part," I explained. "Simply take half of the amount of fluctuation you've identified, and that's the general range for your anticipated annual investment performance when the markets are in a good mood. When markets are in a bad mood, you still have an expectation of making a gain by the end of the year."

"You're saying there is a way to make your account go up, even when the market is going down?" ask Charlie.

"Certainly, but we're getting ahead of ourselves," I cautioned.

"OK," said Rita, "so what happens next?"

Over the next few hours I worked to teach them about what resources and tools they had available. What follows in the rest of this book includes the information I would share with someone like Charlie or Rita... or you. It also includes the combined insight Toni and I have to share about the markets and the tools available to you. We will revisit the topic of a chosen fluctuation percentage, so be sure to jot it down if you haven't already committed it to memory.

In the next chapter Toni will explain how the markets move in cycles. These cycles can significantly affect the way the market behaves over time. Investors who understand their limits for risk tolerance improve their ability to benefit from the progression of market cycles. Her chapter will help you improve on what you have learned here.

Key Points to Remember

→ Investing is individual.

→ Different investors investing in the same assets can still wind up getting different results over time, because they do not react the same way.

→ Investors need to have clear, simple strategies that suit their own personalities and circumstances.

→ Investors need to turn the four keys of the GainsMaster approach to help them build their best strategies.

→ The first key requires that you identify your objectives: specifically, how much loss you want to avoid while investing.

➜ Half of the amount you want to avoid is a good target for your annual performance. You won't hit it every year, but your investing will also produce some very good years where you will exceed your target.

➜ The other three tasks will be based on the information in the remaining chapters.

PERSONAL GAINS

— Toni —

Success Comes with Single-Purpose Focus

Real glory springs from the silent conquest of ourselves.

—ANONYMOUS

These days, many of us feel as though we're living life in a blur. With technology connecting us to everyone, everywhere, personal boundaries have evaporated. Our cell phones constantly ping and ring with e-mails, texts, phone calls, and voice mails.

Indeed, messages of every kind pepper our nights and weekends with a never-ending stream of communications, many related to work. When was the last time you *really* engaged with a person or group of people—or someone fully engaged with you—without the intrusion of e-mails, texts, instant messaging, or "Give me a sec". Someone's on the other line"? Do you answer e-mails while you're on the phone? Do you make calls while you're driving or send the occasional text?

Yes, it's great to send a quick "I love you" or the more popular "ILY." But constant communication comes with a price. Churning multiple tasks, without fully engaging in any single one, splits your attention. Result? Start and finish lines dissolve, and the series of stutter steps you take to get one thing accomplished adds at least 25 percent more time to your time workload.

Added to that, the inner sense of frustration that you're accomplishing *no one thing* runs through your mind's operating system. Those thoughts sap your energy and increase overload and stress.

If you're multitasking to the point of exhaustion, try this: Each morning before your day begins, identify the day's top priority. Assign a start and stop time for the first hour of the day. Then turn off your cell phone and e-mails and work at this task minus distractions for sixty minutes without stopping. Knowing you have a timeline calms your mind, and you can return messages after that time.

Work in thirty- to ninety-minute chunks throughout the day, and take scheduled breaks to answer messages. You may be amazed at your heightened productivity and energy levels.

Success arrives faster if you work with single-purpose focus. And while you are applying yourself, as someone famous once said, "The world will wait for you."

CHAPTER THREE

The Market in Motion
How the Stock Market Travels Through Time

— Toni —

A s you know, there are no straight lines in nature...
Everything in our known universe moves in cycles. Our moon circles our Earth, while our Earth revolves around the sun. Autumn, winter, spring, and summer rotate through each calendar year, with perfect precision. Swirling tides ebb and flow. Water evaporates from our oceans and lakes, rises into the sky on currents of warm air, and soon falls back to earth once again. As humans, we experience cycles in our lives as we move from birth to puberty, to adulthood, to passing.

Defined as an interval of time during which a set of recurring events are repeated, cycles have been studied and observed by experts in astronomy, biology, cosmology, geology, geophysics, history, music, society, commodities, and economics.

Indeed, cycles format our world's operating system. In the financial markets, cycles were first observed in the commodities markets; traders noticed the prices of agricultural products rose and then fell, at roughly the same times, each year. Of course, those price patterns matched seasonal changes in weather, so the cyclical movement made sense then—and now.

Analyze Your Opportunities—
The Ever-Changing View from Above

Imagine that you could observe the stock market's total value from an astronaut's vantage point, high in the sky. Looking down through the clouds, the market's terrain would spread below you in deserts, foothills, mountains, cliffs, peaks, and valleys of continuous rolling action.

Just so, economic conditions in industrialized countries rotate between expansions ("booms") and contractions ("busts," recessions, depressions). We call this rotation the "business cycle."

Its buddy, the "stock market cycle," runs ahead of the business cycle by approximately six to nine months. Why does the stock market cycle trot in front of the business cycle? Because—and please remember this always—*the stock market is a forward-looking vehicle.*

In Figure 3.1, you can see a graph of how the business and stock market cycles travel through time.

During boom times, we enjoy periods of growth fueled by high demand for goods and services. Companies flourish, so they buy more capital equipment and hire more people. Unemployment rates

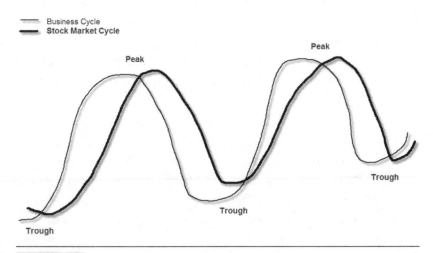

FIGURE 3.1   **Business and stock market cycles.**

fall. People have money to buy "discretionary goods," such as home–improvements, cars, and cruise vacations. Boom times, or expansions, typically last approximately 40–48 months, or up to four years.

HOT TIP

Stock prices move according to future expectations of price movement.

Typically, during the initial stages of expanding economies, interest rates remain low. Interest rates can be defined as "the cost of money." Cheap money induces companies to borrow, so they can purchase more efficient machinery and technology in order to produce more goods and services. Result? They earn more, and higher earnings buoy the price of their stock. Low interest rates also encourage consumers to buy more. Low interest rates mean lower house payments, car payments, and credit-card payments.

Still, all good parties eventually come to an end. And, perhaps you've guessed by now, this is where the "cycle" part comes in. Or, what goes up must come down.

To a greater or lesser degree, economic "booms" are followed by "busts." Think of a big rubber balloon, filled with air. Someone comes along and sticks a small pin into the balloon. It may not deflate all at once, but if that person continues to puncture it, creating a series of pinholes, sooner or later the balloon will shrink. Think: economic contraction.

"Pins" that puncture our economic expansion arrive in many forms. Chief among them is inflation. Defined as the "rising cost of goods and services," inflation can be caused by too much money

HOT TIP

"Economics studies the consequences of the decisions that are made about the use of land, labor, capital and other resources that go into producing the volume of output which determines a country's standard of living" (Thomas Sowell, *Basic Economics*, Third Edition, New York: Basic Books, 2007, p. 2).

chasing too few goods. Remember how much we enjoyed buying homes, cars, and vacations in the rising economy? As we continued that consumer party (expanding balloon), the companies providing those goods and services raised their prices. Result: inflation.

Additional sharp pins that stick holes in our economy and the financial markets can arrive with little or no warning and are known as "exogenous shocks." Economists describe exogenous shocks as disruptive events that cause economic impacts. Examples are wars, pandemics, and financial- and weather-related disasters. The fall of Lehman Brothers (September 2008), the BP oil spill (April 2010), Japan's major tsunami (March 2011), Singapore's ruinous floods (2010–2012)—all of those events disrupted thousands of lives and had an effect on businesses and the global supply chain.

If enough pins puncture holes in our economic balloon, it starts to deflate, or contract. During these economic contractions, we consumers curtail our purchases. To urge us to spend, many companies lower the prices of their goods and services. That causes them to cut down on purchases of capital equipment, and to lay off employees. Of course, when their revenue from sales drops, it lowers their earnings. Lower earnings result in lower stock prices.

These contractions, or busts—which can lead to recessions and even depressions—roll through an average of eleven months. (Nice to know, isn't it, that the expansions last longer than the contractions? That's why we say that the stock market has an upward bias.)

As the steward of your portfolio, you can take one glance at the diagram in Figure 3.1 and instantly know that, as a smart investor, you'll want to enter new stock positions

> **HOT TIP**
>
> The U.S. presidential cycles move in four-year increments and can influence the curve of the stock market cycle.

during the rising action (expansions), rather than at the peaks (market tops) or during the falling action (contractions).

Now, let's talk about the up-moves and down-moves that shape the cycles and the "beasts" that drive the action. Figure 3.2 displays

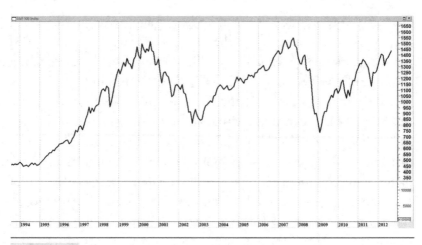

FIGURE 3.2   The S&P 500 Index 1995–2012 displays the cyclical nature of the U.S. stock market.

an eighteen-year chart of the S&P 500 Index, a key benchmark for the U.S. stock market.

Note the cycles that the S&P 500 Index etched through the past eighteen years. Observe how it rushed higher (expanded), and then tumbled lower (contracted). Now you can clearly see how the stock market's cycles evolve, creating valleys and peaks, through time.

See the two peaks in 2000 and 2007? The price paths from those peaks, or "mountain tops," reversed their upward courses and then dove at deep downward angles, taking most stock prices with them. That's why Gordon and I advise you to use protective stops, or manage your risk, on your account positions. Again, you can see that the ride up the mountain is fun and profitable, but the ride down can be detrimental to your wealth.

The Natures of the Beasts

In the late 1700s, the southern tip of the island of Manhattan (New York) was mainly farmland, inhabited by horses, cows, and pigs.

The American Revolutionary War ended in 1783. In 1789, the new United States Congress issued approximately $80 million in government notes. These notes, along with additional bonds, stocks, and orders for commodities and warehouse receipts, were sold to the public, creating an exciting new market.

Many investors helped fund new U.S. companies by purchasing shares of ownership, for which the companies issued stock certificates. The certificates proved the investors' equity ownership, and so secured the debt.

In New York City, traders gathered each weekday under the buttonwood and sycamore trees at 68-70 Wall Street to buy and sell these securities. By 1827, the Merchants Exchange building, erected at Wall and Hanover streets, housed the New York Stock and Exchange Board (now the NYSE Euronext). By 1842, the New York Curb Exchange (later the American Stock Exchange, now the NYSE Amex) opened its doors. Both exchanges enforced strict rules governing the sale of stocks, and Wall Street began its evolution into the center of the global financial markets.

New York City and the Wall Street financial district soon swallowed the farmland, but references to animals remained: bulls, bears, pigs, and sheep. An old market saying goes, "Bulls make money, and bears make money, but pigs get slaughtered."

Bulls attack their opponents by striking up with their horns. So, if you are a "bull," or are feeling "bullish," you believe the stock market will rise. You buy equities and hold them in anticipation of their value increasing.

Bears go after their prey by striking down with their paws. If you are a "bear," or feeling "bearish," you speculate that the market will fall and stocks will diminish in value. Therefore, you're a seller.

It follows that we call rising markets "bull markets" and falling markets "bear markets." When the market climbs 20 percent or more from a major low point for a sustained period of time, we refer to it as a bull market. On the flip side, when the market falls 20 percent from a peak for a prolonged period of time, we call it a bear market.

Who are the "pigs"? You guessed it. Pigs are greedy gluttons who gorge on big, risky positions, with no thought to their objectives or risk management. When the market turns against them, the squealing pigs inevitably get slaughtered.

Sheep follow anybody with a tambourine. If you hear a market guru on one of the financial networks say, "Buy Whizzy Widgets—it's going to the moon!" you know the sheep will buy like crazy without doing their homework. Problem is, when the market reverses and threatens to mow them down, the poor bleating sheep don't know enough about Whizzy to make an effective sell or hold decision. Thus, their accounts get shorn.

> **HOT TIP**
>
> When the market slides 10 percent from its previous high, we also refer to that move as a "correction."

Where you come in: You can see from the chart in Figure 3.2, and you've learned from our prior explanation, that bulls can hold the reins for at least four years at a stretch. During bull markets, you—the savvy investor—will want to strap on your bull horns and stay in the market as long as market values continues to expand. Naturally, bull markets are the easiest times to earn profits.

When a bear market rears its ugly head, Gordon and I see no glory in riding it down to its depths. In the best interests of risk management, we advise that you place protective stops with your broker for each position you maintain in your portfolio. We will show you how to establish those stops in upcoming chapters. The important thing is to *keep the profits you earn in a bull market.* Then, unlike uninformed investors, you won't stand helpless and slack-jawed, watching your positions lose value in bear markets. Instead, you'll simply wait comfortably on the sidelines until high-potential opportunities once again present themselves.

We'll show you several ways to identify, on any given day, who is holding the reins, the bulls or the bears. Then you can assess your opportunities, analyze your risk, and plan to take action with a commonsense plan.

Dueling Market Rulers— Who They Are, How They Move Markets

The absolute rulers of the financial markets are greed and fear. If you think about it, sooner or later, these two titans of emotion involve themselves in nearly every situation or event you can think of.

Greed and fear have ruled the global financial markets from day one. And that's OK. Without these emotions, prices would not move, and profits would not be pocketed.

Bull markets represent greed in motion, and all the variations we can think of, from optimism to euphoria. Optimism, hope, greed, and euphoria drive the markets higher. The more passionately we humans want to own a certain item, the higher a price we are willing to pay.

Bear markets arrive on the back of fear. When the bulls in an extended rising market party too hearty, the neighbors (think *bears*) call the cops. As the sirens approach in the form of increasing volatility, the anxious bulls start to scatter. Smelling the bulls' vulnerability, the bears approach. Snarling and ready to fight, they soon shred the bulls' party site. Ugly headlines blare, the earth shakes, prices wobble. The bulls' anxiety deepens to fear. Fear grows into panic. The remaining bulls run from the party, selling everything they can to lighten their loads.

You, the wise investor, will recognize the emotions in play during different time periods. You will not succumb to them; rather, you will use them to your advantage. Cool and confident, you will recognize the ultimate greed factor, *euphoria,* as a potential time to take gains from winning positions. You identify panic-driven markets as a great time to research for upcoming opportunities, rich with promise. Then you wait until the perfect entry presents itself. No greed or fear here. Instead, you'll act from a well-thought-out plan that matches up with the market's machinations.

Emotion in Motion: Demand and Supply

Say your favorite band, the Rockin' Rascals, is coming to your town this weekend. The local stadium, where they will perform on Saturday night, is nearly sold out. You just found out about the event, and you are frantic to get tickets.

You call the stadium box office. "I'd like two tickets to see the Rockin' Rascals please."

"Sure," a rushed voice replies. "We have two seats left in the E section. Which credit card do you want to use? American Express, Visa, MasterCard, or Discover?"

"Hold it," you say. You've been to plenty of games and performances at the stadium. You know that the E section seats are the worst—the last row in the top bleachers. "Don't you have anything better?"

"Nope. And I've got other calls coming in. Can I put you on hold?"

"Not yet, please. How much are the E section tickets?"

"Eighty-nine per person."

Your jaw drops. "*What?* You've got to be kidding!"

"Nope. That's the price. Can you hold?"

"Wait a minute. Surely you've got other seats that cost less."

"Nope. That's it. These are the only two left in the stadium. Look, if you want to find a scalper for some tickets closer to the stage, take your best shot. But you'll pay even more—through the nose. As for these two tickets, you gotta' take 'em or leave 'em now." *Buzz, buzz.* "I got more lines ringin'. People want these seats. What's it gonna be?"

You groan inwardly. You've wanted for years to see this band live. You've heard this could be their last year performing. If you don't pay up, you might never have this opportunity again. "OK, OK. I'll take them. Here's my credit card number…"

Human nature is such that we want things of which few exist, and we shrug off things of which there are many. To that end, demand and supply influence our emotions… greed and fear… and all the shadings in between.

Just as a dwindling supply of tickets to a concert can cause us to pay higher prices than we would normally pay, the shortage of an attractive stock at low prices causes investors to pay a higher price for it (greed). Those who already own the stock can demand higher prices, because the prevailing belief is that the value will rise. That means few people are selling. Result? The demand is higher than the supply. Of course, those who buy the stock are convinced it will continue to rise in price, or expand in value, into the future.

Now, if a local band that plays regularly at the stadium (ample supply) schedules a performance, chances are that tickets are reasonably priced. Why, you might even purchase good seats at the door on the night of the event. These tickets are in abundant supply and demand is low. Sellers (ticket office and scalpers) cannot demand higher prices than the going rate.

When market bulls perceive that a stock they are holding will not rise in value in the future, they may sell it (fear). For the stock's price to remain steady at current levels, demand must absorb the supply of shares coming into the market.

If, however, supply overwhelms demand, then those who hold the stock and fear its value may shrink must offer it out at a lower price to attract buyers; they have to offer their shares at "sale" prices. Alarm that the stock's price will crumble even further drives sellers to dump more and more shares (supply) on the market. Lower prices continue until new buyers appear to soak up the supply.

How We Measure the Markets— The Major Indexes

OK, if you're not familiar with stock market lingo, you may be thinking, "When you refer to the *market*, what is your measurement?"

Three leading indexes of the U.S. stock market represent the economic barometers of note. Referred to in every major newspaper and Internet browser home page, recited by radio news announcers, and covered by major news networks, these indexes make the global headlines.

The Dow Jones Industrial Average, or the "Dow," as we call it, is the most quoted group of stocks in the world. In fact, if someone remarks to you, "The market shot higher today," that person is probably referring to the Dow's movement.

The oldest of the indexes, the Dow was originated by Charles Dow in 1896. (Charles Dow was also the founder of the *Wall Street Journal*.) Originally containing just twelve stocks, now thirty reigning aristocrats of United States industry comprise this average. You may recognize the names instantly, including AT&T (T), Coca-Cola Co. (KO), International Business Machines (IBM), and Microsoft (MSFT).

The Dow is a price-weighted index. That means the component sporting the most expensive price-per-share weighs in more heavily than the least expensive shares. At present, IBM boasts the priciest shares on the Dow. When that technology titan leaps higher, it nudges the Dow higher, as well.

HOT TIP

General Electric Co. (GE) is the only company remaining in the Dow Jones Industrial Average since its inception in 1896.

Those of us who eat, sleep, and breathe market action, however, think and talk about the "the market" in terms of the S&P 500 Index. The "S&P" is generally considered to be a major benchmark for the U.S. stock market. Market players also refer to it as "the broader index."

Created in 1957 by financial services company Standard & Poor's, this index contains stocks that represent the leading five hundred publicly traded companies based in the United States (The S&P 500 Index now includes a few U.S. companies that have reincorporated outside the United States.) These companies represent a broad swath of economic sectors, including energy, industrial, financial, utilities, consumer discretionary, consumer staples, health care, and basic materials. The index includes companies regarded as common household names, such as Wells Fargo & Co. (WFC), McDonalds Corp. (MCD), and Procter & Gamble Co. (PG).

The S&P 500 Index is a market capitalization—or "market cap"—weighted index. That means the companies are weighted in the index based on their size, rather than their share price. Here's how we measure a company's market cap: *number of stock shares outstanding multiplied by current share price.* ("Shares outstanding" means the shares of a corporation's stock that have been publicly issued into the hands of the public.)

Let's use the General Electric Co. (GE) as an example. Currently, GE has 10.6 billion shares of common stock on the market. The price per share is $20.07. (10.6 billion x $20.07 = $212.3 billion.) So, GE's current market cap is $212.3 billion. Of course, it not only sits on the Dow, the giant, multi-industrial GE is also a component of the S&P 500 Index and other key indexes.

Other key indexes shine in the spotlight during the trading day, including the Nasdaq Composite. This composite is constructed from the more than 5,000 securities listed on the NASDAQ, the second-largest stock exchange in the world behind the NYSE Euronext. Founded in 1971, the NASDAQ stands for "National Association of Securities Dealers Automated Quotations" and is an entirely electronic exchange.

Like the S&P 500 Index, the Nasdaq Composite is market cap-weighted, so index fluctuations depend on moves of the biggest companies represented in the index. In the Composite, technology companies hold sway. You'll hear talking heads on financial news networks referring to it as "the tech-heavy index."

The Nasdaq 100 contains one hundred of the biggest (by market cap) of the Composite's non-financial companies; this index is also market-cap weighted. You know these names—Apple (AAPL), Intel Corp. (INTC), and Google Inc. (GOOG).

Each of the major indexes we just discussed represents a somewhat different slice of the U.S. equities pie. As a smart investor, you'll stay aware

> **HOT TIP**
>
> As long as they meet index criteria, companies can appear on more than one major index.

of the general movements of Dow and the S&P 500 Index. Those who invest in technology stocks will naturally tune into the ups and downs of Nasdaq Composite or Nasdaq 100.

The Dow, S&P 500, Nasdaq Composite, and Nasdaq 100 indexes are considered to be the market's most important indexes. Many more indexes exist, however, that target specific sections of the U.S. stock market. Some people follow the Russell 2000, which lists 2000 small-cap stocks. The S&P Mid-Cap 400 lists mid-caps, and so forth.

"OK," you say. "I get the picture. Stock prices move up and down in cycles. Bull markets go up; bear markets go down." *Yawn.* "But why do I care about which direction the major indexes go?"

You care because in a bull market, three out of five equities will follow the S&P 500 higher. In a bear market, four out of five stocks will follow the S&P 500 lower. Consequently, when our economy is expanding, interest rates are low, and money is plentiful, your stocks—if well-chosen—will surely gain in value along with this U.S. stock market benchmark.

But what if one of those exogenous shocks we mentioned earlier arrives unexpectedly and smacks the market upside the head? In order to preserve your profits, you'll want to manage your risk by checking the placement of your protective stops. To that end, you'll want to keep an eye on the S&P 500 from time to time, and note whether it is rising in a healthy advance or skidding lower. You'll be glad you did.

Now please stay tuned. In Chapter Four, Gordon is going to take your ability to read the market's mood and manner to a higher level. He will show you one key indicator and two confirming indicators that will help give you clues to potential upcoming moves. He will also introduce our GO and STOP signals that tell you when to consider buying stocks and ETFs and when to move to safe havens, or even the sidelines. Enjoy!

Key Points to Remember

→ Cycles are defined as intervals of time during which a set of recurring events is repeated.

→ Cycles appear in a wide range of studies and subjects throughout our society.

→ Cycles in the financial markets were first noted in the commodities space, as the price of grains rose and fell with the seasons.

→ The economies of industrialized nations alternately expand and contract.

→ As a forward-looking vehicle, the stock market cycle typically moves ahead of the business cycle by six to nine months.

→ Market "bulls" believe the market will rise from current levels. "Bears" think the market will fall from current levels.

→ A bull market can be described as one in which major indexes have risen 20 percent or more from recent lows. A bear market refers to the time when the major indexes have fallen 20 percent or more from their highs.

→ The Dow Jones Industrial Average includes thirty of the largest and most prestigious titans of United States industry. The index is price-weighted; the most expensive equities in the index carry the most weight.

→ The S&P 500 Index contains five hundred of the largest U.S. companies by market capitalization. The index blankets a wide swath of sectors that serve the U.S. and global economies. It is sometimes referred to as "the broad market."

→ The Nasdaq Composite contains the equities listed on the NAS-DAQ stock exchange, which number about 5,000.

→ The Nasdaq 100 Index holds the top one hundred non-financial stocks in the Nasdaq Composite, ranked by market capitalization.

→ In bull markets, three out of five stocks follow the S&P 500 Index higher. In market downturns, four out of five equities follow the index lower.

PERSONAL GAINS

Toni

Personal Beliefs Dictate the Directions of Our Lives

When your self-worth goes up, your net worth goes up with it.

—MARK VICTOR HANSEN

Deep below our conscious streams of thought flow the strata of our personal beliefs systems. These belief systems "pull our strings," and direct us to make decisions that influence our lives.

We can compare our network of personal belief systems to our computer's operating system. Microsoft Windows or other such systems operate unseen, supporting the programs we use every day. Let Windows malfunction, though, and our computer will "crash," causing all kinds of mayhem in our business and personal activities.

Just so, our personal beliefs function as invisible—but powerful—forces in our lives. These belief systems form the opinions we have of ourselves. In fact, many decisions we make in our outer lives are based on our personal beliefs and our unconscious desires to fulfill them.

We acquire most of these beliefs in childhood. Did an authority figure tell you that you were smart, honest, and could achieve any goal you pursued? If you chose to believe those statements, you surely display those characteristics today. On the other hand, did an adult tell you that you were lazy, sloppy, or undeserving of good things? If so, it's possible you unconsciously carried those beliefs into your adulthood. Now they lay silent—but not dormant—potentially sabotaging decisions you make and actions you take.

All of us need to "defrag" or de-clutter our personal belief systems on a regular basis. If you like, call this process "mental spring cleaning." Go to a quiet place where you won't be interrupted and sort through the thought processes from which you've been operating. Can you pinpoint thoughts or beliefs you carry through each day that limit your success? Are you dwelling on scarcity, unproductiveness, or low self-esteem? Know that these mindsets do not serve you now and never did. Replace them with statements of prosperity, competence, and confidence.

Next, take a few minutes each morning to review your new positive statements. Each time you catch yourself thinking the "old" thoughts, replace them with the new ones.

When your new personal belief systems take hold, they will redirect your life into a more positive spin, and you can move ahead more easily on your journey toward success.

CHAPTER FOUR

Reading the Market's Mood

— Gordon —

THE STOCK market moves in trends. As Toni explained in Chapter Three, it goes up for a while, and then it goes down for a while. That idea is an observable fact that drives many an investor to attempt making a profit. When investors see prices rise, they hope that the trend will continue. Several times over the past century stock prices have shown the tendency to rise for a longer period of time than they fall.

Just what causes the prices to trend one way or another? Over the years many experts have spent considerable time and resources trying to answer that question, and yet disagreement remains. Here is the point of view I take to help me work with price trends. I believe that underlying all other rationales and calculations about pricing models, the biggest reason prices trend is that a majority of investors have adopted one of two attitudes towards the market: they decide to seek *opportunity* or to seek *safety.*

This is the central insight for turning the second GainsMaster key: evaluating market conditions. When a majority of investors begin to seek either safety or opportunity, they create particular conditions in the market. Those conditions imply that markets will trend either upward or downward for a while longer. That is the big secret, nothing more.

Now I know that some may complain that such a "secret" is obvious. They may insist that the true cause and effect of price changes is deeper than that. Perhaps they will insist that price changes must be modeled with complex mathematical formulae. But since not all investors know or believe the same things about the market, any deeply complex formula for determining investment trends will be a gross approximation at best. I think there is a simpler approach—one with significant value to the individual investor pressed for time in her busy life.

It begins with looking at how other investors naturally behave. Studies show that the average investor prefers to keep his allocations in stocks for about three years or so (Research and Communications Division, *2010 Quantitative Analysis of Investor Behavior,* Boston: DALBAR, Inc., 2010). Recognizing changes early in such periods of investor preference enables me to anticipate that trends will continue as investors cling to their opinions for two to three years longer. If I can interpret simple price data to tell me whether investors have made a recent change toward preferring opportunity or safety, then isn't it reasonable to assume that I can identify what the overall market conditions are likely to be for the next two or three years? My experience suggests that this assumption has merit.

After working with over one thousand individual investors one-on-one, I developed and refined a simple method you can use to better anticipate market trends. I call it reading the market's mood.

Turning Key 2: Evaluating Market Conditions by Reading the Market's Mood

All you need to do to read the market's mood is check three indicators once a month. In fact, for most months you will only need to watch one. To watch the first indicator, you need to read the market's price activity compared to its average. This might sound tedious, but it doesn't have to be. Nowadays charting software makes this very easy by displaying the moving average as a line that follows along above or below the price. When market prices cross that average line, however, you need to look at the next two indicators to confirm whether a major trend change is under way. The two additional indicators are first, volatility, and second, safety-seeking behavior.

Once you can read these indicators, then you can understand that the market's mood will generate what I call GO and STOP signs. I'll be explaining these signs throughout this chapter and also explaining in later chapters how to use these signs.

I am often asked how to tell the difference between a short-term drop in prices and a large-scale change of the market's trend. I admit that, early on in those price movements, it is hard to tell the difference. But that's why I developed the method in this chapter to help myself, and others, have an effective way to read the markets well enough to know the difference. It is my hope that, by knowing how to read the market's mood, you will be able to answer that question for yourself and know what to do about it. When you know how to identify these signs created by the three indicators, you will then be prepared to act on them in a way that will enhance your returns.

When the Market Shows GO and STOP Signs

The market's mood identifies whether investors are interested in taking on risk. I like to say that at such times investors are seeking growth and opportunity. I use these words to make the first acronym, GO, which describes when the market is in an optimistic mood—a mood to take on new risk. When the market is ready for risk, it shows the GO sign.

The other kind of signal identifies when investors prefer to seek safe places for their money. I like to use the STOP acronym to remind me that the market wants safety trades only, please! When the market is in a pessimistic mood, it shows the characteristics of preferring safety over risk. When the market wants more safety than risk, it shows the STOP sign.

To identify these signs, however, you will need to review the indicators I referred to earlier: the average, the volatility, and the safety behavior. Let's discuss each of these indicators one at a time.

Indicator 1: The Twelve-Month Moving Average

The first indicator is the average price. When you think of creating an average out of a collection of numbers, you probably think of adding them all up and doing some division. But with stock market prices, it gets a bit trickier. Price changes take place over time, so instead of a single number for the average, you get a changing number from one day to the next. This changing number is called a moving average.

Toni will explain more about moving averages in the next chapter, but for now it's enough for you to know that a moving average is represented by a line on a chart. The line moves up and down, tagging along behind the market's own price like an ever-faithful golf caddy. Sometimes it catches up to the player, but more often than not it lags behind.

Let's look at how the moving average is represented on a chart of stock prices. For this example we will use the closing prices of the S&P 500 index and display them as a line chart. What that means is that we are going to look at the last published price for each month and simply connect the dots with a line. While it is true that the market prices travel higher and lower within the month, the only price we are concerned with in this activity is the final price each month.

I'll show you two figures—first the market price graph by itself, and second, the same price graph with a moving average applied. Figure 4.1 maps the connection between the closing prices of the S&P 500 for each month. Figure 4.2 is that same chart, but with the moving average added in.

Notice how Figure 4.2 depicts the moving average—the tagalong caddy so to speak—as a much smoother line. The line moves in an offset manner, lower than the line of stock prices during uptrends, but higher than the stock prices during downtrends. This particular

FIGURE 4.1   S&P 500 monthly chart of closing prices.

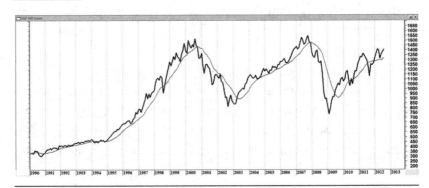

FIGURE 4.2   S&P 500 with twelve-month moving average.

moving-average line tracks the average price over the previous twelve months, so it represents a one-year moving average of monthly prices.

I find this to be a very useful indicator. If you look closely at the chart, you will notice that when the market price crosses over this moving average, a trend change often follows. In the past ten years, this indicator has been extremely useful in helping investors recognize when market conditions have changed.

Now it is true that markets behave differently over time. What happens in the past is never a perfect roadmap for what will happen in the future. After years of study on the subject, I have yet to come across any indicator that is perfectly and profitably right. However, an indicator doesn't have to be perfect in order to be useful.

If you study the historic monthly closing prices of the S&P 500 compared to the twelve-month moving-average line of those prices, you find some interesting details. Since 1928 this indicator has identified a change in trend roughly 60 percent of the time. The other 40 percent were occasions where the price crossed over the moving average, only to cross back over in the opposite direction in the next month or two. What makes this indicator worth your attention is how well it identifies the really big moments when it is important to be right. As you can see in Figure 4.3, the prices cross the moving average line cleanly in four distinct turning points. Knowing about this signal would have enabled you to respond in a timely manner.

The four arrows in this figure point out the key turning-point moments over the last decade. Notice how the price closes below the moving average line just at the top of the market trend in the year 2000, right at a time when so many were willing to say that "this time it's different" in the investing world. Remember how the onset of the Internet made everyone feel as though this moment in history was a really big deal? It was a big deal! The Internet is the single biggest technological boon to investors ever, and as Toni noted in the prior chapter, it has been recognized as a positive exogenous shock. But that doesn't mean investors can't get ahead of themselves. When the market seemed to decide that enough was too much, investors sought safety instead of opportunity and pulled their money back from the

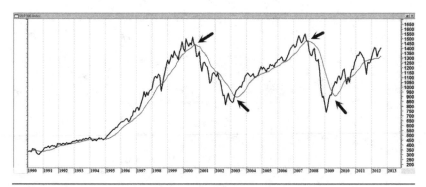

FIGURE 4.3   Four key turning points where the closing prices of the S&P 500 cross over the twelve-month moving average.

markets. When the price crossed the moving average, it was an indicator that a sea change of thought was about to wash over investors.
Boy, did it ever!

Three more signals followed. Later on, at the bottom of the downturn in 2003, the price crossed the moving average again, signaling
a moment in time when the trend reversed and began moving up.
In 2007, as the subprime mortgage crisis was beginning to unravel,
prices crossed the moving average again to signal investor flight to
safety. By 2009 that flight had slowed. When prices crossed the moving average during that year, it marked a moment when investors
began to seek opportunity once more.

The twelve-month moving average indicator is an easy-to-see,
easy-to-understand signal that can alert investors when market trends
are about to change. However, when used all by itself, this indicator
has limitations. In Figure 4.4 you can see that there are three other
times where the indicator made a whipsaw move—it began to change
trend and rapidly realigned with the original trend.

These exceptions to the rule make it clear that signal watchers
need to do a little more evaluation. How could you tell that in 1998
the markets would get over a rapid decline and continue higher? How
could investors know that the unprecedented one-day price swing in
2010—the so-called flash crash—would eventually amount to very
little, and could effectively be ignored? To get a better idea of how

FIGURE 4.4   Three exceptions where a cross of the twelve-month average
did not lead to a trend change.

to evaluate each signal, investors need just a bit more information. That's why I use two additional indicators to help myself read the market's mood: volatility and safety-seeking behavior.

Indicator 2: Volatility

Volatility is the normal fluctuation of prices. Prices move up and down every day—sometimes at random it may seem. But how *much* they move up or down is the measure we call volatility. Reading volatility enables you to collect more information about the market's mood.

Occasionally I have someone ask me why they need to understand how to measure volatility. The answer to that question brings out a story. Reading these measures is a lot like tracking the footprints of an invisible man as you and he are walking in the forest. Imagine that you are walking along immediately behind him and seeing the tracks immediately after he makes them. You can't see or communicate with this man. You can only know where he has already walked. We'll call this invisible man's path "Trend One."

Now imagine that as you follow his footprints an abrupt change occurs—his tracks begin to move in another direction. We'll call this direction "Trend Two." Looking only at the tracks alone, you might not be able to identify *why* the he changed course. But the *why* is important for anticipating whether his tracks will continue along Trend Two or resume Trend One. Imagine, for example, that after the first two or three steps in the new direction, you could look around and see where the man was heading. No doubt the added information could make a big difference in the way you perceive the abrupt change.

To further extend the analogy, imagine that you did look around and that you noticed a woman nearby holding a map. (About now you may be thinking that this fantasy is illogical. After all, what man would actually stop to ask for directions? But stay with me and forgive the humor; there's an important point I'm about to make!)

If you could perceive that the man was making a temporary diversion, perhaps to reassure his inner doubts in unfamiliar surroundings, then you could probably anticipate that the man would return to his former journey on Trend One. Extending this analogy further still, suppose that he lingered near the woman. Isn't it true that the longer he remained there, the more you would begin to anticipate that he would not resume Trend One after all?

Finally, imagine that the tracks suddenly took off in the direction of Trend Two. Not only did his tracks continue the change, but they distinctly spread apart as they go. The man is running! You ask yourself why? You look around and don't see anything ahead that he appears to be running towards, but looking back, you see a charging bear! Under these circumstances it is easy to anticipate that his new trend will likely continue for a while longer.

We can't see a precise identification of all the investors in the market, and we can't always know what they are thinking. But if we look around and watch for details, we can get a good idea of whether to anticipate that a trend change may continue or not.

Volatility helps identify whether investors merely want reassurance or if they are fully panicked. Just like the invisible man's footprints spread out when he is running, market prices move down more rapidly when investors are scared. Even so, not all investors get scared at the same time. When those ready to panic early start selling, there are always others eager to buy up the new, lower-priced shares they see, thinking that they are going to get a bargain.

These dynamics create volatility. Rising volatility is an excellent sign that the market is in the process of changing its mood. As a part of this change in mood, the market's price activity will become notably different from its recent past. In the previous chapter, Toni reminded us that markets are ruled by greed and fear. What most investors don't know is how these emotions can be measured in the price action of the market. Like the tracking analogy, it isn't just the direction; it is also the speed with which the market moves.

Now remember that the market's mood is the collective attitude its participants have about seeking either opportunity or safety. The wonderful thing about the market is that words alone have no effect on prices. In the final analysis, headlines don't matter. Prices change only when investors stop talking and start acting. Any movement of price means someone made a decision. So if we carefully measure the movement and volatility of prices, we can find an opportunity to profit from these potent emotional influences.

The market frequently signals a coming change in its trend by first displaying a change in volatility. This volatility is something I like to refer to as the disagreement between buyers and sellers. Buyers think the price should go higher but sellers thinks it should go lower. This dynamic increases the volatility in the markets. Now when volatility begins to grow, it doesn't necessarily change the trend of prices. This happens in part because it takes a period of time for information to spread and disagreement to grow. The disagreement must spread far enough that a significant portion of market participants change their views of the future and begin acting on them.

Measuring volatility. The measure of disagreement between investors can be quantified by measuring the difference in price between the highest and lowest prices traded in a given time period. It is even more useful to take an average of this measure over a period of time. In the days before personal computing and Internet data feeds, people who actually tried to track this information spent a lot of time burning through pencils, paper, and erasers to be able to measure this information.

HOT TIP

Most charting tools offered by brokerages have a way to display the Average True Range on a monthly chart. While there are also a few free websites that track the Average True Range, most of them don't. Serious investors and traders will find the Average True Range in charting software such as Metastock, published by Equis International. This is the software Toni and I have used to create charting graphics for this book.

This is yet another advantage for the modern investor. Technology has made it far easier to track such data. Reading volatility is as simple as following a line that measures the "Average True Range," or ATR. The stock market shows a remarkable rise in the difference between its highest and lowest prices just before it peaks. The ATR picks this up. It shows the evidence of rising disagreement between buyers and sellers.

When investors are nervous or panicked, their fear-based actions create rapid and volatile price changes. But as these investors settle down, their fear subsides, and the volatility abates. Thus, as investors begin to seek opportunity, the volatility reduces. This often signals the beginning of an upward trend in prices. Once you understand what you are looking for, it is simple to recognize it when looking at price charts. Let me show you some examples of how you could recognize a change in volatility to help you anticipate a change in the trend of prices. The following charts will compare the movement of prices and the Average True Range of those prices.

Examples of volatility change. Let me show you an example of volatility change: the top of the market in the year 2000. This change in the markets is quite easy to see in hindsight, but at the time, it caught many people by surprise (see Figure 4.5).

This chart clearly illustrates the concept of how volatility increases as prices rise towards a top. The top line graphs the S&P 500's closing price at the end of each month from November 1991 to March 2001. You can see that the price is trending upward, and so is the ATR. The rise in ATR preceded the peak in prices by at least three years. That gave the average investor plenty of time to get prepared! But that isn't the only thing you should notice on this chart.

At first glance, you might miss the subtle changes in the chart that occur in the year 1997. Look closely, and you'll notice how the ATR was dropping slightly from 1991 to 1995. In 1996 it rose, but in 1997 the ATR made an even more rapid rise. Prices didn't reach their peak for a long time, but the change marked an important difference beginning in that year. From the end of 1991 to late 1997, the mar-

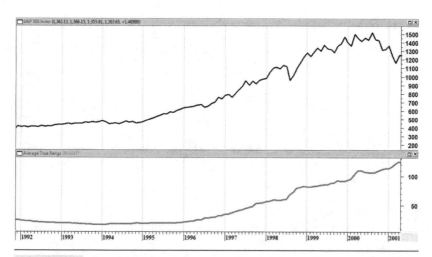

FIGURE 4.5 How the S&P 500 displays greater volatility—more disagreement between buyers and sellers—as the market rises to a peak in prices in the year 2000.

ket was rising without becoming significantly more volatile. Then in 1998 the market's mood began to change. The level of disagreement between buyers and sellers began to increase. That's when the ATR's rise seems to shift gears and the chart shows a more jagged appearance.

It is worthy of note that Alan Greenspan, then Chairman of the U.S. Federal Reserve Bank, remarked in a speech he made at the end of 1996 that the markets were showing "irrational exuberance." It wasn't too long after that when the level of disagreement between buyers and sellers (as evidenced by the ATR) increased significantly. Two years later, the trend in prices changed, and investors experienced something they had not seen in decades—a bear market. What happens next can be seen in Figure 4.6.

Now notice how the ATR begins to decline significantly in 2002. Just about the time most investors have panicked and pulled out of the market, the level of disagreement makes its second notable drop. During the middle of 2003, the ATR fell rapidly, even as prices began to rise. This marked a time when the market mood had shifted again and investors could begin to seek opportunity once more.

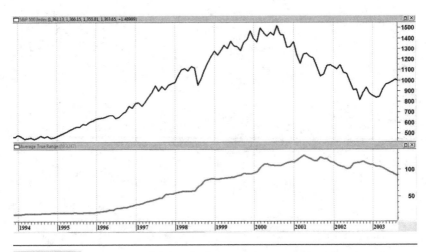

FIGURE 4.6   How the S&P 500 continues to decline in volatility as the market changes trend from bearish to bullish.

Upward trending prices occur in the stock market when the majority of market participants agree that they want to invest their money in stocks and keep it there. This consensus naturally leads to less volatile price activity. When you understand this idea, it becomes easier to see why a decrease in volatility will signal the change in price trend from falling prices to rising prices. Once you know what to look for, then it becomes easier to spot this pattern. Consider two examples that occur in 2007 and 2009, respectively, as shown in Figure 4.7.

I hope that these figures have shown you some examples of how volatility changes confirm the possibility of price-trend changes. Yet while it is important for investors to observe changes in volatility, by itself that indicator is not enough to pinpoint a trend change. To help with this, you need a third indicator, something I call safety-seeking behavior. To understand this indicator, it helps to know about a repeating sequence of events that occurs in the markets. The sequence follows this general pattern: an increasing number of market participants first become uncomfortable and second act on that discomfort by changing their investment strategy.

When market participants begin to disagree about keeping their money in stocks, these two things repeatedly happen: first, prices

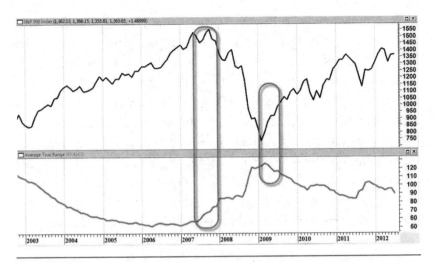

FIGURE 4.7 Two more examples of volatility change at the beginning of a trend change, first in the peak of 2007 and then in the bottoming of the bear market in 2009.

become more volatile; second, market participants take their money out of stocks and commit it somewhere else. Now they could put their money in any number of possible places, but when they specifically choose a place calculated to help them avoid risk, it signals a change in the market's mood. The information from this third indicator, coupled with volatility changes, will give investors a highly reliable method for anticipating the change in trends.

Indicator 3: Safety-Seeking Behavior

You may be concerned that observing and tracking safety-seeking behavior in the market might mean following a whole lot of data. After all, there are a lot of choices for investors. Trying to track where all the money goes could become a complex and time-consuming activity. You will need a way to simplify this research. That's why Indicator 3 focuses on one area as a bellwether indicator: utilities.

Utility stocks are well known in investing circles for one overriding feature: they pay better dividends than most stocks. They also tend to show less volatility over time—or at least that's what most investors perceive. Because these stereotyped expectations persist in the minds of many individual and professional investors, utility stocks remain more interesting to those who are trying to seek safety than to those who are trying to seek opportunity. The perceived degree of predictability that utility stocks offer tends to make them less attractive as a vehicle for growth and more attractive as an instrument for safety. So when investors begin to prefer utility stocks over other stocks in general, that signals that a significant number of market participants are seeking to avoid risk and find a relatively safe place for their money. This makes utility stocks an excellent proxy for tracking safety-seeking behavior.

Measuring safety-seeking behavior. Tracking safety-seeking behavior requires that you evaluate how utility stocks are performing compared to the overall market. This is easier than you might think. Fortunately for us keep-it-simple–oriented investors, there is a single index with a long-running history that tracks utility stocks. You have heard of the Dow Jones Industrial Average, but there is another index similar to it that will work for our purposes. The Dow Jones Utility Average tracks an average of the price of stocks from 15 large utility companies. This lesser-known index will work as an excellent gauge for our purpose in tracking safety-seeking behavior.

All that you need to do is keep an eye on whether the Dow Jones Utility average is rising faster than the S&P 500 Index. The most straightforward way to do this is by simply comparing the chart lines of these two indexes and determining which one seems to be gaining more quickly than the other. When you observe that utilities are rising faster in price than the overall market, you can be reasonably certain that the market participants are seeking predictability over growth and generally trying to avoid risk.

Examples of safety-seeking behavior. When investors want to find safer—or at least somewhat more predictable—investments, many will choose to put their money into utility stocks. Figure 4.8

shows a striking example of how this behavior is on display right at the peak of the market in the year 2000.

In this chart, the upper line denotes the S&P 500 index and the lower line represents the Dow Jones Utilities index. You will notice that within the marked portion of the chart near the center of the figure, the Dow Jones Utilities (DJU) average begins to rise rapidly at the same time the S&P 500 fluctuates in lackluster fashion. This occurs just before the overall market makes a multi-year decline. Notice further that in 2003 the reverse happens. At that time, the DJU is the lackluster line, and the S&P 500 begins trending strongly upward. This signal nicely precedes a multi-year upward trend in the overall market. Another example of this same dynamic occurs again four years later. Consider how Figure 4.9 demonstrates this behavior dramatically displaying itself again just four years later.

In this example you can see how, in 2007, the S&P 500 (the top line) begins to turn down, just at the same time the DJU (bottom line) makes a rapid rise. Once again market participants seek safety

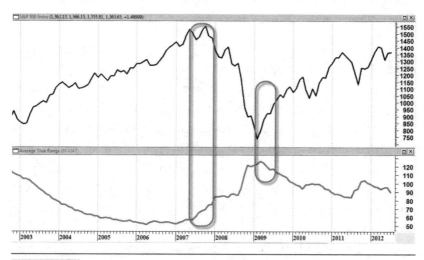

FIGURE 4.8 How utility stocks (the bottom line, ticker symbol DJU) outpace the regular market (the top line, ticker symbol SPX) just before prices fall from their 2000 tops, and how the market outpaces DJU just before prices make a multiyear upward trend.

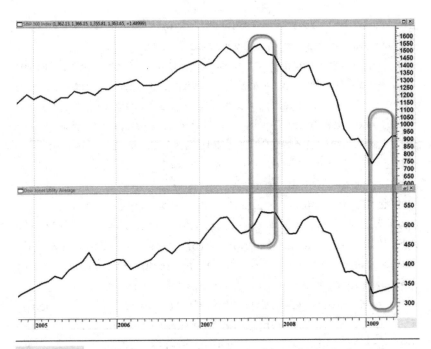

FIGURE 4.9   How DJU did better than the market at the end of 2007, just
before the market began a new downward trend, but did worse in 2009, just
before the market began a new multiyear upward trend.

by moving their money into utility stocks just before a prolonged
downward move by the S&P 500. This time, the movement of money
into utility stocks preceded the worst single-year performance of the
S&P 500 in eight decades. But the same indicator shows us that just
as quickly as it began, the bear market was likely done. By May of
2009, it was very clear that the overall market was moving up in
price faster than utility stocks and that market participants were
no longer trying to seek safety. On the contrary, they were seeking
opportunity.

As you have probably recognized by now, there are plenty of times
when one of these three indicators shows an important change in its
reading, but the market still trends in the same direction. However
when all three indicators signal simultaneously, you have a highly
reliable reading of a change in the market's mood.

Recognizing the GO and STOP Signs

The market's mood identifies whether investors are interested in taking risk. When the market is seeking opportunity, it shows the GO sign. The other kind of signal identifies when investors prefer to seek safe places for their money. When the market wants more safety than risk, it shows the STOP sign.

The first indicator, the twelve-month moving average, is the key signal to watch. The next two indicators confirm this signal. If neither of these signals accompanies crossing of the moving average, then you can be patient and expect the trend to resume. What you are looking for is a combination of indicators. First you look for prices to cross the twelve-month moving average, and then you look for the confirming GO or STOP sign.

The market flashes the STOP sign when the level of disagreement in the markets increases at the same time that a large number of market participants actively seek safety. The market's mood has then turned sour, and it's not a good time to be buying stocks. But when this first occurs, the market has increased its daily volatility. It may not turn down right away. Some investors may have come late to the party, so to speak, and they may begin buying up stocks as prices fall.

These late-responding investors keep the higher volatility of prices continuing and also keep prices from falling into a downward trend—at least for a little while. But eventually more and more people begin to sell out of their stocks and run to the perceived safety of utility stocks. That's why I like to wait to see two full months of Indicator 3, safety-seeking behavior, before declaring it a STOP sign.

Over the past eighty years, a sustained downward trend has been preceded by both increased volatility and a move toward utility stocks—the STOP sign—about 90 percent of the time. Getting practice recognizing STOP signs is a critical skill. To get your first taste of building this skill, look at the charts in Figure 4.10 and Figure 4.11 to see if you can identify the combined signals from indicators 2 and 3. See if you can tell whether these signals are likely to precede upward- or downward-trending prices.

I'll do the first one for you. It's a GO sign, and it occurred near the end of the year 1993. The first set of arrows in Figure 4.10 show the point near the end of 1993. At this time the S&P 500 (top window) was rising, the Average True Range (center window) was declining, and the DJU (bottom window) was not keeping up with the S&P 500.

Notice the arrows aligned with Box 1, placed at the end of the year 2000, show that stocks are trending downward (shown in the top window), the Average True Range line is sloping upward, and utility stocks (shown in the bottom window) remain high. If you thought that this would indicate that the markets were ready to seek safety, you are right. Box 1 is a STOP sign. The market's mood turned pessimistic at that time. But the markets were not in a down trend yet. They were just getting started. What happened next has gone down in history as the bursting of the dot-com bubble.

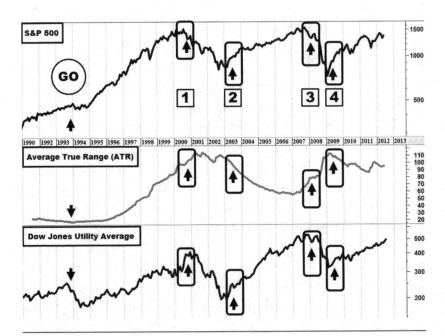

FIGURE 4.10   Five points in time where the key characteristics gave important clues about what the market would do next. The first one is a GO sign, but what about the others?

As you consider Boxes 2, 3, and 4 in turn, see if you can identify what the key characteristics are telling you at each of those points. Figure 4.11 reveals the market signals so that you can see if your analysis of these charts matches what you had reviewed in the previous figure.

How did you do? Did you anticipate these answers? Let's walk through them. When you look at Box 2, you don't need to make the analysis complicated. What you see is that, in that period of time, regular stocks had begun to move upwards, the ATR was falling, and utility stocks, while they were going up at the time, were not moving higher as rapidly as other stocks. This pattern gave a clue that the market was showing a preference for seeking opportunity rather than safety. That qualifies as a GO signal. The year was 2003, and what followed this GO sign was a four-year upward move in stocks.

Turning our attention to Box 3, we recognize a signal that has features similar to Box 1. At that time the S&P 500 had begun to decline, while the ATR had been on the rise for the entire year before; the ATR was continuing to rise, while at the same time, the DJU had held its ground. That's all it had to do for the signal to be initiated.

Remember that Indicator 3 is not that the DJU must rise, but rather that it must fare better than the S&P 500. So if the DJU does rise, it must rise faster than the S&P 500, and if it falls, it must not fall as fast as the S&P 500. In this case the DJU was fluctuating in a sideways pattern, while the stocks of the S&P 500 were actually trending significantly lower. When compared with the rising ATR coincident to that time, this generated a very timely STOP sign that coincided nicely with Indicator 1, a cross of the 12-period moving average.

The signal could have helped you protect your money from the rapid decline in price which followed shortly after. That move was unusually swift and severe compared to what most market participants had experienced. Even the Dot-Bomb era seemed mild by comparison.

In Box 4 we have a timely marker that gave a clear signal for those who were able to see it. While investors were still reeling from the pain and uncertainty left over from the crash of 2008, the market

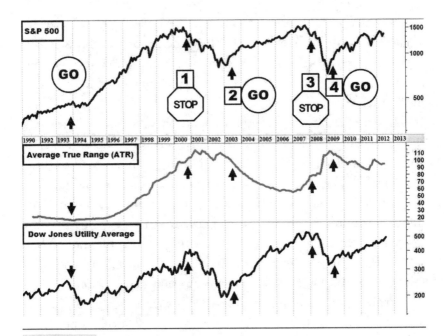

FIGURE 4.11   The remaining times when the key characteristics of the market gave signals about the market's mood and likely future direction.

HOT TIP

If you found it difficult to pick out STOP and GO signs based on the previous charts, don't worry. Toni and I have developed a website for you, www.investtowinthebook.com, which maps out the current GO and STOP signs. A quick review will be all you need to determine what the current market mood seems to be telling us.

---

index rapidly made a turn early in 2009. The turn was quick, and the response was potent. But by the end of the month of May the market was flashing what may have been the best GO signal in the entire decade. This GO Sign also happened to precede the crossing of the 12-month moving average.

S&P 500 stocks rose rapidly and outpaced the DJU for both of the two months preceding May. At the same time, the ATR indicator was clearly falling. A new bullish trend was about to begin. For the two years that followed the GO sign, stocks rose more rapidly than any time since the 1930s rebound from the Great Depression.

Combining the Indicators

Earlier I explained that Indicator 1, the twelve-month moving average, was an excellent, simple way to watch for trend changes in the market. I also explained that the problem with using Indicator 1 by itself was that it was prone to false signals—temporary fluctuations in the price action. But now that you understand how a GO and a STOP sign are generated, you can recognize that you have a way to filter out many of the false signals. The procedure for doing so is as follows:

Step 1: Watch for a cross of the twelve-period moving average.

Step 2: Evaluate whether the market has flashed a corresponding GO or STOP sign.

Step 3a: If there is a GO sign, then adapt your investing in anticipation of a new upward trend.

Step 3b: If there is a STOP sign, then adapt your investing in anticipation of a new downward trend.

Step 3c: If the price of the S&P 500 has crossed the twelve-period moving average line and neither a GO nor a STOP sign has been flashed, then expect the previous trend to resume.

These steps form a simple procedure you can follow once a month to read the market's mood. Doing so will effectively help you adapt and prepare for whatever conditions the market may show. Figure 4.12 shows all three indicators combined. This will give you some indication of how you might have read the market's mood over the last decade.

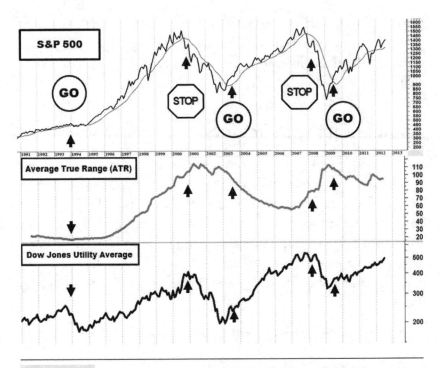

FIGURE 4.12   All three indicators combined will help you identify trend changes and filter out false signals.

Using the indicators together to help you read the market's mood is the best way I know to help you be prepared for the next major change in the trend of prices. The combination of evidence about volatility and safety-seeking behavior makes a powerful combination. When reviewed in conjunction with the twelve-month moving average, it makes a powerful signal to help you adapt to the market's mood. It takes just a minute or two once a month to check these charts. If you don't know how to read charts very well, don't worry. In the next chapter Toni will show you the necessary basics of chart reading.

Key Points to Remember

→ The twelve-month moving average shows a useful indication of a potential trend change.

➔ True trend changes in the market are more frequently dictated by investors' preference for seeking opportunity or for seeking safety.
➔ Investors show a repeated pattern in how they respond: namely, if their investments are going up they move slowly, but if their investments are going down they move faster, creating more market volatility.
➔ Volatility can be measured by using the Average True Range (ATR). Increasing volatility (ATR) implies that investors are becoming more nervous.
➔ Investors display a preference for seeking either growth or safety. This preference can be seen with a comparison between regular stocks (tracked by the S&P 500 index) and utility stocks (as tracked by the Dow Jones Utility Index).
➔ The combination of ATR measurements and the comparison between utility stocks and regular stocks provides GO signs (signals that investors are looking for growth and opportunity) and STOP signs (a signal that investors are looking for safety trades only, please).
➔ When GO or STOP signs accompany or shortly follow a cross of the twelve-month moving average on the S&P 500, a major market turning points is likely.

PERSONAL GAINS

— Toni —

Build on Your Strengths

Know thyself means this, that you get acquainted with what you know and what you can do.

–Menander

Each and every one of us is born with a unique set of valuable traits and talents. Some of us, with encouragement in childhood, discover these talents and nurture them into successful careers. Many of us, though, do not become aware of our strengths and natural talents until much later in life (if at all).

Our society tends to focus on people's weaknesses. As is often pointed out in the corporate workplace, "She has an opportunity for improvement in that area."

Most of us accept the challenge to work on our shortcomings—perhaps we resolve to be more considerate, sympathetic, or time-efficient. Once we've attempted to reverse our personal defects, however, it's gratifying news to find out what behavioral therapists recently discovered: people have several times more potential for growth when they work on developing their strengths.

Imagine this: You are known in your workplace and community for your "people person" skills; you are an excellent manager, and your staff excels under your leadership. On the other hand, technology torments you; detailed reports and spreadsheets result in long hours of agony.

Considering your ROI, or "return on investment," where would your time best be spent? Should you spend extra hours learning how to produce neatly executed spreadsheets? Or would it be wiser (more fulfilling, more productive, and more profitable) to dedicate your time to beginning new initiatives, building new teams, and aiming for a higher leadership position? Clearly, the latter is the more intelligent choice.

As mentioned earlier, many of us go through our lives doing all of the usual things: we attend school, get a job, start a family, and work to build successful lives. We would have a lot more pleasure, more feelings of fulfillment, and more success (and downright joy) if we also allocated time to build on our strengths.

Have you taken the time to discover and sort out the positive characteristics and talents that are uniquely yours? Have you targeted your best traits and invested time in developing them?

In *StrengthsFinder 2.0*, author Tom Rath states, ". . . our studies indicate that people who *do* have the time to focus on their strengths every day are *six times as likely to be engaged in their jobs* and more than *three times as likely to report having an excellent quality of life in general"* (Tom Rath, *StrengthsFinder 2.0*, New York: Gallup Press, 2007, p. iii).

Perhaps you are a fantastic organizer, a good communicator, or a conscientious motivator. Maybe you have a "green thumb," kids adore you, or you can run like lightning. Whatever you do well, know that you can build on your strengths and talents to contribute to your personal growth potential, fortify your family, and support your social networks and communities.

CHAPTER FIVE

Your Investing Edge
The Art of the Chart

— Toni —

W HEN YOU—THE savvy investor—begin to research a stock as a potential investment, you will encounter two basic methods of analysis: fundamental and technical.

Say you have decided to buy a late-model, pre-owned car, and you've located one you are considering. Analyzing a company's fundamentals could be compared to looking under the hood of the car. Just as you inspect the engine and its parts to make sure it's clean and well-maintained, when you examine a company's "numbers," you look at the company's financial information, such as balance sheet information, earnings, and price ratios. (Gordon will show you quick and effective methods for evaluating company fundamentals in Chapter Six.)

But let's continue our examination of the car. After checking under the hood (or hiring a mechanic to do it), you walk around the outside of the car, looking for dents and any signs that the vehicle had been in an accident. In the same way you give an automobile's exterior a visual once-over for signs of former trouble, you look at a price chart to discover whether the stock's price is currently rising or falling. We can also see the stock's price history over time and determine whether the stock price moves up gradually in an orderly fashion (desirable as an investment) or if tends to hop straight up and down in irregular moves like a kangaroo on speed (not desirable as an investment).

Technical analysis is the art and practice of interpreting price charts, or "price pictures." Since a picture is worth a thousand words, when you glance at a stock's price chart, you can see the path that price has taken over time. Knowing where price has been can help us project which direction it may potentially take next. And that's a gratifying feeling.

"Hold, it, Toni," you say, rolling your eyes. "I'm smart, but learn 'technical analysis'? Isn't that stuff for geeky people who have lots of time on their hands?"

Not necessarily. Reading a price chart is not as difficult as it sounds. And if the very thought of evaluating a price chart sounds intimidating, answer this: Can you look at a picture of a black line displayed on a white background and tell whether the line is moving up or moving down? Of course you can. So, you can read a price chart.

> **HOT TIP**
>
> Technical analysts believe all of a company's fundamental information is manifested in the stock's price action.

This is the cool thing about price charts: being able to evaluate a price chart with even a modicum of accuracy (is the line moving up or moving down?) can make you, and save you, a lot of money. What you learn in this chapter will set you apart from the vast majority of investors, who buy and sell without a solid understanding of the market's inner workings. And it's an integral part of this book's GainsMaster approach, Key 2, *Evaluate market conditions.*

Traditionally, two types of people participate in the financial markets: traders and investors. They are both in it to profit. The difference is in the time frame they use to earn those profits: traders intend to earn their profits in minutes to months. They want to "get in when the gettin's good" and jump out when the stock, or the market, acts knarly. Investors, on the other hand, plan to hold their stock positions for years, sometimes for decades. (Remember the McDonald's example we discussed in an earlier chapter.)

OK, rewind to traders. (And yes, there are some very profitable short-term traders out there, but you won't see their names in the press. They stay under the media radar and keep their strategies to themselves.) Those traders who target trading time frames of minutes to days haven't the time to slog through pages of company fundamentals. They need accurate information—*fast*.

That means, instead of reading pages of words (company fundamentals), these traders look at the stock's price chart. They evaluate where price has been, perhaps over the course of the current year, and where it is now. Has price risen from this month last year to the current time? If so, has it moved in an orderly pattern? Is it rising or falling now? A trader believes that everything he or she needs to know is reflected in the stock's price action. Or as the Wall Street saying goes, "Price is truth."

Now, let's turn to investors. Traditionally, investors check out a company's fundamentals. *Period.* That's how stockbrokers have operated for years. "If a company has good fundamentals, its stock will survive, and even thrive, through good and bad markets," they tell us. *Maybe. Maybe not.*

> **HOT TIP**
>
> Price charts show us human emotions on a screen. Optimism, greed, euphoria, anxiety, fear, and downright panic—all are shown on a stock or index's price chart.

We've already learned that the economies of developed nations rotate through cycles of bull and bear markets. Those expanding and contracting market moves influence stock price. Fundamentals notwithstanding, stock prices can drop off sharply, depending on the severity of the economic headlines. Those of you who have participated in the market for more than a few months know that in ugly market downturns, the very best babies get thrown out with the bathwater. With our risk-management strategy, you need not be one of the handwringers that watch the value of their portfolios shrink by 30 or 50 percent during a market downturn.

Added to that, if the headlines are making you queasy and you'd like to know how the stock market feels about those headlines, wouldn't it make perfect sense to pull up a chart of, say, the S&P 500

Index or the Dow Jones Industrial Average and interpret the market's mood and manner? That way you can make prudent decisions that line up with your time horizon and risk parameters.

Let me put it this way. Before you purchase equity shares, perusing your target company's earnings is indeed wise and necessary. Once you've established good fundamentals, we also advise that you also devote a few minutes of your time to the stock's price chart. The chart will tell you if the stock is currently in a favorable buying environment or not.

We believe that when you plunk your hard-earned money into an equity position, you stand the best chance of high profit potential when you utilize the best parts of both the fundamental and technical worlds. That way, you base your decisions of whether to buy, sell, or hold on the most sensible, well-rounded information available.

Before we start looking at the pictures, though, let's briefly discuss the single most important component of any financial asset—at any given moment of time—*price*.

Price: The Master of the Universe

Imagine a tornado-like tunnel of energy, whirling through space. At the tunnel's top, global and geopolitical events, economic conditions, the forces of supply and demand, and interest rates spin furiously. They funnel down into the sphere's vortex, igniting sector trends,

> **HOT TIP**
>
> On Wall Street, individual traders and investors are known as the "dumb money." Typically, the "dumb money" buys at market tops and sells at market bottoms. Financial institutions, with their huge banks of research and information analysis, are dubbed the "smart money." While these definitions can be accurate, don't get your feelings hurt. With a little moxie and homework, we can be just as shrewd and smart as the "smart money"!

earnings, and investor sentiment. The vortex narrows, spiraling down... until all elements converge into a single point: *price.*

Price is the agreed upon value of an object in a given moment in time. It is consensus of opinion. Price represents a present perception of value that both the seller and buyer agree to *right now.*

As we've mentioned before, the stock market is a forward-looking entity. As investors, we buy and sell our stock shares depending on how we see the *future* of the underlying company unfolding.

Maybe you've been holding shares of Bossy Bank and earned a nice profit on it. Now, however, you've heard banks are headed for an unstable quarter. You'd like to take Bossy's current gains and look for greener pastures.

I, on the other hand, have been watching Bossy for some time now. I am convinced its earnings will grow and its shares will move higher.

In the world outside the stock market, as long as seller and buyer agree, the seller usually receives for an item what that item is worth *at that moment in time.* Were that true in the financial markets, then I would pay you the amount for your shares dictated by Bossy's fundamental information and its book value.

Investments are different. Whether we're speaking of a work of art, a classic auto, a rare stamp, or shares of stock, we buy with expectations that, wisely chosen, our investment will increase in value.

That means, if I purchase your shares of Bossy Bank, I will purchase them at a higher price, or a premium, than their fundamentals and book value (book value = dollar value remaining for common shareholders after all debts are paid) dictate. (Were Bossy's earn-

---

HOT TIP

Failures in the financial sector can cause extreme mayhem in the equities markets and cause economic downturns to wallow longer than failures set in motion by other sectors, such as technology. That's because financial institutions represent the "heart" of a country's economic health.

ings negative and its fundamentals appalling, the current stock price might be listed at a discount to the fundamental value. In that case, I wouldn't want that stock.)

The variable between a stock's *real* share price dictated by fundamentals, versus the price investor participants *expect* it will be worth in the future, causes price fluctuation. To the degree greed and fear forecast expectations for future price value, they propel stock prices higher or lower.

How We Plot Simple Line Charts

When you see stock price charts displayed in newspapers, books, and other media, you will note the historical price action on those charts presented in three basic formats: line charts, bar charts, and candlestick charts. (Additional types include point-and-figure, tick charts, and others, but we'll leave them for another time.)

For those of you who are new to price charts: charts have an "X" and "Y" axis.

In Figure 5.1 "X" (you read it from left to right, just like this sentence) displays time (days, months, years), usually along the bottom of the chart.

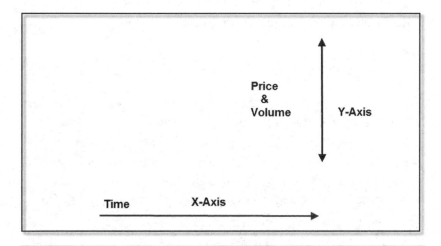

FIGURE 5.1   Price charts, basic formula X- and Y-axes.

"Y" shows price action and volume measurements, which move up and down on the vertical axis.

Line charts are the simplest to interpret. To plot a daily-price line chart of a stock (or other financial asset), we record the closing price of that stock each day. (In the U.S., the stock's closing price is the last price recorded when the stock exchanges close each weekday at 4:00 p.m. Eastern time.)

Were we creating a price chart by hand, as technical analysts did in the old days, before computers and charting software programs, we would take our pencil and put a dot on a paper price chart, indicating the stock's published closing price each trading day. Then, we would connect the dots. The resulting line shows price moving higher or lower.

The two charts that follow, Figures 5.2 and 5.3, are daily line charts of General Electric Co. (GE) and the Walt Disney Co. (DIS), respectively.

You can see how the prices of these two securities change over time. During bull markets and a positive company outlook, price happily trends higher. When bulls and bears buy and sell at about the same pace, price dances through time in a demure little sidestep. During times of market stress or company angst, price dives lower.

Weekly line charts are created by connecting each Friday's closing price, known by market players as "the weekly close."

HOT TIP

In the financial markets, "closing" prices carry a lot of weight. Whether you refer to the end-of-day closing price or the weekly (Friday) or monthly close, that particular price tells us a lot about the mood and manner of the market. Think: the close = commitment. If investors' expectations deteriorate regarding the future value of a stock, then they will sell their shares before the market closes for the day, weekend, month, or quarter.

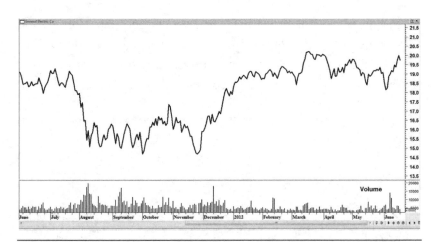

FIGURE 5.2   A daily line chart of the General Electric Co. (GE), over the span of one year.

The price line you see connects the closing price for the stock each day. Note the prices listed in the column on the far right side of the chart, which give you a reference point for the price line. Under price, you can see volume spikes (in the volume scale), which measure the number of shares traded each day. The months and their days (time) appear beneath the volume scale. Chart courtesy Metastock.

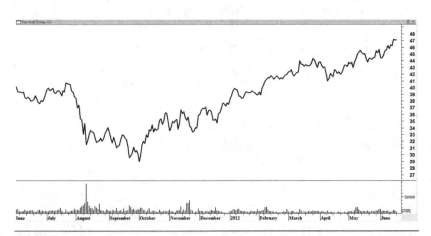

FIGURE 5.3   A daily line chart of The Walt Disney Co. (DIS).

Note that from October of the year shown, the stock increased in price from its lows of about $29 per share, to $47 per share in June. Those were sweet gains for this Dow component! Chart courtesy Metastock

In Figures 5.4 and 5.5, you can see weekly line charts of GE and DIS, respectively. By connecting only one price for each week (Friday's closing price), we can view a longer time span of price action (fewer closing prices take up less space).

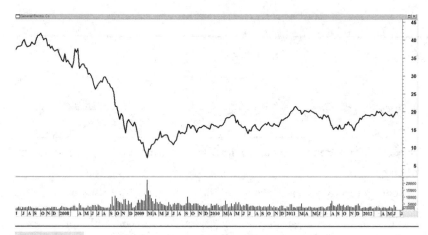

FIGURE 5.4   A weekly line chart of GE.

Instead of one year's price data on the screen, now you can see five years of price action. This gives you a much bigger picture of GE's price history. Chart courtesy Metastock

FIGURE 5.5   A weekly line chart of DIS.

Glance at the previous chart of GE over the same time period, and then note the difference in price strength displayed by DIS. While GE manages to bounce off of its bear market lows in 2009 and more than doubles by 2012, DIS reverses from 2009 lows and rises more than 200 percent to current highs. Chart courtesy Metastock

Monthly line charts show a line connecting a stock's closing price on the last trading day of each month. Figures 5.6 and 5.7 exhibit GE and DIS price movements on monthly line charts.

"Seasonal" or quarterly line charts display a line connecting each quarter's closing price. Yearly line charts present a line that links the closing prices on the last trading day of each year.

HOT TIP

For those new to the stock market, here's what you need to know about quarters. In the business and financial world, there are four quarters in every year. Obviously (with twelve months in a year), each quarter contains three months. The first quarter, or "Q1," runs January 1–March 31. The second quarter, Q2, spans April 1–June 30. The third quarter, Q3, covers July 1–September 30. And the final, or fourth, quarter, Q4, is October 1–December 31.

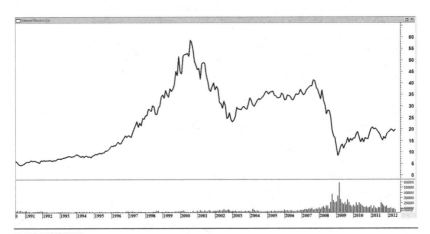

FIGURE 5.6   **A monthly line chart of GE.**

Talk about a revealing picture! The giant multinational company rose from $4.60 in 1991, to $60.50 in the year 2000. Then, along with most equities, GE gave back it is huge gains in the bear market of 2000–2002. It showed strength again during the bull market that lasted until 2007, and then gave way again in 2008. By 2009, we can see a compressed picture of the price action we saw in the preceding weekly and daily line charts. Chart courtesy Metastock

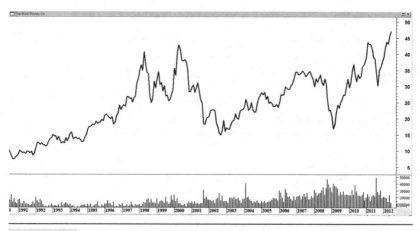

FIGURE 5.7   **A monthly line chart of DIS, spanning the time period**
1991–2012.

Note how the price action and the volume, differ from those of GE in the previous chart. While DIS celebrated the same bull markets and endured the same bear markets as did GE, you can see how the media and entertainment stock acted with a different mood and manner. Each stock trades differently, with its own "personality." The more you look at price charts, the more you will recognize differing "personality traits" among different stocks. Chart courtesy Metastock

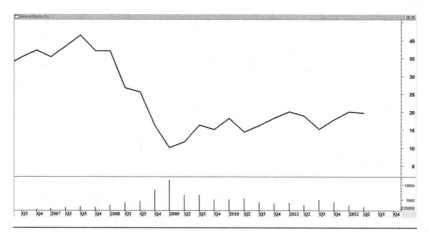

FIGURE 5.8   **A quarterly line chart dating from Q3 of 2006 through Q1**
of 2012.

Translation: time span shows GE price action as it moves from quarter to quarter. Shown is price from the last day (closing price) of the third quarter of 2006, September 30, through the last day of the first quarter of 2012, June 30. Chart courtesy Metastock

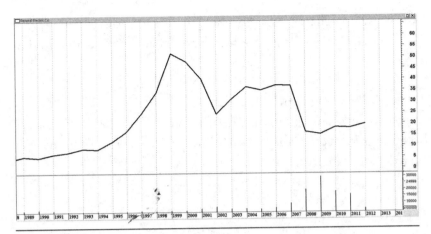

FIGURE 5.9   A yearly line chart of GE from 1989 to current times.

Comparing charts (yearly to quarterly), you can see repetition coming into the time periods. Although it's advantageous for investors to be able to evaluate the "big picture," once you can assess a stock's price back to the 1990s or 2000, you have enough information to analyze its current strength or weakness. Chart courtesy Metastock

In Figures 5.8 and 5.9, you will see GE's price action displayed on a seasonal (quarterly) and yearly chart, respectively.

For our purposes in this book, we will use mostly daily, weekly, and monthly line charts. These are the easiest time periods to access in chart programs and software. Besides, they tell us everything we need to know in powerful pictures of a stock's price action.

A Quick Reference to Bar Charts

In *Invest to Win*, Gordon and I are going to use line charts (just discussed) and Japanese candlestick charts (on the menu next). Still, I cannot skip the classic price chart formation known as the "bar." Until candle charts nudged most bar charts to the sidelines, bars were the standard time measurement used by technical analysts. You may see bar charts from time to time, and you'll want to know how to interpret them.

Figure 5.10 shows how the bars on bar charts are configured. The vertical line represents the stock's price action for a day (daily chart), week (weekly chart), month (monthly chart), and so forth. Check out the caption under the chart to learn what the bar configuration means.

Figure 5.11 exhibits a daily bar chart of GE. Note how the bar chart differs visually from line charts.

Now, let's move on to candlestick charts. Candlesticks help us to see the price picture more clearly and to divine what other market participants are thinking.

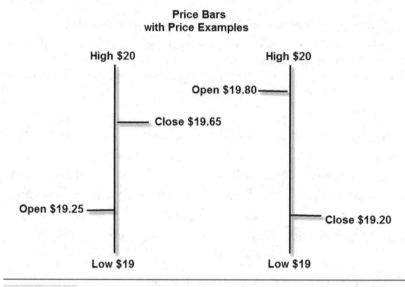

FIGURE 5.10   **The price bars used by technical analysts on bar charts.**

Each bar might represent a day, week, month, quarter, or year (or whatever price period is being used) in a stock's price action. The vertical bar always represents the stock's price move, between the high and the low of that time period. The horizontal line on the left side of the bar represents the stock's opening price. The horizontal bar on the right side of the bar represents the stock's closing price. On the first example (left), we can see that the stock opened the trading day (or whatever period is being measured), at $19.25. At some time during the trading day it fell to a low price—or "low" of $19, with a high of $20. The stock closed the day at 19.65—higher than the opening price of $19.25. On the second example, we note that the stock opened the day at $19.80. Subsequently, price fell to a low of $19 and rose to a high of $20. The stock's price "closed down," however (below its opening price), at $19.20, incurring a loss for that day.

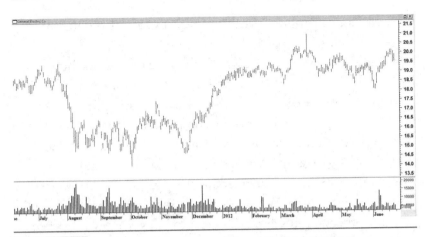

FIGURE 5.11   Daily bar chart of GE. Each bar shows the "HLOC," as we say in market-speak, or the high, low, open, and closing price of each day.

Chart courtesy Metastock

How Candlesticks Shine Light on Our Charts

While line charts give us an instant, easy-to-define picture of an index or stock's price history and bar charts deliver the basics, Japanese candlestick—or "candle"—charts add interesting details to the price action. Candle charts are also easy to read, once you tuck under your belt the basics of how to read them. (Of course, if you already know how to interpret candle charts, you can skip this section.)

Japanese candlestick charts date back to the early rice traders, in tenth-century Japan. We owe a debt of gratitude to my good friend, market expert and educator Steve Nison, who had ancient Japanese candlestick texts translated into Western terminology and so brought this fascinating chart technology to the West. Steve likes to say that candle charts help "light our path" to trading and investing success. While we will cover the basics of candle patterns in this text, if you'd like more in-depth information and learning tools, please go to candlecharts.com.

Candle charts display signals that—when read accurately—can be highly beneficial to us as investors.

- Basic candle patterns reveal the market's "mood and manner," be it optimistic or pessimistic.
- Candle patterns can broadcast early price reversal warnings. Example: a stock's price preparing to reverse from a downtrend into an uptrend (we'll learn about trends in an upcoming section). You'll see examples of this on the charts that follow.
- Finally, our ability to interpret candle patterns helps us manage risk. For instance, when we see a long, black candle appear after price makes an extended move up, the signal can warn that price is weakening. While we may or may not want to pocket some profits on this event, it's great to know we have access to a signal that warns us of an upcoming price shift, or reversal. As we know, managing risk is vital to investing success.

How Candles Are Structured

A candle, or candle "line," as a single candle is sometimes called, is simply a price bar—all "gussied up." To transform a bar into a candle, we enclose the space between the bar's opening and closing price into a rectangle. The rectangle is called the "real body." When the low price of the candle extends down from the real body, or the high price of the candle extends up from the real body, we display it with a line extension, called a "shadow." Figure 5.12 shows how candles are formed from the same high, low, opening and closing prices that complete bars.

Please know: When the candle's closing price is higher than the opening price, we color the real body clear, or white. If the candle's closing price is lower than the opening price, we color the real body dark, or black. And here's an extra benefit of using candle charts versus bar charts: If you are like me . . . and perhaps just a bit, ah, over 40 years old . . . the white and black candles make the price pattern easier to see.

Now, let's look at a couple of elementary, but high-powered, candle patterns that can help you predict what the market is "thinking." While there are hundreds of candle patterns to investigate (you'll find them on candlecharts.com), at the moment, we will address the candle formations that occur most often on our charts.

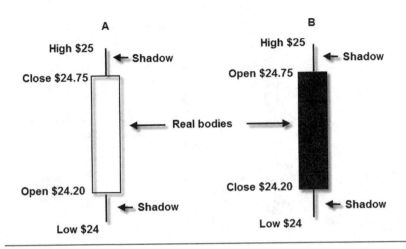

FIGURE 5.12 Examples of two chart candles, along with their high, low, opening, and closing prices.

As you will note, Candle "A" closed higher than it opened, so the real body is clear, or white. Candle "B" closed lower than it opened, so the real body is black. Alternatively, some online brokers or charting software programs color the white, or positive, candles green and the dark, or negative, candles red.

Tall white candle: Real body opens at, or near, the low and closes at or near the high. During that time period, investors feel positive about that stock.

Tall dark candle: Real body opens near, or at, the top of the candle (high), closes at or near the bottom (low); we know investors view the stock negatively, and are selling it.

White or dark candles, tall or short: Completed candle shows opening and closing prices at, or near, the same level, which indicates indecision among the buyers and sellers. This is especially true if the candle completes its pattern with long shadows extending above and below the opening and closing prices.

Figure 5.13 illustrates the basic candle formations we just discussed.

Now let's look at candle charts displayed in daily, weekly, and monthly time frames.

Chart Time Frames: By the way, please remember that whether we're referring to a bar or candle chart, a "daily" chart displays each trading day as a single candle.

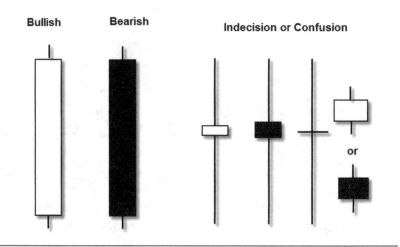

Bullish   **Bearish**   **Indecision or Confusion**

FIGURE 5.13   Basic candle formations and the signals they broadcast.

The first candle on the left signals bullishness—plenty of buyers fueled the price rise and closed the candle near its high. The second candle, however, indicates that the bears are out in force; they closed the candle near its low. The next sequence of candles shows market players are indecisive; neither the bulls, nor the bears can overpower the other and close the price near its highs or lows. The small candles on the far right display narrow price ranges, again telling us that neither the bulls nor the bears were inspired to move price to wider-range highs or lows.

On a weekly chart, a single candle represents the culmination of prices in the five days that make up that week. That means that of those five days, the weekly candle forms from the highest high, the lowest low, the Monday opening price, and the Friday closing price.

On a monthly chart, a single candle represents one month's worth of price action. So, that candle's high reflects the highest price of the month, the candle's low represents the lowest price of the month, the candle's opening price reflects that of the first trading day of the month, and the candle's close shows the closing price on the final trading day of the month.

Figure 5.14 shows a daily candle chart of the Microsoft Corp. (MSFT). You can see how the tall, white candles (prominent buying or demand) fueled the price moves to the upside. Toward the right side of the chart, you can see how the appearance of more dark candles (closing prices lower than opening prices showing sellers) drove the software giant south.

Figure 5.15 displays a weekly candle chart of Lowe's Companies (LOW). Once again, you'll note that the white candles (price closes above the open) drive price higher and the dark candles push it lower.

Figure 5.16 exhibits a monthly chart of Dow component International Business Machines Corp. (IBM). Here you can clearly see how the white or clear monthly candles powered IBM to the upside, while the dark, or bearish, candles smacked IBM lower, especially in the recessionary bear market of 2008.

Your takeaway: Particularly on the monthly chart, as long as most of the candles are clear, or white, and price continues to move upward, you are making money. When, however, a long, dark candle appears to close out the current month to the downside, you may want to assess your risk, begin to monitor price movement more closely, and adjust your plan to assure you keep your profits safe.

FIGURE 5.14   A daily candlestick or "candle" chart of the Microsoft Corp. (MSFT), over an approximately four-month time span.

Note that each trading day is represented by a single candle. Note also how the tall, clear or white candles propel MSFT's price higher from levels of about $25 (left side of chart,) all the way up to $33 (mid-March). Then price begins to soften, and more negative or dark candles begin to appear. When we see dark candles closing on their daily lows, we recognize that "Mister Softee" (as traders call MSFT) needs a price rest. Chart courtesy Metastock

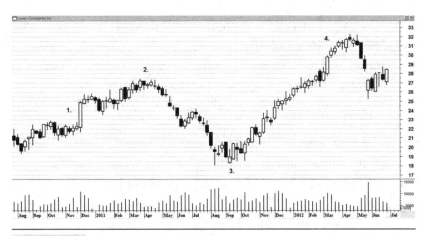

FIGURE 5.15   A weekly candle chart of Lowe's Companies (LOW), over an approximately two-year span.

1. Looking from the left side of the chart, you can clearly see how the home-improvement chain struggled to move higher from August to April, doing so with alternating white and black candles. Note the wide range (tall) white candle in December. This candle indicated strong bullishness and helped to fuel LOW to higher prices. 2. Notice how the candles become "shorter" here, or narrow in price range, indicating that market players feel more indecisive about LOW. Subsequently, price fell. 3. In August, we see falling dark candles, a bearish signal. Toward the end of August, at the bottom of the fall, we see a final, wide-range, bearish, dark candle. When bears could drive price no lower, the candles reversed; in September, bullish white candles appeared. The bulls held strong, and tall, white candles reversed LOW's downtrend into an uptrend. 4. Note the strong trend higher, propelled by the majority of positive, white candles. LOW advanced from summer lows of $18 to a spring highs of $32, nearly a 70 percent advance. When we see the wide-range black candle appear in May, however, we know LOW's price party is over, at least for the moment.

Chart courtesy Metastock

As you study these three charts (Figures 5.14, 5.15, and 5.16), you will become more adept at recognizing the signals candles broadcast. That skill will help you become a more successful investor.

Your Best Money-Making Friend—The Trend

In earlier chapters, we discussed the subject of stock market cycles and how we can see their cyclical patterns on charts. Now, let's saddle up and ride parts of these cycles to rip-roaring profits.

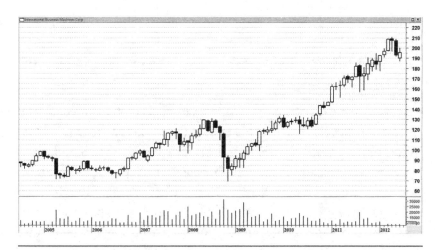

FIGURE 5.16   A monthly candle chart of International Business Machines Corp. (IBM) dating back to 2005.

You can clearly see how the technology behemoth sidestepped into 2007, then rose to its then-highs of about $130. Note the back-to-back (white, dark, white, dark) stutter steps at those highs, indicating indecision and confusion. The market has no patience for indecision, so via long, dark candles (on the back of Lehman's downfall), IBM plunged with the broad market in 2008. Now, notice the long lower shadows on the final two black candles of the 2008–early 2009 plunge. Those lower shadows tell us buyers are arriving. Then, in March of 2009, the first small white candle appears, helping to reverse the downtrend into an uptrend. From March onward, IBM rose from its lows of about $70, to recent highs of $210, rewarding investors who entered early with more than a 200 percent profit in three years. Chart courtesy Metastock

---

HOT TIP

The longer the timeframe on a chart, the stronger the signal. Translation: candle signals (such as a long, dark candle) on monthly charts are more powerful than those on weekly charts. Candle signals on weekly charts hold more sway than those on daily charts.

When you look at Figure 5.17, you will recognize the cycle formation. This time, however, we've labeled different sections, or stages of the cycle, to differentiate them from each other: 1. Base or Accumulation, 2. Uptrend or Mark-Up, 3. Top Reversal or Distribution, and 4.

Downtrend or Mark-Down. Once the Downtrend or Mark-Down stage is complete, the cycle begins again.

Here's what you need to know about each of these stages of the cycle:

■ **Base or Accumulation:** In earlier chapters, graphics of economic and business cycles labeled this part of the cycle the "trough." If we were looking at the Dow Jones Industrial Average or the Standard & Poor's 500 Index, and if the trough were very deep, it may well have signaled the bottom of a recession. If we're looking at a trough on an equity chart, we know a number of factors can lead to price falling to extended lows—perhaps even to prior lows from some years before. A contracting economy may or may not be a contributing factor (job losses, slowing manufacturing and hiring). Then we consider sector challenges, such as lack of demand (falling oil prices, or tumbling home values). Finally, a stock's company may encounter deteriorating fundamentals via bad management, lack of innovation, or perhaps

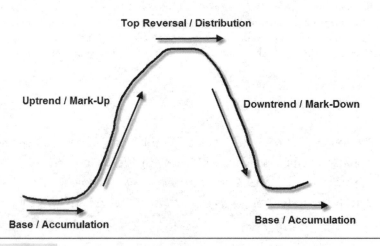

FIGURE 5.17   The cycle formation, this time relating to stock prices.

This drawing illustrates an idealized price cycle. Of course, stock prices and their trends do not always move in precisely the same measured and orderly fashion. Still, with enough practice, by using this pattern, you will learn how to recognize bases, uptrends, top reversals, and downtrends on charts of all time frames. Trend recognition is a great knowledge tool for the savvy investor.

real ugly situations such as "accounting irregularities." If the company survives its challenges, the stock price will then begin to "base." That means price moves sideways, or up and down within a relatively tight price range. (The tighter and more orderly the price range, the more promise it has when, or if, it breaks to the upside.) In this base, the bulls are buying. The bears are selling. And, since they are doing so at an even pace, price bumbles along sideways, in a stutter step. At some point in the base (which could sidestep through weeks or even months), if investors see fundamentals and outlook improving for this company, then bulls may begin to accumulate more shares. Investors' *expectations* ride on the assumption that if they buy now, they are acquiring the stock at a bargain-basement price. They *expect* the stock price will rise in the future and increase in value. And if the stock shoots higher, *viola!* They're rich! (Unless, of course, said stock plunges south. On a general basis, I may wait to buy when the stock rises above its 12-month moving average, thus "taking more of the worry out of being close.")

■ **Uptrend or Mark-Up:** An uptrend is defined on a chart as price making a series of higher lows and higher highs. Please memorize this definition. Put it on a sticky note where you can see it. Why? *Because, as successful investors, uptrends are our stomping grounds. Uptrends present the fields of opportunities where you and I want to invest!* The uptrend, or mark-up, represents the second phase, or stage, of a price cycle. When enough buyers soak up enough shares at the base prices, sellers begin to demand higher and higher prices. Result? The stock rises in an uptrend. As long as price continues to etch higher highs and higher lows on its chart, the shares are "marked up," and sellers can demand higher prices.

■ **Top Reversal or Distribution:** Let's say that Whizzy Wireless has tripled in price in the last two years. (It's risen in an uptrend from its base price at $10 per share to its current price at $30 per share.) Now, it's meandering sideways, teetering on its high price perch. Whether from an overheated economic environment, sector weakness, or because Whizzy's price and fundamental valuations are considered too high, buyers have stopped buying with enthusiasm. After a time, price slips downward. Enter Johnny-Come-Lately and his friends, who buy, and price jumps up again. In reaction, Nervous Nellie investors who have been holding Whizzy see another chance to sell at a higher price—and they do. Price dives again. As the bulls and bears disagree (Gordon talked about this bull-bear disagreement—which causes volatility, or wide price swings—in Chapter Four), Whizzy's price swings—up to current highs, then down to nearby lows—get wider. Now poor Whizzy encounters a good chance of "rolling over," or sliding into a downtrend. Stocks experiencing these top reversal patterns (think: price peak), such as Whizzy is right now, are subject to "distribution." The smart money or institutional money (which moves the markets) may be quietly selling millions of shares and taking profits. These professionals have no intention of sticking around to find out which team—the bulls or the bears—is going to win *this* battle. They will take their 200 percent profits, thank you very much, and go hunting for other opportunities. Now, please know that if you follow the strategies we outline in later chapters, your positions may get "stopped out" during this stage. Just like the "smart money," you will automatically sell your Whizzy Wireless shares with a profit. *Very smart, indeed.*

> **HOT TIP**
>
> The stock market dislikes uncertainty and volatility. Just as people run indoors to escape a thunderstorm, when the bulls and bears disagree too hotly, investors sell their stocks and flee to safer instruments, such as bonds.

- **Downtrend or Mark-Down:** If the price is subjected to enough distribution, and subsequently pitches of a cliff in a dive here, then it tumbles down into the mark-down phase, or a downtrend. *A downtrend on a chart is defined as price making a series of lower highs and lower lows.* Anxious sellers, who want to get rid of their shares, are forced to offer them out at lower and lower prices. Once price has fallen to the level where investors finish selling—in market lingo, we say "sellers are exhausted"—the stock price begins trading in the sideways pattern (short up and down hops) that indicates a fresh base. And another cycle begins. . . .

One of the most rewarding aspects of being able to interpret simple bases, uptrends, top reversal patterns, and downtrends is that you can look at these "price pictures" and know what the market is "thinking." With a little practice, your ability to spot bases, uptrends, tops, and downtrends on charts will give you an incredible edge over other investors, who haven't this knowledge. This information also helps you to plan intelligently, and to manage your risk, which maximizes profits and minimizes losses.

Figure 5.18 shows the history of a textbook cycle experienced by AT&T Inc. (T).

Next, let's take out a microscope and change our focus to a weekly chart. Figure 5.19 displays T's uptrend, in which it nearly doubled in price (from $22 to $43). Now you can see the uptrend in more detail.

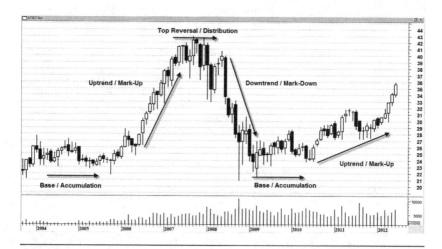

FIGURE 5.18 Monthly chart of AT&T Inc. (T) and its four-year price cycle.

Of course, you can see all the sturdy white candles that built the telecom giant's climb from $23 to $43, and then the dark, bearish candles that grabbed T's price and shoved it back down to $21. Since we like happy endings, note that after T's price fell and the cycle was complete, a new base formed. T soon started a fresh move into another uptrend, and another opportunity for investors to profit. Chart courtesy Metastock

Why do you care? Preference and investing style, that's why. Some investors monitor their positions weekly; others prefer to glance at a monthly chart. During times when the market threatens to swoon, those who usually monitor monthly charts may want to observe weekly charts for a closer view.

As we wind down our important discussion about trends, let's look at a *daily* chart of a portion of T's uptrend. Each time we move from a longer-term time frame into a shorter-term—say a yearly chart to a monthly chart, a monthly chart to a weekly chart, or a weekly chart to a daily chart—it's like observing the larger time frame under a microscope for a close-up.

Many investors rarely refer to the "close-up" details delivered by daily charts. Still, since we're on the subject, you may want to check out Figure 5.20. The chart displays a portion of the uptrend we've examined in AT&T's full price cycle, this time on a daily chart.

As noted in Figure 5.20's caption, you can see on the chart how T's uptrend climbs to higher prices; yet it doesn't shoot up in a straight line. Like a mountain climber, price has to "rest" after each move-

FIGURE 5.19   **Weekly chart of AT&T Inc. (T) price action and a close-up of the uptrend shown on Figure 5.18.**

Note how the stock climbed in stair-steps from its lows on the left side of the chart ($22), to its highs at $43. Once there, T's price began to experience wide price swings and long, dark candles. Those are sure signs of trouble ahead. Chart courtesy Metastock

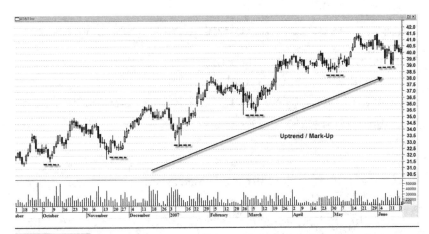

FIGURE 5.20 Daily chart that shows a portion of T's uptrend illustrated in Figure 5.19.

Now, though, the trend is "under a microscope." With each day represented, the uptrend on this chart shows more detail. Also, note that price is like a mountain climber. Although price does move higher and higher, it has to rest in between climbing periods. We call these resting periods "pullbacks," or "retracements." Notice how each pullback low (dotted lines) is higher than the one before. This fulfills part of our uptrend definition: higher highs and *higher lows*. As long as our stocks are in an uptrend, we can be comfortable holding them. Chart courtesy Metastock

ment up. Price can "rest" by moving sideways or "consolidating." Or it can rest by retracing a small part of its previous move up. In order to keep its designation as an uptrend, however, it must continue to climb in higher lows and higher highs.

HOT TIP

When price climbs in an uptrend, the "higher lows" are more important to us, as investors, than the "higher highs." If price falls to a price lower than the previous low, it means that investors are not buying the stock—even as it falls to "sale" prices. That's why a "lower low," particularly on a monthly chart, signals it's time to apply risk tactics.

Moving Averages: Simple Lines That Say a Lot

Now we're going to add a couple of simple indicators to our charts to help us make more efficient and profitable decisions. First, let's talk about one of my favorites, the moving average. Gordon introduced moving averages in Chapter Four. Now we'll discuss them in more detail.

Moving averages—as I'm fond of saying—are like your favorite uncles. They are reliable, calm, and when asked, contribute a straightforward opinion that is always helpful. On a chart, a moving average is a single line indicator that connects closing prices and averages them over a designated time period. Viewing these line(s) on a chart relative to price gives us perspective as to the current "health" of our target stock. If our stock's price is trading above the moving average, we can say the stock is strong and generally trending higher. If our stock's price is laboring below the moving average, we deduce the stock is weak. Finally, when price has been dancing above a moving average(s), but then stumbles and tumbles to levels below that average, we need to take note and possibly respond with risk management.

The easy-to-read signals emitted by moving averages have made me—and saved me—money countless times. Once you become familiar with them, I think you'll agree they are dandy decision-support tools.

Moving Average Definition: Again, a moving average is a single-line indicator. The resulting line shows us the average price of the security over a certain time period. If a security's price is trading above the moving average, then we know it is trading above its average price for the designated time period of the moving average. We can assume the stock is "healthy." If, however, the security's price is trading below the moving average, we deduce that the stock is trading at a discount to its average price for the moving average time period.

How Moving Averages Are Calculated: A moving average is calculated by adding the closing price of a security for a number of time periods (e.g., fifty days) and then dividing this total by the number of time periods. Nowadays, our chart software calculates moving aver-

> **HOT TIP**
>
> Moving averages act as swell trend lines. Habitually, these lines provide a rising "ramp" for healthy stocks that are trending higher. They can also act as "ceilings" for unhappy stocks in the process of trending lower. As long as your stocks are "walking up" atop a rising moving average, your positions are in good shape.

ages for us. Still, if we were to calculate it by hand on a paper chart, as they did in the old days before computerized charting software, this is how we would calculate a 50-day moving average on a daily chart: First, we sum our stock's closing prices for the preceding 50 days. Next, we divide that sum by 50; this would give us the average price during the preceding 50 days. Now we place a dot for that price on the chart above today's date (just as we did with line charts earlier in the chapter). The following day (tomorrow) we would repeat the same calculations: add up the previous 50 days' closing prices, divide by 50, and put a dot for the resulting figure on the chart. Finally, we draw a line to connect the dots and *Shazam*, our moving average appears.

Your Moving Average Toolbox

If you've worked with moving averages before, you may have your favorites. In this book, we are going to plot selected moving averages on our charts. The lines we have chosen fit our investing strategies and meet our criteria—they are simple and effective.

In fact, rewinding to our car analogy at the beginning of this chapter, we could imagine that we are taking a test drive with our new car on a country road. We know that the center line painted on the middle of the street is, for the most part, not meant to be crossed. As long as we stay on the right side of the center line, we are safe. However, if we cross to the left of that line, we might cause an accident.

Just so, as long as our stocks, for the most part, stay on the "right" side (above) of our designated moving averages, they are in demand

and attract buyers (expectations are bright). Let them stray to the downside of those lines, though, and nervous sellers will dump supply on the market, causing the price to fall (expectations are cloudy).

Figure 5.21 shows a monthly chart of the Intel Corp. (INTC) with a 12-month moving average plotted onto the price pattern. The 12-month moving average is an efficient all-around line to plot on monthly charts and one we will use in our system for entries and risk management and exits.

Since the time period on Figure 5.21 spans fourteen years, you can see how the moving average rises under price during uptrending months and pressures price downtrends when the stock moves lower. It's best to stay on the right side of this powerful moving average!

Figure 5.22 displays a weekly chart of the Intel Corp. (INTC). This chart spans three-plus years of price action using the 14-week moving average. Once again, you can see how the moving average line offers support when the stock price rises and buyers are in control, and acts as a hot blanket when sellers push price lower. If you

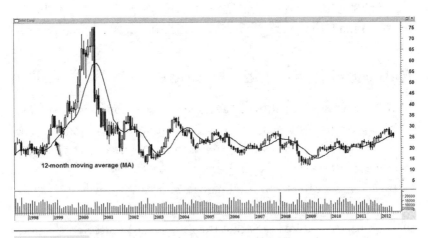

FIGURE 5.21   A monthly chart of Intel Corp. (INTC) with a 12-month moving average plotted over price.

Note how the moving average acts as a "ramp" for INTC's price to "walk up" when the stock trends higher. Conversely, you can see that when INTC weakens and drops below the moving average line, the line acts as a "ceiling" until the stock gains the strength to climb above it once again. Chart courtesy of Metastock

like to evaluate weekly charts, you can use the 14-week moving average in your investing strategies.

Figure 5.23 presents a daily chart of our INTC with two very well-known moving averages, the 50-day and 200-day lines. Commentators on financial networks will talk about these moving averages on the major indexes, the Dow Jones Industrial Average, the S&P 500 Index, and the Nasdaq Composite. The moving averages will take the biggest spotlight when the S&P 500 Index falls below either of these two averages.

HOT TIP

Many times a stock's downtrend will ride south for a shorter period of time than does its uptrend. That's because bull markets typically last longer than bear markets (thank goodness!).

Institutional traders and investors also watch the 50- and 200-day moving averages. Many times they will buy a stock (with good fundamentals) when its price bounces off the top side of the 50-day MA. (Think of the 50-day MA as a trampoline.) Also, these institutions may sell a stock that stumbles below its 50- or 200-day moving average.

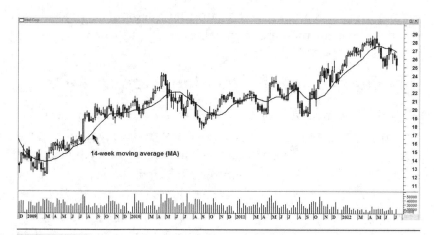

FIGURE 5.22 **A weekly chart of INTC's price action in a three-year period.**

Plotted on the price pattern is the 14-week moving average. This is a good all-around average that indicates when the semiconductor stock is attracting buyers (above the MA) or attracting sellers (below the MA). Chart courtesy Metastock

FIGURE 5.23 A daily chart of Intel Corp. (INTC) with two major moving averages plotted on it: the 50-day moving average (MA) (dotted line) and the 200-day moving average (MA) (solid line).

You can see that once the giant semiconductor company rose off of its lows in October (lower left), it scooted above both of its major moving averages and mostly held above the 50-day MA until May. Note how the 200-day MA rises at a more gradual angle, beneath the 50-day line. When INTC falls below the 50-day line, many investors think "caution." When a stock slides below the 200-day MA (which INTC hasn't currently accomplished), these investors may sell their positions. Chart courtesy Metastock

Some of you may want to monitor daily charts of the major indexes and equities. If you do, these are key moving averages to watch.

Moving Averages as Decision-Support Tools

Now that you are aware that moving averages offer a calm, straightforward perspective on a stock's price action, let's plug in a quick strategy session. We'll focus on the moving averages we just discussed and use them as decision-support tools for buying stocks.

Say you have targeted a stock that you may want to purchase. In conjunction with checking out the company's fundamentals (again, a discussion of that information is coming up), you will want to evaluate a weekly or monthly price chart of that stock. Preferably, you want your target stock's price moving in an uptrend, or at least beginning to rise out of a base.

How can we simplify this identification process? Check to see if your target stock or ETF is *trading above its rising 12-month moving average on a monthly chart.* For those who prefer using weekly charts, look to see if it is *trading above its rising 14-week moving average on its weekly chart.* As mentioned, in our approach, we will use the 12-month moving average. However, you can use either one of these criteria as an entry support tool. If the stock trades below its moving average, you may want to consider waiting until (if) it rises above that line.

What's the point? The point is, when you enter an equity position, you want to choose stocks that are attracting buyers—not sellers. You don't want to buy a losing stock, and then lose even more money for goodness knows how long. I've seen this happen to investors on countless occasions. When I was new to investing and couldn't read charts, it happened to me. And I'm willing to bet that you know someone (I hope not you) who has bought equity shares only to watch them tumble in value for what seemed like for darned ever. Let's not go there. And if you've been "there," you need not go there again. Now we have a moving-average strategy that helps to point us in the right direction. After that, it's up to us to manage our risk.

Which chart time period do I choose—the monthly or the weekly? You can check monthly charts on a monthly basis, or monitor weekly charts for a more detailed view of price action of indexes and your equity and ETF positions. That's for you to decide. Their signals are similar, and either will work to your advantage.

Figure 5.24 shows a monthly chart of the American Express Co. (AXP), with its 12-week moving average.

You can see how the moving average acted as a guide to show when price trended higher and bulls controlled the stock. When price tumbled to the downside, however, and the moving average matched it in a cliff-dive, it was not the time to purchase shares of the credit card giant. In fact, when AXP closed below its 12-month moving average for one to two months in a row, we suggested exiting the position and taking profits. We can monitor the stock to purchase shares again, if desired, when price reverses to the upside, begins to trend higher, and rises above the 12-month moving average.

Figure 5.25 displays a weekly chart of American Express Co. (AXP), with its 14-week moving average. As you can see by the arrows, the moving average rose upward, and the stock traded above the line for

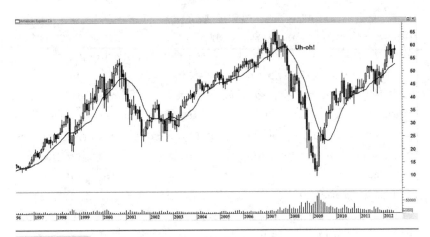

FIGURE 5.24 **The American Express Co. (AXP) spanning about 15 years.**

Note how the 12-month rising moving average indicated the years when the stock trended higher and offered a profitable investing opportunity. Woe to those who bought, however, when the moving average plunged to the downside. Chart courtesy Metastock

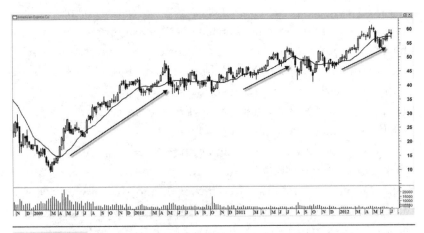

FIGURE 5.25 **A weekly chart of American Express Corp. (AXP) that spans three-plus years of price history.**

As you see, the moving average rose higher about 70 percent of the time. This tells us that AXP attracted buyers and offered investors a dandy opportunity to profit.

Chart courtesy Metastock

the majority of the time. Investors who purchased shares of AXP during these upmoves surely took home sweet gains.

Using moving averages as decision-support tools for entries can give added strength to your investment choices and your results. We'll talk more about these tactics as we go.

Now that we've focused on the "technicals," or how to evaluate price action on charts, in Chapter Six, Gordon is going to talk about the "Fabric of Fundamentals." He'll show you straightforward techniques for appraising company earnings so you can judge a company's present strength and future expectations for growth.

Key Points to Remember

→ To research a stock as a potential investment, investors use two basic methods of analysis: fundamental and technical.

→ Fundamental analysis entails examining a company's financial statements.

→ Technical analysis represents the art and practice of interpreting a stock's historical price charts.

→ The current price of a stock represents the perception of value agreed to by both buyer and seller.

→ Line charts consist of single lines that connect the closing prices at the designated time period (daily, weekly, monthly).

→ Bar charts display a high, low, open, and close for each designated time period.

→ Japanese candlestick charts use high, low, open, and closing prices, like the bar charts, but fill in the spaces between the open and close with a white or dark rectangle, called the "real body."

→ Equity prices move in cycles that include Base/Accumulation, Uptrend/Mark-Up, Top Reversal/Distribution, and Downtrend/Mark-Down phases.

→ Most investors will focus on the Uptrend/Mark-Up phase as their field of opportunity.

→ Moving averages are single-line chart indicators that display a security's average price over time.

→ Basically, when a security's price is trading above a major moving average and the average line is trending higher, that security is "healthy" and attracting buyers. When a security trades below the moving average, that security is "weak" and attracting sellers.

→ Moving averages act as decision-support tools; we can support our "buy" decision when our stock target's price trades above a rising moving average. When price trades below a falling moving average, we may choose to avoid that stock for the time being.

PERSONAL GAINS

— Toni —

Resiliency—Your Essential Skill for Success

That which does not kill us makes us stronger.

—Friedrich Nietzsche

I suspect that for most of us, these are challenging times. Happy? Sure. Hectic? Definitely! Change is all around us, and for many people, that change is happening way too fast. (Technology doubles in advancement approximately every eighteen months.) Feelings of "overwhelm" can lurk around every corner. Added to that, personal, career, health, and financial obstacles jump into our paths on a regular basis.

In my life journey, one skill I find myself pulling out of my quiver more and more often is *resiliency*. When we are resilient, we recover from life's setbacks quickly, and with minimal scars. When we are resilient, we maintain our health and energy throughout disruptive times. When we are resilient, we are open to new ways of working and relating to others. In other words, we cope with life's adversities, learn from them, and move forward with a stronger sense of purpose.

When confronted with disasters, resilient people suffer the same feelings of despair, grief, loss, and anger as those around them. But they don't blame others. Also, they don't stay stuck in negative emotional states. Instead, they look forward: they look for ways to solve their current problems that will lead to better-than-before situations. They expect to create "new and improved" life conditions, and they work toward them with single-focus purpose. Finally, resilient people maintain a healthy sense of humor. After all, laughing at oneself and with others can be the fastest way to lighten, or even cure, most any negative happenstance.

I've noticed that the more resilient I become, the more I enjoy life. My ability to *resile* (the verb for resiliency) has made me stronger, healthier, and more confident. In this day and age, I believe resiliency is a vital life skill. The more we hone this skill, the happier and more successful we will be.

Analyzing Company Performance

Fundamental Research for Investors

— Gordon —

MOST PROFESSIONAL investors buy a stock only after they have thoroughly analyzed the company behind it. The typical individual investor has little hope of duplicating this effort effectively. Even if an investor has the knowledge, she rarely has the time. If that sounds like you, read on. This chapter offers helpful advice to the time-constrained investor looking for opportunities.

The GainsMaster approach guides an investor to make decisions first about himself, next about market conditions, and then about individual companies as investment opportunities. To efficiently analyze the financial fundamentals of a single company, you must concentrate on what matters most; otherwise you can get lost in the ocean of data, facts, and figures associated with company reports.

Reading charts and analyzing market moods may help an investor answer the question, "What *could* the price of the stock be before long?" Financial analysis has a different purpose. Most financial analysts weave together a picture of a company's financial standing in hopes of answering the question, "What *should* the price of the stock be?" In reality you need both types of analysis, because the first question, once answered, tells you *when* to buy a stock, but the purpose of answering the second question is to tell you *what* to buy.

Now this chapter assumes that you have the desire and ability to select individual stocks for your own portfolio. It is true that stocks, as a class of investment, perform quite well when the market is in a positive mood, especially compared to bonds. In bull markets, stocks tend to outperform bonds and show significantly less risk than commodities, so putting your money in stocks is a reasonable thing to do if you think the market is likely to remain in a good mood for a few years. But it isn't the only choice you have.

In today's investing world, you don't have to buy individual stocks to get the good returns stocks provide. As Toni discusses in Chapter Eight, you can invest in Exchange Traded Funds (ETFs), which allow you to participate in the gains of general stock market indexes like the S&P 500. If your task is limited to selecting an ETF, your ability to analyze the market's mood and read charts becomes much more important than knowing how to research the fundamentals of an individual company.

The reason Toni and I advocate that investors learn how to select individual stocks is so that they can overcome the limited gains available in index investing alone. The value of Apple Computer's stock grew by two thousand percent over the last decade. Few if any ETFs are capable of matching that feat. Just one good stock pick can help you handsomely outperform the markets all on its own. When you are investing in individual stocks, however, you need ways to observe the overall financial strength of the companies behind them.

Most people assume that financial analysis is laborious drudgery. The stereotypical effort of extracting information by poring over balance sheets and income statements conjures up images so tedious that most novice investors gasp in fright if they so much as imagine themselves making the attempt. But they needn't fear that they will be submerged in spreadsheets and drowned in data. Financial information is far more accessible and comprehensible now than ever before. Investors can research information about a company wherever they find themselves with access to the Internet. In a matter of minutes, you can weave together your own tapestry of potential when analyzing almost any company. In fact, with a little refinement in your efforts, you can quickly arrive at the answer to the question, "Could the value of this stock increase if other investors came to see the future of the company as I do?" Even a simple look at a few key details will enable you to understand enough about a company's current financial position to determine its future prospects. The simplest way to accomplish this is to focus on the fundamental details that represent the culmination of all the efforts a company makes. That's why in this chapter I will explain a simple method of analyzing fundamental information that focuses on two critical areas of evidence used for forecasting a company's financial prospects: Growth and Opportunity.

The Tasks of Fundamental Research

You've probably heard the words that most investors assume do not apply to themselves. I'm referring to the words that stand out like the Surgeon General's statement on the side of a cigarette carton but are crafted for the investing world. These words are often included when you hear or read something that discusses investment opportunities. They go something like this: "Investing involves risk, and you could lose some or all of your money." They are appropriate, if imprecise, words of caution.

The first task you undertake in doing fundamental research is to help yourself find a way to avoid the fate these words imply. As I mentioned in Chapter Four, market prices shift from a downward trend to an upward trend when the market's mood also shifts, from safety seeking to opportunity seeking. During times when the market has made this transition, many companies have much lower stock prices than they had in the previous year or so. In such times many companies have had their business models severely tested. Some businesses may not survive another year or two beyond this point, but among those that do, there will be excellent investment opportunities. Reviewing the financial fundamentals of a company is one way to limit your chances of losing all the money that you have committed to a single stock.

The second task in your research is to build a list of stocks from which you can select your investment candidates. You will create this list by finding stocks that fit the fundamental criteria you establish. Once you have this list, you can review it for changes on a periodic basis—perhaps once a month. You'll want to have about twenty or so on this list so that you can have that many to choose from. If you have this list on hand and review it periodically, then you'll be able to recognize changes in these stocks over time. Those that improve the fastest are likely to continue to do so if the market improves, so keeping an eye on these stocks over time is a useful exercise. Stocks that do not improve after a month or two are simply dropped from your list and replaced by new ones.

Accomplishing both these tasks may sound like a very time-consuming exercise. In times past, it took seasoned professionals hours, or even days, to put together such a list. Times and tools have changed. Yet another of the great advantages for individual investors is the available research they can find in a matter of minutes with access to the Internet and a well-refined procedure. I'll walk you through just such a procedure in this chapter. This will give you some ideas for doing your own research on a regular basis in a more productive way than you might have thought possible.

Look for the Green—
Recognizing Signs of Growth

Like an eager farmer looking for the first light-green shoots of plant growth to come out of the dark dirt, so do investors and analysts watch for signs of growth in companies. The term "growth" simply means that a company experiences enough success that it measurably increases the amount of business it is doing. Analysts spend a significant amount of time trying to read a company accountant's reports and determine precisely how much growth, and what kind of growth, a company had during the reporting period (usually three months).

Analysts and professional investors scrutinize two measures of growth. These measures are often referred to as "top-line growth" and "bottom-line growth." The names have reference to the numbers positioned on a balance sheet where a company's income is listed at the top, expenses are then listed and subtracted, and the amount at the bottom is the profit left over. Top-line growth represents gross revenues, or in other words, the total sales made by a company. Bottom-line growth represents the net profits left over after expenses and taxes are subtracted from the sales. The bottom-line growth also has a more common name: earnings.

Earnings growth. Earnings are the main point of focus in all financial analysis, and the growth of earnings is the most important evidence to observe. For a company to earn a single dollar of profit is a significant achievement. Just imagine a one-of-a-kind machine that is large, complex, and has many intricately moving parts. That image is a good analogy for any publically traded company. If you were to look at any particular department within the company, you'd find people faced with day-do-day challenges. But if you focus on the output of all those people working to overcome the challenges in front of them, it boils down to a single number. Any single department can have large enough problems to throw off the company's inner machinery and wipe out profits. When the bottom-line number is both positive and larger than it was the last time the company reported its earnings, it is an indicator that the company and all its departments are working in order. If earnings grow larger, it means that the company is capable of finding a way to do more of what it wants to do. If you focus on the growth of earnings, you are observing the key output that implies the value of all other efforts. It is the most economical point of data for you to spend your time reviewing.

By saying this, I do not mean to discredit or discourage the use of all other fundamental financial data. Certainly there is value in learning to study the balance sheet, income statement, and cash-flow statement of a publicly traded company. Being able to sort through those details can give you a means of occasionally being able to spot problems well before they become evident in the stock price. But as an individual investor, you will have difficulty recognizing whether those problems represent something on which you need to act in a timely manner.

Consider the following example. Learning how to dig into the cash-flow statement will allow you to track the trends in two useful measures, cash-from-operations and cash-from-financing. Now this can provide useful insights if you want to take the time to look at it. In 2007, before the financial crisis hit, Goldman Sachs, Lehman Brothers, and Morgan Stanley, the biggest investment banks on Wall Street at the time, all showed evidence of systemic problems that can now be clearly seen in hindsight by looking at those two numbers. As early as 2003, these companies were beginning to show that cash-from-operations was down and cash-from-financing was up. That trend continued for four years until the financial crisis, which wiped out Lehman Brothers and altered the future of the investment banking industry.

So why would I not advocate looking for that kind of data? It isn't that I don't think it useful, but in my opinion, it isn't timely enough for the individual investor. That data showed up four years ahead of time, and during the first three years of that activity, Lehman Brothers stock increased by 132 percent.

The year before it went bankrupt, however, its quarterly earnings growth declined. This coincided with a time in which the market's mood turned sour. These two indicators allowed investors to confirm the need for a timely exit as the price began to decline. The more you know about fundamental analysis, the better informed you can be; however, for those individuals who are not schooled in finance or economics, it is important to be economical with time spent on financial research. Focusing on earnings growth is the research tactic most likely to render timely information for individual investors.

In my opinion, there are three pitfalls from relying on such a method for analyzing a company's stock, namely: the speed of the market, a company's natural aversion to bad news, and a false sense of security.

The first pitfall is the speed of the market. Price trends change well before actual problems appear in the statements printed once every three months—today's investing world moves much faster than once per quarter. Long before a company's woes become public and obvious to someone reading the balance sheet, the price of the stock may have fallen 30 percent, 50 percent, or more. Consider that even a decade ago Enron's stock fell 50 percent in just eight months before its CEO resigned in sudden fashion. In that time there were only two quarterly reports issued, and there was nothing in the company's accounting statements to suggest that bankruptcy was just over a year away. As fast as the fall of Enron was, the fall of Lehman Brothers in 2008 was even more rapid. In the same time it took for Enron's share price to be cut in half, Lehman Brothers' went from sixty dollars per share literally to zero. The speed of information and investor response gives no investor the leisure to wait things out until the next quarter's business report.

The second pitfall is the hyper-sensitivity of the company's officers toward the appearance of any bad news in the company's statements. These statements will put the company in the best possible light within the framework and standards of generally accepted accounting principles (GAAP). GAAP standards are meant to make publicly-traded entities as transparent as possible, but even these standards couldn't warn investors quickly enough about the problems inherent to the business models of either of the two companies mentioned.

The third pitfall, based on the other two, is the false sense of security that an over-analyzing perusal of such statements can create for an investor. I have heard many investors tell me stories as their justification for holding on to their investments while share prices dropped and continued falling. I've heard many fanciful hopes about how the stock will rise once a certain transaction is completed or a government policy is enacted or some other such external event occurs. The company must be a good buy, they say, based on the data they

> ## HOT TIP
>
> We focus on earnings growth as an aggregate of business effective-
> ness. In the movie *Moneyball,* starring Brad Pitt and Jonah Hill, there
> is a scene that captures the essence of focusing on earnings growth
> in fundamental data. Pitt's character, Billy Beane, a Major League
> Baseball team's general manager, and Hill's character, Peter Brand, a
> newly hired assistant who studied economics at Yale, explain to the
> team's staff why they want to acquire a particular player. Their ratio-
> nale is that the player in question has a high on-base percentage—a
> statistic that measures how often the player actually gets on base
> compared to how many times he takes a turn at bat. One of the staff
> points out that his stats are skewed, because the player often gets on
> base without making a hit. Pitt's character fires back with a ques-
> tion, "He gets on base a lot. Do I care if it's a walk or a hit?" After the
> silence from the staff, the general manager turns to his assistant for
> the answer. "Pete?" he asks. The stats-loving assistant responds dryly,
> "You do not." Now admittedly there is a chasm of difference between
> statistics and real live humans, but in the investing world, dollars
> and dividends are not well correlated with that divide between the
> perception of reality and reality itself. Similar to the way *Moneyball*
> elevates the value of the on-base percentage stat in baseball, I echo
> those who advocate the notion that earnings growth is the single sta-
> tistic on which the attention of the individual investor is best spent.

have wrung from the inner bowels of these statements. The business is solid; it's just an anomaly. When relying on a study of untimely financial statements, a researcher's hope that things can turn around often requires turning a blind eye to the ugly reality staring back at him from just a single item: earnings growth has slowed or stopped. There are far too many investments out there that offer better busi-ness results.

Three particular characteristics of quarterly earnings reports can signal the kind of growth that attracts investors. First, earnings growth attracts new investors at the moment a company first shows earnings, where before it has had none—or at least none for a while. Second, earnings growth is also attractive when a company shows growth for a string of consecutive quarters. Last, earnings growth is attractive when it exceeds the expectations that the company or independent financial analysts have set for that particular quarterly report. Any of these occurrences will attract enough new investors that the company's stock price will likely rise.

Measuring earnings growth. A publicly traded company reports its earnings to all investors who hold shares of the company. Each quarter when this is done, a company has to give some measure of its earnings that is meaningful to those investors. Since no two companies are exactly alike, the numbers of different measures may vary greatly in size and meaning. One particular standard that the finan-

HOT TIP

The P/E ratio measures how much money an investor is willing to spend to theoretically participate in one dollar of annual earnings. For example, if a company earned $5 per share over the course of the year, and the stock were priced at $50 per share, then it could be said that investors were willing to pay $10 for every one dollar of earnings. Another way to say this would be express the value in terms of time. A P/E ratio of ten would also means that investors are willing to theoretically wait ten years to get their money back based on the current rate of earnings. This assumption is truly theoretical because shareholders of publically traded stock do not participate in direct distributions of the company's profit based on these shares. Some companies pay dividends, which is a form of profit sharing. But the dividend distributions are not uniform from one company to another. Yet, while the assumption behind the P/E ratio is theoretical, analysts consider the P/E ratio among those tools they consider highly useful in measuring the value of a company.

cial industry has settled on to help put earnings reports in an appropriate context for shareholders is to quantify earnings in terms of stock shares. To report earnings this way, analysts divide the amount of money earned that quarter by the number of the company's shares. That measure is called earnings per share, or EPS.

These events are attractive to investors who are looking for ways to see their money grow and for that growth to be returned to them. As investors buying shares of a company's stock, we look for any evidence we can find that helps us believe earnings growth will continue and give us our money back with some measure of increase.

Another commonly used measure of earnings is a ratio found by dividing the share price of the stock by the earnings per share. This, not surprisingly, is referred to as the price-earnings ratio, or P/E ratio. Investors use the P/E ratio to determine how expensive a stock is compared to the amount of money the company brings in. The P/E ratio is a convenient measure and has a variety of uses in fundamental analysis.

Identifying EPS Growth Signals. With these definitions in mind, it becomes simple to identify which kinds of growth measures are attractive to investors. Earnings reports that show any of the following will be considered good news by most investors and will likely lead to a rise in the price of the stock:

- EPS reported to be larger in the latest quarter than in the previous quarter
- EPS reported to be continuing an upward trend of growth
- EPS reported to be positive for the first time, or for the first time after any length of time where the company lost money
- EPS reported to be larger for any number of consecutive quarters
- EPS reported to be larger than any previous report
- EPS reported to have increased over previous reports at a faster rate than ever before
- EPS reported to have increased at an amount or rate greater than analysts estimated

Of all these in the previous list, I find the first one the most influential in helping spot stocks likely to begin or continue an upward trend in price. If the EPS number is higher in the most recent two quarters than in the quarter before, it shows that the company is operating well for now and has some success it can build on. It is true that the last bulleted item in the list will make the stock rise, sometimes dramatically, but this tends to be a short-term effect, lasting only a few days at most, as investors adjust to the surprise and factor in the news it brings.

Another important factor for earnings reports is that we also want to see a trend of such data over a longer period than just a few days. We want to see earnings rising in a pattern of growth that continues. Some companies might have a seasonal pattern to their business, and so they always make more money in one quarter than in the other three. For those companies you don't need to see growth rising each quarter, but you would still expect to see earnings trending higher each year.

Let me give you an idea of what I mean. If you were to see a company's earnings graphed out and wanted to be able to recognize what strong earnings look like, what would you look for? Figures 6.1 and 6.2 show some examples.

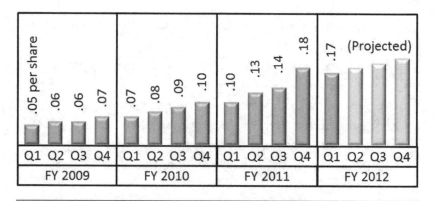

FIGURE 6.1   Earnings for Rackspace Hosting Incorporated (RAX).

This company showed a steady increase of earnings growth for three years.

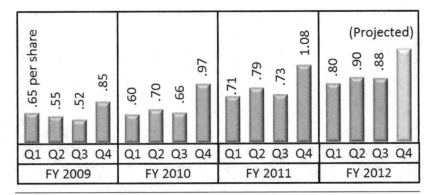

FIGURE 6.2   **Earnings for Costco Wholesale Corporation (COST).**
Though this company always has a strong fourth quarter, the trend of the chart is higher each year. Each of the quarters outperforms the previous year's number.

In Figure 6.1 you can see a graph of earnings for a company called Rackspace Hosting Incorporated (RAX). This company has been steadily growing its earnings for the past few years. Not surprisingly, the stock price has moved significantly higher along the way. In Figure 6.2 we see a different story. The earnings graph for Costco Wholesale Corporation (COST) shows a climbing trend in earnings year after year, even though the fourth quarter of the year is noticeably higher than the other three. Investors don't penalize the company in the first quarter of each year because they know that the business is seasonal—affected heavily by Christmas shoppers.

On the other hand, companies with poor earnings records have very different-looking graphs. Some show a pattern of decline, while others show no pattern at all. Investors aren't likely to be patient with a company who makes less and less money each year (or loses more and more). Investors prefer predictability when they can get it, so they would consider a company that fluctuates between surprisingly good earnings and surprising losses to be unattractive. Consider the two examples in Figures 6.3 and 6.4.

Figure 6.3 shows a graph of the earnings trend for a company named Hutchinson Technology Incorporated (HTCH). As you can see on the graph, this company has consistently been losing money

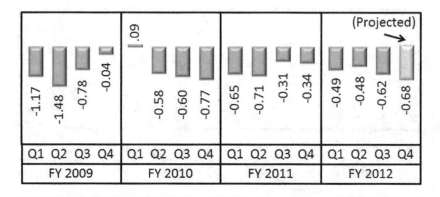

FIGURE 6.3   Earnings for Hutchinson Technology Incorporated (HTCH).
The company reported losing money from 2009 through 2012. After a brief glimmer of hope in 2009, investors were left disappointed.

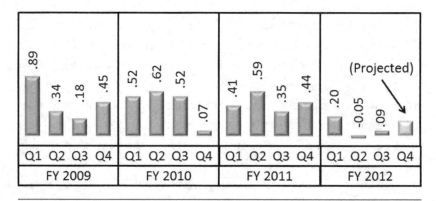

FIGURE 6.4   Earnings for Bill Barrett Corporation (BBG).
The earnings for this company fluctuate, but you can see for yourself how the quarterly results are trending lower.

each year. You don't have to try hard to imagine what happened to its stock price during the period of time depicted by these graphs (2009 to 2012). The price fell by more than 90 percent.

Figure 6.4 shows a more subtle story. While it is true that the company, Bill Barrett Corporation (BBG), has actually been making money most of the time, you can clearly see that the trend for its earnings slants in an unfortunate downward drift. The stock price moved upward from 2009 through 2010, but in 2011 investors lost patience. When the company reported a decline in its earnings in the last half of 2011, investors began to flee. By mid-2012 the stock had lost more than half its value.

Because growth is a key element for us to observe, we would do well to build one or more of these measures into our procedure for identifying stocks. The procedure I will show you does just that. But before I can explain the procedure, we must turn our attention to the second critical area of observation: looking for evidence of opportunity.

Watching for Blue Skies— Recognizing Evidence of Opportunity

The first signs of growth, whether in nature or finance, must necessarily be followed by favorable conditions so as not to endanger recent progress. It is little wonder that the financial world can so easily adopt a metaphor or two from agriculture. Both represent man's efforts to significantly invest time, labor, and personal identity in creating an increase from the resources used to start the endeavor. These efforts are significant enough that we don't want to squander them, so we must survey our surroundings to know the likelihood of meeting with success. Investors can discern favorable conditions for success by observing three pieces of evidence: the comparison of P/E ratio to future P/E ratio, the measure of insiders buying the stock, and the measure of institutional investors buying the stock.

The Forward P/E Ratio

One measure that analysts use to help investors anticipate future earnings growth is called the forward P/E ratio. This number is calculated by taking the average of several financial analysts' estimates of what the company's earnings will be in the coming year. These analysts are not employed by the company in question; they simply make a living researching that company and a few others. Professional investors pay significant fees for the detailed research of these

analysts. The highlights of their reports are made publically available.
This average estimate is then divided by the current price of the stock.
A good score for the forward P/E ratio would be one that is lower
than the current P/E ratio score. Since the forward P/E ratio is based
on the current stock price, one could expect that if the company's
earnings grew and the stock price stayed the same as it is today, then
mathematically, the forward P/E ratio score should be lower than the
current P/E ratio.

Insider Trading: Bad for Martha, Good for Investors

When looking at a company's fundamental financial data, there isn't
anything on its balance sheets that explains what the opportunity
for a company is. The purpose of the financial data is not to lay out
marketing plans or an overview of the company's business strategy, so
investors need to look for more subtle kinds of evidence that the company is surrounded by conditions of opportunity. For this evidence,
we, as potential investors in the company, can look at how other
people view the company's opportunities. In particular we should

observe those who have a better look at the company's future and its opportunities—namely, the company's officers, who would be considered insiders.

Insiders include anyone who has access to key data about the financial performance of the company before it shows up in public reports. This would include, but is not limited to, the company's board of directors, senior management, and individual shareholders who own more than ten percent of the company. When you hear about insider trading in the news, it is usually referring to illegal activity. But insider trading is perfectly legal if done within the prescribed time frames.

Several academic studies have made the claim that a strategy of merely following insiders as they legally buy shares can outperform the markets. The studies refer to moments in time when insiders are allowed to buy but must hold on to stocks for a specified minimum period. These holding requirements basically make it very difficult for an insider to truly and knowingly buy or sell with the intent to deceive investors into thinking the stock is better than it is. Therefore, we can use this principle as part of our decision-making procedure. Insiders know more than we do, and we can leverage their knowledge. If insiders are willing to spend their own money buying their own stock, it might be that they are taking an educated, calculated risk, the same kind we'd take if we knew what they knew.

It follows that if insiders are legally buying shares, that action is evidence of opportunity as viewed by those who can see it better than the average investor. This is useful evidence we can include in our procedure for identifying stocks that go on a watch list. But we don't have to limit our insight to optimistic insiders. There are other kinds of individuals who can provide similar evidence of opportunity.

Institutions: Investors with Commitment

Individuals who invest money professionally on behalf of other people are referred to as institutional investors. These are the men and women who manage mutual funds, pension funds, or something similar. They control an unusually large proportion of the money in the markets, perhaps at times even a majority of the invested money active in the markets.

Most of these investors have rules that they place on themselves—rules you want to know about—which require them to stay in a position for more than one year. When they purchase a stock for the first time or add more shares to their existing collection, they hope not to have to part with them for more than a year. The implications of that decision are important. If institutional investors begin taking or increasing positions in a stock and they are unlikely to reduce that position in the stock for at least a year, their actions invite others to join them. If many other institutional investors do the same, it is because they likely all see an opportunity.

These investors have access to much greater resources of knowledge, research, and experience than most other individuals in the market, so when they make a commitment to buy a stock, they don't do it lightly. They have brought their best resources to bear on that decision. It makes sense that we should pay attention to their actions. Their commitment is evidence of opportunity for the company's success, and in turn, for its stock price to rise.

Fortunately, there is a way to take advantage of not only institutional investor activity, but also evidence of opportunity from both insider trading activity and P/E ratio scores. Internet-based searching tools are easy to use nowadays. With such tools, you can generate a list of stocks that meet these criteria in just a few minutes.

Get a Jump Start on Fundamental Research— Stocks to Consider in a GO-Sign Market

In the next chapter, Toni will explain some of the best resources for stock research and information. But I want to introduce you to at least one online resource that can reduce the effort it takes to gather fundamental financial research in just a few mouse clicks. That resource is FINVIZ.com. If you haven't ever heard of or visited this website, then you'll want to, because it is the answer to your question.

What question? The one you are probably asking yourself about this point in the chapter. "How am I going to check through all the detail in this chapter in just a few minutes once a month?" The answer is that you are not. FINVIZ.com will do it for you. Let me explain how.

This website is designed to help you quickly sort through financial information in a number of ways. But you only need to follow a single path through this website to accomplish the main task at hand in this chapter, namely: building a watch list of stocks whose companies show signs of growth and evidence of opportunity, thereby steering clear of any possible bankruptcy. There is much more you can do with this site, but you'll have to browse through the rest of it on your own time. I'm going to show you how to use it to perform the task this chapter has prepared you to accomplish. It begins with the screening tool on the website.

Screen Your Calls:
Picking Stocks by Appointment Only

You could spend time evaluating every hot stock tip you get from your brother in law or the latest round of advertisements in your e-mail's spam folder, but you might find it a better use of your time to narrow your focus to just a few stocks each month. The following method will show you how to set up an automatic search of over six thousand stocks and return a list of a few dozen to you in a single mouse click. It will take a few more clicks than one to set it up the first time. However, if you want to save time, you can simply rerun the search each month. There are other websites where you can do similar things, but among those that are free, I didn't find any that were easier to use than this one.

Using the screening tool on FINVIZ.com, I like to set eight filters within the various criteria available. Once I have these filter settings established, I save the screen and later rerun it in an instant. Because the screen is based on growth and opportunity, I call it my GO screen. Table 6.1 describes the filters and the values I chose for them.

See if these settings give you some ideas for setting up a screen you might prefer to use.

Filter Name	Setting to Use	Rationale
P/E ratio	Profitable > 0	So long as the P/E ratio has positive number, then the company hasn't lost money over the past year.
Forward P/E	Over 10	The average P/E score for an S&P 500 company is 18, but below 9 the score implies problems of some kind. While forward P/E should be lower than regular P/E scores, it shouldn't be too low.
EPS growth qtr. over qtr.	Over 10%	Double-digit growth in the most recent quarter catches investors' eyes every time.
Sales growth qtr. over qtr.	Over 10%	Earnings growth over 10% means good execution of business, but combining it with similar sales growth means there is an opportunity for more good things to come.
Insider transactions	Very positive > 20%	There might be lots of reasons why insiders will sell, but there is only one reason they will buy shares of their own company: they see opportunity.
Institutional ownership	Over 50%	If more than half of the stock is owned by institutional investors, then you can bet that they consider the company a sound investment, with little chance of it going bankrupt in the foreseeable future
Average volume	Over 200K	The more shares you plan on buying, the more important this setting becomes. In general, you want a stock liquid enough to allow you to get out without your order changing the price of the stock when you sell.
Price	Over $5	You can set this level at a higher price if you don't feel comfortable buying stocks below a certain price.

TABLE 6.1 **Screening criteria used to search for growth and opportunity stocks in GO-sign markets**

Identify What to Buy When the Market is in STOP Mood

As I mentioned in my previous chapter, market participants are sometimes in a pessimistic mood. During those periods of time, your goal as an investor is simple: don't lose money. Earnings growth and business opportunity are no longer key factors, so instead we need to search on something else. You could simply move your money out of any stocks or mutual funds and sit in cash through those periods, but recent years of quantitative easing have made investors realize that the value of their cash cannot be taken for granted.

Many investors want to begin chasing commodities like gold or silver. Others want to consider investing in foreign markets during these times. But there is no guarantee among any of those investments that prices will rise while stocks are going lower. In fact, many commodities will simply fall lower in price at a rate faster than the stock market will. If you can achieve any measure of growth in your investments at all during a persistently down-trending market, you will likely outperform the market and be prepared to continue doing so when things turn around.

During such times, it is useful to look for relatively safe stocks that pay dividends. You will want to find a stock that delivers an automatic payment, a dividend, to its investors every year, and at the same time doesn't move around in a risky fashion. To identify such stocks, I suggest that you consider a screen with the following criteria or something similar. Because I am looking for safety trades when I use this screen, I call it my STOP screen. I want the screen to give me, you guessed it, "safety trades only, please."

Using screens like the two I've described will generate a list of 10 to 20 stocks each month. You can use those stocks as your watch list and determine a good point at which to buy using Toni's chart-reading methods described in the previous chapter. Using the market mood method in Chapter Four, you can switch between the GO screen and the STOP screen. This will allow you to generate a new list of fundamentally sound investing ideas each month with very minimal effort. Table 6.2 provides a list of criteria used to search for stocks in STOP-sign markets.

You can find earnings information and many other resources for screening stocks on various websites. In the next chapter Toni will explain to you what information resources you have and where you can find more information about the fundamental and technical details of a company and its stock price. The resources she describes will help you mesh your understanding of how to measure a company's value with an analysis of stock prices, thus helping you weave together the information you need to build a sturdy investing strategy.

Filter Name	Setting to Use	Rationale
Dividend yield	High > 5%	You can set this measure as high or as low as you like, but you should set it high enough to outpace inflation if possible.
Institutional transactions	Over 5%	You want to know that institutions are acquiring a stock or exchange trade fund. In pessimistic times, many institutions will buy these kinds of stocks.
Beta	Under 5	This filter setting is not a point of fundamental research, but is rather a technical aspect of the price. Beta is a measure of how a given stock moves compared with the overall market. With a beta score under .5, the stock's daily movement is likely to be half as large as the market's, on a percentage basis. This setting will help you identify stocks whose price is unlikely to fall as fast as the market averages.
Average volume	Over 300 K	A liquid stock or ETF means that you can change your mind at any time and get out of the investment without losing as much money in transaction costs.

TABLE 6.2   Screening criteria used to search for stocks in STOP-sign markets

Key Points to Remember

→ Fundamental analysis attempts to answer the question, "What should the price of the stock be if all investors interpret the data the way I do?"

→ Earnings growth is the key indicator of a well-run business.

→ The speed of the market may send the price of a stock down well before problems are reported in the financial data.

→ Fundamental data can be helpful, but it is easy to get caught up in a false sense of security when studying that data.

→ Insider buying activity is a good indicator that the company has an increased degree of opportunity.

→ Using an online financial research website (like FINVIZ.com), you can generate a list of growth and opportunity stocks to periodically review.

PERSONAL GAINS

— Toni —

Gratitude: A Powerful Tool for Prosperity

Gratitude is not only the greatest of virtues,
but the parent of all others.

—CICERO

Most of us don't stop to think about it, but it's true: feelings and emotions act as powerful channels through which we direct our lives.

One of the most influential emotions is the feeling of gratitude. When we live from an active mindset of appreciation and center on the good that surrounds us, we automatically find that we encounter more peace and happiness, better health, stronger confidence, and higher levels of prosperity.

Of course, each of us encounters frustrations and negative circumstances that we'd like to wish away. Complications, it seems, are part of life. The trick is to avoid focusing on them. Why? When we insist on focusing on the negative parts of our lives, we attract more of the same thing. That means we limit ourselves, our opportunities, and our happiness.

We all have long lists of things for which we can be thankful. Most people in the world haven't a roof over their head or enough to eat. If you are reading this book, however, it may be safe to say that you have a home, food, loved ones, friends, and to one degree or another your health. Look around right now. I am sure you can spot many things or people that enrich your life. Look inside yourself. What are your strong traits? Are you grateful for them?

Here's a quick, simple process I perform each day. It works—I promise you. Every night before you go to bed or when you wake up in the morning, write down five personal character traits, people, or situations in your life for which you are grateful. Then take 60 seconds and concentrate on them, embracing them with deep and authentic feelings of gratitude. During the course of the day, make it a habit to identify the good in people and places.

After a few days, you will notice your approach to life has changed. Gone or minimized are feelings of fear, judgment, blame, inadequacy, and negativity. It's difficult to feel like a victim, become angered, or feel undeserving when you are busy recognizing the good in the world around you. You'll feel lighter, happier, laugh more, and enjoy each day more.

Learn to live from an active mindset of gratitude. You will experience more abundance and prosperity, and a more fulfilling life.

CHAPTER SEVEN

Mind Your Own Business
What You Need to Succeed

— Toni —

ARE YOU ready to take a mental break? In this chapter, we're going to leave the realm of analysis and journey into the hands-on projects that include choosing a broker, evaluating analyst ratings, and exploring websites and print resources for the best and most straightforward research.

Even if you're an experienced investor, I suggest that you glance over the chapter contents. You may see a nugget of helpful information that will bring you additional gains.

Choosing Your Investment Broker

The U.S. Securities and Exchange Commission (SEC) rules that when you buy and sell financial securities, you must use a broker registered with that government agency to serve as the channel through which your transactions are conducted. The registered broker acts as the "middleman" between you and the financial exchange on which the stock (or other asset) trades. The broker also maintains records of each of your purchases and sales. If you haven't yet opened a brokerage account, the following section will help you choose one that's right for you.

When we say brokerage "houses" or "firms," we are referring to companies such as Charles Schwab, TD Ameritrade, E*TRADE, Fidelity, and a host of others. You can also open an account with an "independent broker," meaning an individual who runs his or her own money management business. However the independent broker must be affiliated with a registered brokerage firm.

Besides recording all of your securities purchases and sales and providing you with monthly statements detailing your account balances, brokers provide advisory services and may offer limited banking services (check writing, electronic deposits and withdrawals, credit/debit cards, and interest-bearing accounts). They also broker other securities, including exchange-traded funds, options, mutual funds, bonds, and other investments on your behalf.

Brokers make their money from investors through brokerage commissions, which are the fees charged every time they execute a buy or sell order for us. Brokers also charge interest on margin accounts (more on this later in this chapter), and they add charges to our accounts for performing administrative tasks, such as those related to Individual Retirement Accounts (IRAs).

Make sure your broker is registered with the Financial Industry Regulatory Authority (FINRA) and the Securities Exchange Commission (SEC). To protect the funds in your account in case the broker goes out of business (yes, it happens), the broker should be a member of the Securities Investor Protection Corporation (SIPC). To check your broker's registration, use the respective websites: FINRA, finra.org; SEC, sec.gov; and SIPC, sipc.org.

You'll find two basic categories of brokerage firms: full-service brokers and discount brokers.

Full-service brokers. If you prefer not to go it alone and would feel better supported by having investing advice and personal service, then you'll want to check out a full-service broker. Most money center banks offer in-house full-service brokerage departments; examples include Merrill Lynch (owned by Bank of America) and Wells Fargo Advisors. Other full-service brokers include Morgan Stanley Smith Barney, Raymond James, and Edward Jones.

Once you open an account with a full-service firm, they will assign a representative to your account (called a stockbroker, registered rep, account executive, or financial consultant). This representative will offer advice to you regarding specific stocks and other investment vehicles. A good advisor will ask you to define your investing goals and then devise a plan using a selection of investing vehicles that should help you achieve those goals.

Many times, these advisors will suggest that you build a "balanced" portfolio, divided between stocks and bonds. (Gordon will discuss variations on the balanced theme in Chapter Ten.)

Of course, when you open an account with a full-service broker, please remember that the advice, guidance, and additional services come with a price. Brokerage transaction fees and advisory fees are more expensive than those of a discount broker. And you may be required to open an account with a minimum of $5,000 or higher.

Also, remember that stockbrokers are salespeople. They have bosses to please and families to feed. Generating commissions from selling investing instruments to you and other clients is their job and their source of income. When your full-service advisor recommends a stock or other asset, ask why he or she chose that particular vehicle. Then make sure you are satisfied with the answer.

Keep in mind that *no one* is more interested in your well-being—and that of your money—than you are.

Discount brokers. Are you reasonably proficient on the Internet? Would you prefer to journey into the investment world independently, without guidance or hand-holding from an investment advisor? Then you'll want to open your account with an online discount broker. These firms include Charles Schwab, Fidelity, TD Ameritrade, E*TRADE, Scottrade, OptionsXpress, and many others.

Online discount brokers offer convenience and low commissions. When you decide to buy a stock or ETF, you can hop online and go to your discount broker's website. There, you can bring up an order page, populate the boxes with your order information, and click the "buy" or "sell" button. Within a nanosecond (or thereabouts), the position appears in your account. And because you bought or sold minus investment advice from a broker professional, the commissions may cost less than $20 per trade. (Full-service brokers can charge upwards of $100 or more to execute your trades. More shares traded = higher commission.)

In addition, most online brokers offer access to online research and webinars (online seminars) that teach lessons targeting investing techniques. Since these brokers know you are "on your own," and since they prefer "sticky" clients, meaning clients who stay with them for long periods of time, it is to their advantage to offer educational resources that help you become a successful investor.

Another plus: short-term traders gravitate to online brokers, since they demand low commissions and fast trade executions. And since traders also depend on price charts to make their trading decisions, many online brokers provide good charting programs.

HOT TIP

Through industry consolidation, many online discount brokers have added more conventional services, including portfolio planning, and brick-and-mortar offices where you can get face time with an advisor.

Remember, if you open an account with an online discount broker, you will have to take full responsibility for the stewardship of the account. You create the strategies and tactics, conduct the research, and execute the buy and sell decisions.

If you choose to open your investing account with an online broker, make sure to "test" call them before funding your account. How fast do they answer the phone? How long do you have to wait to speak to a representative?

Say your Internet connection goes down or your computer crashes, and you want to sell one of your stock positions quickly. Don't you want to be able to reach your broker on the phone and get your business done swiftly and professionally? I do. So before you open an account, make a trial call, or two. If you are put on "hold" for several minutes, that is not acceptable. Look for another broker.

Selecting Your Account Category

When you open an account with your broker, you'll choose from two basic categories: *cash account* or *margin account*. Please know that with either account type, your broker may require a minimum deposit. That sum could range from $500 to $10,000, depending on the broker and the classification of the account.

A *cash account,* also referred to as a Type 1 account, is just that. You deposit a sum of money and then begin investing. It's the same as if you put $100 in your wallet and headed off to the mall. You can only purchase $100 worth of products. Say you buy a shirt—and then return it. You will receive the purchase price of the shirt back in cash. Then you can buy something else. But no matter what, you cannot exceed $100 in purchases. Ditto a cash account. IRAs are cash accounts.

A *margin account*, known as a Type 2 account, gives you more leeway. Once you qualify and are approved by your broker, you can open a margin account. This means your broker will extend credit to you, up to 50 percent of the cash in your account, so you can buy more securities.

Here's the good news: Say you decide to buy shares of Brawny Builder and you need $8,000 to complete the transaction. Problem is, you only have $4,000 cash in your account. If you have a 50 percent margin account, that $4,000 cash gives you an extra $4,000 buying power. *Shazam!* Now you can purchase the Brawny shares that you wanted.

Here's the downside. Your broker charges interest on the money lent to you. Usually the rates are reasonable, so that's not the main hitch. The main hitch is this: what if, when you buy shares of Brawny, it maxes out your margin (think: credit line)—and then Brawny's shares fall and you take a 20 percent haircut?

This is the part when you get a phone call from your broker (or a large red message on your online account page). He or she will tell you in a solemn voice that you have a "margin call." Your account is "over margin" and will be "frozen" (you can sell shares, but you can't buy new positions) until the call is cleared. You'll have to wire funds to cover the dollar amount over margin (meaning the amount above the 50 percent loan). Or you'll have to sell securities in your account to make up the amount. And if you're obliged to sell a portion of Brawny shares, which have shrunk in value, you'll take a hefty loss.

> ## HOT TIP
>
> These days, if you enter in your online account an order to buy securities that takes you over your margin limit, a notice should pop up that stops you from doing so. When technology fails, however, margin calls still occur. It's your responsibility to keep track of your buying power.

"Whoa, Toni," you say, "You sound like you have experienced a margin call."

Yes, indeed, I have. Back in my early days of investing, I made a dopey move: I maxed out my margin limit on a hyped-up stock. Right after I bought those shares, the stock's price fell like a boulder off a cliff. To cover the margin call, I had to sell that stock position at a huge loss. Talk about a learning experience! Still, the pain taught me to use margin sparingly. In other words, if you decide to use part (never all) of your margin allowance, remember to use it as a blessing, not a burden.

Getting Familiar with the T+3 SEC Rule

While we're on the subject of your investment account type, here's a final item you need to know about. *The T+3 rule,* enforced by the SEC, says that investors must settle their security transactions within three business days. This settlement cycle is referred to as "T+3," meaning "trade date plus three days."

To expand a bit, the rule dictates that your brokerage house must have payment for securities you purchase no later than three days after you execute the order. If you purchase securities in your account, the cash amount, with or without margin availability, has to appear in your account within three days. When you sell securities, it typically takes three days for the proceeds from that sale to appear in your cash account. While this rule may not sound like a big deal, the implementation can become a bit dicey. You'll see why in our example.

Example: Let's say that on Tuesday, you buy 100 shares of Shady Software, total cost: $3,000. On Wednesday morning, you sell those shares for the same cash amount and decide to buy $3,000 shares of Wacky Widgets. Can you use the same $3,000 you sold Shady shares for to buy Wacky? *No.* You have to wait T+3. Or since you sold Shady on Wednesday (trade date) you must to wait three more business days to use those funds. Thursday is the next day after the trade date. Thursday and Friday are business days, but Saturday is not; Monday will be the third day of settlement. Tuesday, you can use the $3,000 to buy Wacky.

In this day and age, you should not have to worry about attempting to use unsettled funds too early. If you place a "buy" order in your online account that can only be filled with unsettled funds, a warning message should pop up that tells you (1) you don't have enough cash to complete your trade, or (2) you are using unsettled funds for this purchase; if you complete the purchase and decide to sell *these* shares before the settlement date, your account will be frozen. In the second case, if you go ahead with the purchase, be sure you intend to keep the position for at least three days.

When you open an account with a broker, ask your brokerage firm for a list rules pertaining to your type of account. Although by law, brokerages must enforce SEC rules, many firms add specific restrictions of their own.

HOT TIP

Most brokerages will pay you interest on the unused cash in your account. Some will give you a choice between placing the funds in a money market account or in a tax-free municipal money market account.

Evaluating Broker Recommendations

You're watching your favorite show on your favorite financial network. The shiny announcer addresses his guest, the man sitting across from him, who is an analyst from Big Bad Brokerage.

"This economic environment is volatile. Where should we put our money now?"

The guest, impeccable in his three-piece suit, flashes a dazzling, California-white smile. "We've just put out a 'strong buy' on Stealthy Semiconductor. It's cheap here, with plenty of free cash flow and new products in the pipeline."

"Sounds good," the announcer says. "We see Stealthy trading at $36 here. What's your price target?

The suit leans forward in his seat. His tone is earnest. "We think Stealthy can get to $46 by the end of the year."

This is the part when folks in the viewing audience spring from their sofas, run to their computers, log on to their brokerage accounts, and buy shares of Stealthy. *Bad idea. Maybe* Stealthy *will* gallop 25 percent higher by the end of the year, although that's an optimistic call for any stock. Or maybe it will gain a fraction of that. Or maybe semiconductors will suffer an ugly quarter and Stealthy's price will fall like a boulder off a dump truck. Just because an analyst "rates" a stock a "Strong Buy" or "Buy" does not mean the stock will absolutely, positively grow in value.

During the market meltdown in 2008–2009, many brokers kept "Strong Buy," "Accumulate," and "Hold" ratings on the stocks of companies that lost *all* of their value. Instead of issuing "Sell" ratings on stocks of companies that were obviously headed for bankruptcy, these brokers kept their positive ratings intact and let investors who counted on the ratings lose trillions of dollars.

Fast-forward to one day last week. On the financial network I was watching, an announcer noted to a highly-regarded analyst, "The stock we're discussing has lost eighty-nine percent of its value over the last five years. There are no buyers for the company in sight. Yet, your firm still maintains a 'Hold' rating on its stock. Why?"

The nattily-dressed analyst squirmed in his seat. "Well, yes, I guess we do. Ah, in hindsight I suppose we should have lowered it to a 'Sell.'"

A jolt of incredulousness shot through me. I thought of all the unknowing investors who held that stock in their accounts because of that rating. These folks imagined the ratings were taken seriously by the firm that issued them. That certainly was not true in this case.

Yes, some brokerage firms hold their ratings to a higher accountability. And yes, an analyst's rating (advice) holds more weight than a "hot stock that's going to the moon" recommendation from the guy you sat next to on the plane or your best friend's dental hygienist.

The best use of analyst rankings: Use them to confirm your own research. After I research a stock and determine that I would consider purchasing shares, I turn to the analysts' rankings. You should be able to go to your broker's website and click on a tab that says "Research," and then another that says "Stocks." When you bring up an "Overview" or "Snapshot" (or similarly named) page of your target stock, you should see a list of five or six analyst ratings. The ratings may include the standard ones listed below, or they may simply state "Buy," "Hold," or "Sell."

Standard Broker Recommendations

- **Strong Buy** and **Buy**: The highest ranking. The analyst projects to the world that this stock has what it takes to compete with its competition and rise to the top. Caveat: please do not use this rating as a substitute for completing your own research. Instead, use it as a pleasant confirmation of your own due diligence.

- **Accumulate** and **Market Perform**: The second-highest rating, this tells you the analyst is less excited about the stock and so won't rate it at the tippy top. She expects it to perform at the level of its peers and perhaps keep up with the pace of the S&P 500 Index.

- **Hold** or **Neutral**: With this rating, the analyst projects a "ho-hum" attitude.

- **Sell:** Because of the bear markets of 2000–2002 and 2008–2009, when analysts' refusal to issue "Sell" ratings on companies facing certain collapse came under scrutiny, more and more analysts are now putting out sell recommendations. It's about darned time.

Where it gets confusing: if you check out enough stocks and their analyst ratings, you will see contradictions. On a single stock, one analyst will rank it a "Buy," while another will rate it a "Sell." *Now what?*

HOT TIP

Brokerage firms sell stocks to their clients. That's how they make a living. If you were selling a product, would you issue a "Don't Buy" rating on it for everyone to see? No, you would issue a "Strong Buy" or "Buy."

If you check out the stock's price chart, you may see that its price has fallen in a downtrend. That price tumble may have caused the "Sell" rating. Now, if you still want to purchase shares, before you do, please find out why the stock fell so hard. Some reasons are valid (we discussed them in Chapter Five). Read up on the company's news (we'll discuss news resources in this chapter) and find out what took the company down. On the chance you come upon phrases like "accounting irregularities," or "accounting fraud," don't walk away . . . run! And stay away for a long time.

What about the "Buy" rating? You'll want to click on the link to the analyst's report, if possible. If the report is dated more than six months or a year ago, then I would disregard it. And remember, there are two sides to every story.

Again, instead of using analysts' ratings as gospel to buy stock positions, use them as a validation of your own research. I feel the most satisfied during the occasions when I research my target stock, then check the ratings and find all "Strong Buy" or "Buy" ratings from the analysts listed. Those positions can turn out to be strong winners.

Now, let's talk about the various media you can access to gain knowledge about stocks and the companies they represent.

Tuning into the Financial Networks

Investors who want to stay updated on the markets will tune in to the financial television networks at least once a week, for an hour or two. CNBC, Fox Business, and Bloomberg are the best known. It is true that these networks broadcast valuable information that can help you with your investing decisions. Still, as we noted in the previous section, latching on to a talking head's stock recommendation can lead to reward—or remorse.

Please know that most financial guests, be they company heads, analysts, or portfolio managers, have their own agendas: Naturally, most company CEOs who are interviewed will declare that everything is rosy, no matter what. If an analyst represents a brokerage or investment bank that has a bullish outlook on the market, that analyst will have to repeat the company mantra; ditto portfolio managers.

Also, after being a highly active participant in the financial markets for the last eighteen years, I can state unequivocally one fact: *no one can say for sure which direction the market will take next.* Could we forecast Katrina before her disastrous debut on the shores of Louisiana? Could we forecast the BP oil spill? The Japanese tsunami? I think not. Yet each of these "exogenous shocks," as economists call them, delivered huge impacts on different sectors in the financial markets.

Bottom line: The financial networks are treasure troves of financial news and information. We are best served, however, by using the news and opinions they broadcast as decision-support tools for our investments—not as the final word.

HOT TIP

In the financial world, "exogenous shocks" refers to significant events caused by factors outside our usual environment. These events affect the market in positive or negative ways. Positive example: the Internet. Negative examples: energy shocks, global crises, and credit crunches.

Let's Mine the Web

Everything you probably ever wanted to know—and a lot of stuff you don't—is on the World Wide Web. Want to peruse websites devoted to your money and investing? No problem—those sites number in the tens of thousands.

Can immersion in this seemingly endless sea of information be intimidating? *You bet.* To overcome that syndrome, let's talk about selecting a few websites that will serve you well and provide the information that will help you establish and maintain a profitable portfolio.

Since we mentioned the financial news networks in the last section, let's start there. As media giants, these network nabobs have invested big bucks in their websites, and they hold a wealth of information you can use to prosper.

CNBC: www.cnbc.com
Fox Business: www.foxbusiness.com
Bloomberg: www.bloomberg.com

Now let's jump to more of the most popular financial websites. Yahoo! Finance, MarketWatch, and FINVIZ are three favorites. (Gordon gave you great earnings scanner advice in Chapter Six about using FINBIZ.com). The following lists a selection of web destinations and their URL addresses that will provide you with a ginormous amount of information about the financial markets, including news, economic and earnings announcements, investing advice, charts, tutorials, scanners, and more.

Yahoo! Finance: finance.yahoo.com
MarketWatch: www.marketwatch.com
FINVIZ.com: www.finviz.com
Briefing: www.briefing.com
Benzinga: www.benzinga.com

If you are not familiar with these sites, I suggest you spend a few minutes wandering through them and clicking on their headings.

Find the sections that hold the most value for you, and then return to them periodically to stay updated.

Online Charting Programs
MetaStock: www.metastock.com
TradeStation: www.tradestation.com
FreeStockCharts.com: www.freestockcharts.com
StockCharts.com: www.stockcharts.com

Another dandy resource resides right in front of our noses... our online broker's website. Once you've logged into your account, you can click on a tab that says, "Research" (or something similar), and a dashboard (fancy tech word for "menu") should pop up. The dashboard will offer tabs on everything from U.S. and global market news to index levels, sector action, different asset class (commodities, currencies, bonds) movements, charts, alerts, and a host of other subjects.

What may be important to you: On this page, if you are researching a stock to buy or checking up on your current positions, you should be able to type the stock's symbol in a box labeled "Symbol," or "Symbol lookup." That will take you to the stock's page.

When I'm researching stocks, I spend a lot of time on individual stock pages. After I glance at the fundamental information, I gravitate to the "Earnings" tab to check out the earnings graph and see how it matches up with the bulleted "EPS" points that Gordon listed in Chapter Six. (You can use these graphs in addition to those on FINBIZ.com.) I might also check when the next earnings report is due and bone up on any recent news about the company.

HOT TIP

Have you ever waded through financial research on the Internet, only to find yourself mired in the State of Overwhelm? Climb out of that muddy place by targeting two to four resources for your research and ignoring the rest.

Again, your broker's website should furnish you with a wealth of investing information. If you haven't done so already, take some time to explore it.

Read All about It—Financial Newspapers

I confess. I still love the feel of a *real* newspaper in my hands. I like the way it sounds when I fold it in half. I like the way the scent of the newsprint mixes with the aroma of my morning coffee. *This is your time*, it says, *your morning ritual. This is the hour you take out of your day to discover what's going on in the world.*

Whether you're a "real" paper devotee or prefer to go online, you can settle into a plethora of finance-focused columns and articles in these four iconic newspapers: *Wall Street Journal, Barron's, Investor's Business Daily*, and the *Financial Times.*

■ *Wall Street Journal* (or WSJ), www.WSJ.com: Published six days a week (Sundays excluded), WSJ features world news, business and finance, markets and investing, and articles on health and human interest. The weekend edition includes a fantastic section devoted to subjects from books to science to commerce to technology. If you don't receive WSJ every morning on your doorstep, consider subscribing to the weekend edition or occasionally picking one up at the newsstand.

■ *Barron's* (owned by *Wall Street Journal*), www.Barrons.com: Published once a week, on weekends. Alan Abelson's column, "Up and Down Wall Street," is full of dry wit and insights, and worth the subscription price. Indeed, all of Barron's columnists are erudite and offer valuable perspectives on the economy, companies, and stocks. For added value, the "Market Week Pullout" offers a compact and concise summary of the past week's market action.

■ *Investor's Business Daily* (or IBD), www.investors.com: Published Tuesday through Friday mornings, with occasional Monday Special issues available on Saturday mornings. You can learn a lot about investing from this valuable resource, as its main theme is to teach responsible investing. William O'Neil, the paper's founder, is a great believer in technicals (charts), and you'll find stock charts dominate the articles. The stock tables feature proprietary ratings, such as "IBD Composite Ranking," which ranks stocks on a scale of 1 to 100, compared to their peers. Other ratings pertain to earnings, and they reveal helpful information that can initiate, or validate, your research.

■ *Financial Times* (or FT) www.ft.com: Published in London and issued Monday–Saturday, FT bills itself as "The world's most authoritative business voice..." Indeed, I find it refreshing to read global news minus the U.S. perspective. I recommend you read this resource at least once a month; you may be surprised at what you learn.

Print and "e" (electronic) editions of magazines devoted to finance and investing also act as valuable information and learning resources. Examples are *Smart Money, Kiplinger's,* and *Forbes.*

In conclusion, you can readily see that at your fingertips reside all the facts, data, and tools you need to become a profitable investor. I'm sure it will serve you well.

Now, speaking of tools, in the next chapter we're going to talk about those much-heralded investing instruments, exchange traded funds. These funds provide some dandy benefits, and I'm eager to tell you about them. See you there soon...

Key Points to Remember

→ The U.S. Securities and Exchange Commission (SEC) rules state that when you buy and sell financial securities, you must use a broker registered with that government agency to serve as the channel through which your transactions are conducted.

→ Brokers make a good portion of their money from investors through brokerage commissions, which are the fees charged every time they execute a buy or sell order for us.

➡ If you are approved by your broker for a margin account, your broker will extend credit to you for up to 50 percent of the cash in your account; that means you have more buying power to purchase additional securities.

➡ *The T+3 rule* enforced by the SEC says that investors must settle their security transactions within three business days.

➡ Most brokerages will pay you interest on the unused cash in your account.

➡ Financial analysts' ratings applied to equities, such as "Strong Buy," "Buy," "Accumulate," "Hold," and "Sell," may be best used as decision-support tools to confirm your own due diligence.

➡ With the aid of financial television networks, the Internet, and print media, we are surrounded by virtually all of the information you could ever need about the markets and investing.

PERSONAL GAINS

— Toni —

Create and Sustain a Vibrant Self-Image

If we all did the things we are capable of,
we would astound ourselves.

—THOMAS EDISON

Were you to reflect on your personal self-image, "who" would you see?

Psychological study reveals that the most successful people are those who have positive self-images.

Are you enjoying life? Are you satisfied with your relationships, business and social progress, and your levels of health and energy? If not, you may want to take a few minutes to think about the self-image you hold of yourself, in your mind.

We all hold different concepts of ourselves in each of our daily "roles"—whether it be mom or dad, business or job, host or hostess, hobbyist or athlete. Still, all of us retain general "overviews" of ourselves that weave through each role we experience.

Here is an interesting fact: We cannot outgrow the image we have of ourselves—not for any length of time. Certainly, all of us can surprise ourselves and others with moments of great strength and fearlessness. But if our mental tapes constantly repeat messages such as, "I'm not as good as everyone else," then we move through our daily lives with self-imposed limitations. These limitations can impede our ability to achieve desired goals and to live a happy life.

If you want to transform your self-image to a more positive one, you'll need to *choose* and then *practice* thinking about yourself in a different way. First, you'll want to mentally and emotionally remove the "old" image and replace it with a positive one. *Choose:* Perhaps the "new" you maintains a position of strength in everything you do. Perhaps you are more patient, wise, and caring. Maybe you are energetic, smart, and successful. *Practice:* Next, you will want to mentally review your new image each morning, and remind yourself of it as you move through your daily activities.

Your personal self-image is a key component that drives the way you live your life. If you create and then sustain a more positive self-image, you will find your life more fulfilling and more enjoyable with every day that passes.

CHAPTER EIGHT

Exploring the World of Exchange Traded Funds

— Toni —

I F EVER a new kid burst onto Wall Street and immediately won the "Most Likely to Succeed" designation, it would be the exchange traded fund (ETF). Since the first one hit the Street in 1993 (S&P 500 SPDR, symbol SPY), ETFs have won the hearts and wallets of institutional and individual investors the world over.

As you read this, someone on Wall Street with a twinkle in his eye is creating yet another ETF—while down the Street, another professional shoos an underperforming fund out to pasture. Nearly 1,500 of these vehicles exist to date, sporting over a trillion dollars in assets.

Gordon has already mentioned several ETFs in past chapters. And as you've seen, these funds fit extremely well into our GainsMaster approach. Many investors enjoy the versatility of ETFs to the degree that they allocate their entire portfolio to a selection of funds. Others mix funds with individual equity selections. Those who like the simplicity of "indexing," or buying a fund that represents a major index, can easily do so by purchasing shares of funds such as the SPDR Dow Jones Industrial Average (DIA), the S&P 500 SPDR (SPY), or the PowerShares QQQ (QQQ) (Nasdaq 100 Index).

If you want to purchase shares of ETFs for your cash or margin account or IRA portfolio, you'll want to consider your financial goals, your diversification requirements, and your tolerance for risk. Take some time to determine what asset classes and categories best suit your needs.

I will talk briefly about how ETFs fit into asset allocation methods later in this chapter. Gordon will outline asset allocation strategies in Chapter Nine. Some of you will want to apply the approach that dictates holding index and equity ETFs during bull markets and then switching to bond (fixed income) funds during bear markets. With ETFs' versatility, this tactic is easily implemented.

The goal of this chapter is to acquaint you with exchange traded funds and introduce you to the main fund families and their premier funds. For those of you who are familiar with ETFs, this chapter may include ETF sector-related information that will expand your knowledge base—and thus your ability to invest to win.

ETFs: What They Are

An exchange traded fund (ETF) contains a basket of stocks or other securities that track a particular index, or theme. These funds trade throughout each trading day, like a single stock. They represent every major asset class, including equities, bonds, commodities, and currencies.

You can invest in ETFs that follow any major equity index, such as the Dow Jones Industrial Average (DIA), the S&P 500 Index (SPY), the Nasdaq 100 Index (QQQ), the SPDR Mid-Cap 400 Index (MDY), the Russell 2000 Index (IWM), and others. Style-focused funds target "growth" and "value" equity indexes. Sector funds concentrate on sectors of the S&P 500 index, such as financial, energy, or health care. If we drill down to industry groups (subsets) in these sector funds, we find funds dedicated to businesses such as transportation, biotech, or semiconductors. Slice industry groups into smaller pieces, and we discover ETFs that follow such specialized fields as nanotech, ocean-going shippers, or the sovereign debt of emerging markets.

If your investing objectives are more conservative or the market issues a STOP signal, you can shift to bond or fixed-income ETFs. Examples include Treasury bond ETFs, such as the iShares Barclays Aggregate Bond Fund (AGG), iShares Barclays 7–10 Year Treasury Bond Fund (IEF), or the popular iShares Barclays 20+ Year Bond Fund (TLT). iShares and other fund sponsors also offer a wide selection of ETFs that track municipal bonds, corporate bonds, junk bonds, and more.

When interest rates remain low, you may also want to check out ETFs that follow various REIT (real estate investment trusts) indexes; these funds can yield delightful dividends.

For more excitement (sometimes more than you want), you can trade *commodities* ETFs that march to the tune of oil, natural gas, metals, grains, cotton, coffee, cocoa, or even livestock prices. (Gains from commodities-based ETFs are taxed differently than gains earned from equities-based ETFs; check with your broker for details.) I advise a thorough knowledge of commodities trading before entering these funds; they can be very volatile.

Since their introduction a few years ago, *currencies* ETFs have exploded in popularity. The once-mysterious territory of the world's biggest market, the currency or Forex (foreign exchange) market, is now accessible to individual investors. With a few keystrokes, we can bring up the CurrencyShares Euro Trust (FXE) and observe the value of the euro versus the U.S. dollar or check out the Currency-Shares Canadian Dollar (FXC) versus the U.S. dollar. Many more currency pairs and baskets are available, but as with commodities,

---

HOT TIP

In 1993, State Street Advisors, a large global money manager, partnered with the Amex (American Stock Exchange, now the NYSE Amex) to launch the first ETF, the Standard & Poor's 500 Depository Receipt, or the SPYDR (ticker symbol SPY). Traders nicknamed the fund "the spider."

it is vital you have expert knowledge on these asset groups before investing in these funds.

Not only can you monitor shares of an ETF that represents the currency of a foreign country—you can consider shares in a (equity) fund targeting a country's largest publicly traded companies. Have you studied the Australian economy and believe it's ready to trend higher? Check out the iShares MSCI Australia (EWA). Does Brazil show signs of heating up? Check out the iShares MSCI Brazil (EWZ).

If you'd prefer to target a global region, such as South America, or emerging markets, you can find a wide selection of equity ETFs that spotlight every global region imaginable.

ETFs: How You Can Benefit

Investing with ETFs includes some dandy perks. Consider the following:

- Unlike mutual funds, which you can only buy or sell for that day's closing price, ETFs trade all day on the stock exchanges, just like single stocks.

- ETFs provide diversity *within each share*. Diversity = risk management. Say the market issues a GO signal. You expect the biotechnology industry group to outperform, so you purchase shares of the Select Sector SPDR Biotech ETF (XBI). The next morning when the opening bell rings, one of the fund's component stocks falls by 15 percent—the victim of a failed drug trial. Although the XBI may notice the loss by a few cents (depending on that component's weighting in the ETF), it will not fall drastically. Investors who own the individual stock, however, will be reaching for their Maalox bottles.

- Investing with ETFs reduces research time. Instead of wading through prospectuses (yawn) that detail the innards of mutual funds or researching individual stocks, ETFs simplify the process. Do you need to know what the fund contains? *Absolutely.* But we'll tell you how to do that, plus provide a list of the biggest funds, on our website www.investtowinbook.com.

▪ Picture this: Technology stocks have flown higher for the last three months. With our GO signal in effect, you researched the big stocks in this group early on and have chosen one with good fundamentals and chart pattern. Still, the entire group soared to the clouds this quarter—*except yours*. Had you purchased shares of the SPDR Technology Fund (XLK) or one of the other technology-focused ETFs, you would have enjoyed the ride up. This is not to say you would have achieved the same returns as did the leading stock in this group. But you would not have missed the entire run. Bottom line: If a sector decides to rally, a portion of stocks in that sector will outperform and others will underperform. To catch a great percentage of the rally, you may want to consider purchasing shares of the related sector ETF.

▪ If you compare the fees of index-tracking mutual funds to index-tracking ETFs, you'll find the ETFs sustain lower expense ratios. Additional expenses, such as accounting, marketing, and distribution, are generally lower for ETFs, which translates to lower fees.

▪ The ETF tax structure adds to their investing appeal. In a typical open-end mutual fund, a bear market can cause a flood of redemptions (people pulling their money out of the fund). In order to cover his obligations, the fund manager may have to sell stock shares. That can trigger end-of-the-year capital gains taxes for you—the fund shareholder. Conversely, the structure of an ETF dictates that it is traded on an exchange, just like a stock. You log capital gains on profits (at the end of the year) if *you* sell your ETF shares—and not until.

Later in our ETF discussion, I'll show you ETF strategies that you may come to think of as additional benefits to investing with these funds.

ETFs: What Are You Getting Into?

I've seen it over and over... traders and investors glance quickly at an ETF label and assume they know what the fund is about. Then they jump into shares, only to find out the hard way that they've lassoed a wild tiger.

Listen to Fred's story: Fred's co-worker told him that the value of the U.S. dollar was falling. Pacing the floor and gesturing frantically, Fred's co-worker went on to say that the only "real" currency is gold. Didn't Fred have any gold or at least the GLD ETF in his portfolio? *Uh, oh.*

Fred panics, runs to his computer, jumps into his online account, and immediately buys a hundred shares of the SPDR Gold Trust (GLD). For the next month, Fred watches slack-jawed as his GLD shares rocket higher, then reverse and tumble lower. Up, down, up, down. *Gulp.*

Fred, who has a low appetite for risk, bought "gold" to alleviate his fear of losing value in his dollars. His mistake: he didn't stop to research. Had he done so, he would have realized he purchased shares of a commodity ETF, which can be a relatively high-risk vehicle.

Had he completed due diligence on the wide selection of ETFs that are gold-related, he could have found similarly based shares that traded with narrower price swings and thus met his personal risk parameters.

> **HOT TIP**
>
> One reason commodity ETFs are so volatile: commodities trade around the clock with global developments affecting their prices. Just so, the asset value will change overnight, while you are sleeping.

How would he complete this research? First, he would have gone online and checked out the GLD thoroughly at the SPDR website (www.spdrs.com). Fred would see at the top of the GLD page that he was buying shares in a fund that closely follows the daily price of gold bullion. Each share of the GLD is based on the price of 1/10 of an ounce of gold. (As a matter of fact, the fund holds physical bars of gold bullion representing its value in assigned bank vaults.) While that's all good, Fred needed to know that gold is a commodity, and as mentioned before, commodity funds can be volatile.

Once Fred checked out the GLD and understood what it contained, he could have evaluated a monthly or weekly chart of the ETF, noting its price moves. Finally, after assessing his own investing goals and considering how he would manage the position's risk, he could have either purchased shares with confidence or looked up other gold-linked funds. The iShares Gold Trust (IAU) also trades based on the "physical" (current, not future) price of gold. However, one share is based on a much smaller (1/100) portion of gold. Although it is still volatile, percentage-wise, the lower price means Fred could have started with a smaller initial investment.

Further, Fred could have explored gold miners' shares, such as the Market Vectors Gold Miners ETF (GDX), or its sibling, the Market Vectors Junior Gold Miners ETF (GDXJ); both funds are equities-driven. Although miners' shares at times underperform their commodity cousins, if the price of gold is rising, these funds can still deliver good value.

ETFs are attractive investing vehicles. Their titles make it look easy to jump into a specialized field. Please don't jump, though, until you ascertain exactly what asset group the fund targets and what its components are. Then determine whether they meet your investing objectives and risk requirements. Finally, ask whether the fund is poised to succeed in the current market environment. If those criteria come together, you are good to GO.

ETFs: Where to Find Them

Exchange traded funds reside in fund "families" that sponsor them. Since ETFs have risen to such heights of popularity, everyone-who-is-anyone-at-all in the financial world seems intent on constructing an index and creating an ETF to sponsor.

For our purposes, we will explore three fund families that offer the advantages of seniority, stability, and varied selections in different asset categories: State Street Global Advisors SPDRS, Barclay iShares, and Invesco PowerShares. Their websites are as follows:

Select Sector SPDRS: www.sectorsp-
   drs.com
Additional SPDRS: www.spdrs.com
iShares: http:.ishares.com
PowerShares: .invescopowershares
   .com

Additional ETF families mentioned:

Guggenheim (Rydex) .rydex-sgi.com
Market Vectors: .vaneck.com
Wisdom Tree: .wisdomtree.com

General Websites with ETF information:

Morningstar.com: .morningstar.com
SmartMoney.com: .smartmoney.com
ETF Trends: .etftrends.com
Yahoo Finance: finance.yahoo.com

> **HOT TIP**
>
> ETFs track underly-
> ing indexes con-
> sisting of tens to
> hundreds to thou-
> sands of securities.

For an expanded listing of ETF websites, visit us at www.invest-towinbook.com.

ETFs: Consider the Weighting Categories

In *Invest to Win,* we will talk primarily about strategizing with index, sector, and fixed-income or bond ETFs. Please know that even though funds have similar names, their underlying indexes may be "weighted" differently.

Many types of weightings currently exist, and more are being developed. They include: capitalization (or "cap") weighting, equal weighting, fundamental weighting, and revenue weighting. (If we "weight" a minute, someone on Wall Street will think up yet another category.)

Each of these weightings comes with advantages and disadvantages. When you understand the differences, you can apply them to your strategies to obtain the best results from the market.

Cap-weighted. To date, the majority of equity ETFs are market cap-weighted. Cap-weighted funds give the biggest companies the highest portions of the underlying index; mid and small-cap companies in the index receive smaller shares according to their capitalization size. Say the global economy is chugging forward, and you believe the energy sector will reap profits. Cap-weighted ETFs such as the Energy Select Sector SPDR (XLE) or the iShares DJ U.S. Energy Sector Index Fund (IYE) are the obvious choice. The largest companies in this space, measured by market cap, hold the highest weightings. Right now, Exxon Mobil Corp. (XOM), Chevron Corp. (CVX), and Schlumberger Ltd. (SLB) reign at the top of both funds

With the bigger, brawnier stocks at the top, these funds can move nicely higher in bull markets. That's the good news. Here's the challenging news: when the markets reverse to the downside, the over-valuation of large-cap stocks in these ETFs can cause them to fall harder. One tactic in the energy sector: allocate part of your energy shares to the PowerShares S&P Small Cap Energy Portfolio (PSCE). With different components from those in the XLE or IYE, you will get exposure to the smaller, sometimes faster-growing companies in this space. Another tactic: dedicate part of your energy shares to an equal-weighted fund in that sector.

Equal-weighted. Just like it sounds, equal weighting under-weights every large-cap stock and over-weights each small-cap stock, so all stocks are weighed evenly. The weightings are rebalanced periodi-

---

HOT TIP

In cap-weighted ETFs, the construction of the underlying index will have a significant impact on the fund's performance. The bigger a stock's weighting, the greater the influence it has on the ETF's performance. Good idea: For clues as to which way your fund may be headed next, keep an eye on the top three components in your cap-weighted ETFs.

cally. These funds tend to do well when small caps flourish. That scenario usually takes place following an economic downturn and in the early stages of the recovery. Fans of equal-weighted funds, such as the Rydex S&P Equal Weight ETF (RSP), which follows an equal-weighted index of the S&P 500, believe that the strategy can beat the market by eliminating cap-weighted growth bias. For information on more equal-weighted (EW) ETFs, go to the Guggenheim (Rydex) website listed earlier and under "Fund Finder," click on "Guggenheim ETFs."

> **HOT TIP**
>
> Legendary value investor Benjamin Graham said, "In the short run, the market is a voting machine, but in the long run, it is a weighing machine."

Fundamental-weighted. Sometimes called "intelligent" or "smart" ETFs, these indexes focus on one or more fundamental factors, such as book value, cash flow, revenue, sales, or dividends. The companies represented in the ETF could be revenue-weighted (based on top line sales), earnings-weighted (based on high profit margins), or dividend weighted (based on payment of cash dividends). These ETFs often carry higher fees than major index, market-cap, or equal-weighted funds, as they are more actively managed.

Examples of fundamental-weighted ETFs are PowerShares FTSE RAFI US 1000 Portfolio ETF (PRF) (large-caps) and PowerShares FTSE RAFI US 1500 Small-Mid Portfolio ETF (PRFZ). Earnings-weighted ETFs include Wisdom Tree Total Earnings ETF (EXT) (total U.S. market). If you believe that fundamental indexes will outperform their traditional market-cap colleagues, you can use these types of ETFs along with, or instead of, traditional broad-market ETFs. Please know, however, that because of their construction, fundamental-weighted funds involve higher portfolio turnover (thus higher fees) and lower tax efficiency than market-cap funds.

High-beta and low-volatility. Also called "factor-driven ETFs," high-beta ETFs consist of stocks that show the highest sensitivity to market moves (beta). Low-volatility (price fluctuations) funds follow stock indexes that produce quieter price swings while striving to keep pace with the broader market. Naturally, high-beta ETFs can give dandy returns in strong bull markets, but in high-risk markets, low-volatility (low-beta) ETFs can be a better choice. Examples: Power-Shares S&P 500 High Beta Portfolio (SPHB) and PowerShares S&P 500 Low Volatility Portfolio (SPLV).

Understanding Net Asset Value (NAV)

At any given moment, an ETF has two values: (1) the market price of the fund that you and I use to buy and sell and (2) the actual value of the underlying index, or net asset value. In volatile markets, a few ETFs or ETNs (mostly commodity-related) will trade at a premium or discount to their net asset value. While this dynamic is not of great concern to most investors, when you decide to buy an ETF, you may want to check the price spread between the market price and NAV on the fund's website to make sure they are closely aligned (within a few cents of each other).

A Quick Look at Exchange Traded Notes (ETNs)

You may have heard of—or traded—the ETF's cousin, the exchange traded note (ETN). While these instruments trade similarly to ETFs on the exchanges, they are constructed differently. ETNs are debt securities (notes) designed to exist for a limited period of time (normally ten to thirty years). At that point, they will pay investors a return, based on the performance of an index or other benchmark.

The risk: Because ETNs are debt instruments, it's possible (not probable) that the issuer could not make its debt obligations. At the moment, many ETNs hold commodities. Please make sure you fully understand the characteristics and risks of ETNs before you purchase.

If you'd like to investigate ETNs, you can look at one of the most prominent ETN families, Barclays iPath ETNs, which can be found at www.ipathetn.com.

Let's Sample ETF Sectors

For those of you who are new to ETFs, or sector funds, let's take a quick look at the Select Sector SPDRS. They are highly liquid (trading millions of shares each day), and their cap-weighted indexes contain companies that represent household names. If you want to go comparison shopping, iShares features similar cap-weighted sector ETFs.

You can find the widely held suite of Select Sector SPDRS at www .sectorspdrs.com. The Select Sector SPDRS ETFs divide the S&P 500 into nine categories, or sectors. Remember, each sector contains different industry groups, which boosts the funds' diversification abilities. The following lists the Sector SPDRS in alphabetical order and a brief explanation as to what types of market environments each sector enjoys.

Note that in the descriptions, I've included "top holdings." Please know that an ETF's top equity components shift in ranking from time to time, according to their market capitalization. So, when you read this the top holdings may not be identical to those listed here, because weightings may change. My goal in citing them was to familiarize you with typical equity icons that reign over each sector. (Be sure to check the fund website for current listings before you purchase shares.)

Select Sector SPDRs

■ **Consumer Discretionary (XLY)** Industry groups represented in this sector include products we typically purchase more of when the

---

HOT TIP

Just as there is no point in investigating each one of the nearly 9,000 stocks listed on U.S. stock exchanges, it makes no sense to scrutinize every ETF in the fund universe. As Gordon advises, simply develop a short list of funds that serve your investing goals.

economy is flush and employment is high: autos, consumer durables, apparel, hotels, restaurants, leisure activities, media, and retailers. Top holdings: McDonalds Corp. (MCD), Walt Disney Co. (DIS), and Home Depot, Inc. (HD).

▪ **Consumer Staples (XLP)** Businesses in this sector produce consumer products that most of us need on a continuing basis: food and drug retailers, beverages, tobacco, and household and personal products. Also known as "non-cyclicals," many of these companies can do well in any economic climate. In addition, you may see the XLP pop when market uncertainty causes investors to run to dividend-paying "staple" stocks. Top holdings: Procter & Gamble Co. (PG), Coca-Cola Co. (KO), and Philip Morris International Inc. (PM).

▪ **Energy (XLE)** Energy companies in this fund explore for, develop, produce, and service the oil, natural gas, and coal industries. Because we use energy sources for manufacturing and growth, you'll find that expanding global economies and rising GDP (gross domestic product, the total of goods and services produced in a single country) numbers fuel the rise of this sector and the XLE. Of course, there are many other catalysts that boost energy prices, including indigenous shocks, such as storms and wars. Current top holdings: Exxon Mobil Corp. (XOM), Chevron Corp. (CVX), and Schlumberger Ltd. (SLB).

▪ **Financials (XLF)** Taking a large slice out of the S&P 500 Index pie (currently 14+ percent), this sector cuts a broad swath through U.S. financial firms, ranging from investment management to commercial and investment banking, insurance, and REITs (real estate investment trusts). I often say that our financials represent the backbone of the U.S. economy. (This is true in most industrialized countries.) As long as our financial firms remain in good health, our economy can stay vigorous. If they begin to trend lower, investors do well to start thinking defensively. Top components include Wells Fargo & Co. (WFC), Berkshire Hathaway 'B' (BRK.B), and JPMorgan Chase & Co. (JPM).

■ **Health Care (XLV)** As you can imagine, companies in this sector focus on pharmaceuticals, biotech, health-care equipment and services, and providers. While the health-care sector can trend nicely higher in bull (GO signal) markets, many investors also run to this space as a defensive move when the markets get anxious. Of course, as the baby boomers age and demand more medical services, the health care arena may become a good staple for our portfolios. Top components include Johnson & Johnson (JNJ), Pfizer Inc. (PFE), and Merck & Co. Inc. (MRK).

■ **Industrials (XLI)** This sector covers a long list of industry groups. Many of the reigning icons are conglomerates, meaning they develop and manufacture goods in more than one industry, such as General Electric Co. (GE) and Honeywell International Inc. (HON). Industrials include: aerospace and defense, building products, construction and engineering, commercial supplies and services, electrical equipment, and all means of transportation and transportation infrastructure companies. We can think of industrials as "cyclicals," meaning they typically perform the best when we are in a bull market and the economy is expanding. Bear markets and contracting economies take the steam out of this sector's earnings.

> **HOT TIP**
>
> Consumer "durables" are products that last more than three years. Examples: automobiles, homes, and appliances.

Current top components include General Electric Co. (GE), United Technologies Corp. (UTX), and United Parcel Service (UPS).

■ **Materials (XLB)** Materials comprise one of the smallest slices of the sector pie; at the moment they represent only 3.35 percent. When you think of "materials" companies, think of the raw and manufactured resources needed to create our homes, buildings, offices, and everything we touch and use each day. Basic materials companies focus on industries such as chemicals, construction materials, containers and packaging, fertilizers, metals and mining, and forest and paper products. Like industrials, materials stocks do best in bull (GO

signal) markets and expanding economies. In recessionary economies, demand for materials backs off, which puts a lid on these companies' earnings. Current top holdings: E.I. DuPont de Nemours &
Co. (DD), Monsanto Co. (MON), and Dow Chemical (DOW).

▪ **Technology (XLK)** In contrast to the materials' small slice of the
S&P 500 sector pie, technology often weighs in with the biggest slice.
At the moment, this bad boy garners 23.53 percent of the entire pie.
Industry groups within this sector involve computers and periph-
erals, software, semiconductor equipment, IT consulting services,
diversified telecommunication services, and wireless communication
services. Because most technology companies spend a lot on research
and development, they do best when interest rates are low. Naturally,
they also do best in expanding economies when the demand for new
technology is high and companies have high IT budgets. High-rank-
ing components include Apple Inc. (AAPL), International Business
Machines (IBM), Microsoft Corp. (MSFT), and AT&T Inc. (T).

▪ **Utilities (XLU)** As you can imagine, the utilities sector includes
companies that generate, transport, or distribute natural gas or electricity. Like materials, utilities amount to only a small slice of the
S&P 500 sector pie—presently 3.56 percent. Since utilities companies
incur huge expenses for developing and maintaining their services,
they thrive in low-interest-rate environments. In addition, the XLU
(as a utilities index) broadcasts unique signals that can give us insight
as to the mood and manner of the market. Gordon discussed this

HOT TIP

When you purchase shares of a sector fund that you may rotate in
and out of more frequently than, say, a fixed-income fund, you may
gain a (small) price advantage buying and selling shares in a "liquid" fund that trades at least 200,000 shares per day, average daily
volume.

in Chapter Four; we'll talk more about utilities and look at its chart in the following section. Current XLU top holdings: Duke Energy Corp. (DUK), Southern Co. (SO), and Exelon Corp. (EXC).

Asset Allocation Strategies Using ETFs

As we've just seen, ETFs are ideally suited to asset allocation. They track major indexes, offer a variety of asset classes, and charge low fees.

With those benefits in mind, let's discuss two standard approaches to asset allocation, strategic and tactical. Assuming you've established your investment objective and ascertained your risk tolerance, we'll start with the approach known as strategic allocation.

Strategic allocation is a more passive approach, relying on asset diversification. As Gordon will show you in upcoming chapters, this approach does not require much time or attention to manage.

Here's a brief example of this approach: If the S&P 500 SPDR (SPY) is trending higher, trading above its rising 12-month moving average in a GO signal, then you may want to start by allocating a portion of funds to the SPY, itself, or to a similar fund, the iShares S&P 500 Index (IVV). With large-caps in place, you might then add S&P 400 Midcap ETF (MDY) and then perhaps the iShares S&P SmallCap 600 Value Index Fund (IJS). While it does track the S&P 600 Index, the IJS seeks to perform a version of value investing within the small-cap world.

For the bond portion, you may consider such fixed-income funds as the iShares Barclays Aggregate Bond Fund (AGG). For those who like to keep a small store of gold shares to help guard against inflation, you may consider adding shares of the iShares Gold Trust (IAU), which we mentioned earlier in this chapter. Another inflation fighter mentioned earlier is the iShares Barclays TIPS Bond (TIP). (Gordon will discuss portfolio planning and strategic allocation more thoroughly in Chapter Twelve.)

You can consider the strategic allocation approach as your macro approach (majority of your portfolio) and leave it at that. Or you can use this approach as your core portfolio and add a tactical asset allocation approach as a "satellite."

The tactical approach tends to be more aggressive and more hands-on. With it, you can pursue "risk-on" assets, such as sector ETFs. A quick analysis of targeted monthly charts will tell you whether the current market environment is issuing a GO signal or advising you to wait for a better entry time.

Here's the first step I take before allocating funds to a new position: I evaluate a chart of the S&P 500 SPDR (SPY). If the SPY is trading in an uptrend (higher highs and higher lows) above its rising 12-month moving average, then I know the overall market is strong—a GO. During times when the SPY trends down below its downward-sloping 12-month moving average, and the market issues a STOP signal, I choose to wait on the sidelines.

Many new investors jump into the market on impulse. They don't know to take the simple step just described. Sometimes the impulse move lands them in a soft pile of pillows. And sometimes it plants them squarely in a pit of hornet's nests.

Taking a few minutes to implement the simple "evaluate-the-SPY" step will save you money and keep you from getting bitten by the market. Then you can translate what you see into our simple GO and STOP signals.

Figure 8.1 displays a monthly line chart of the SPY. We can see clearly that when that benchmark ETF rose above its 12-month moving average, the market was strong. And when the SPY reversed to the downside and the moving average came down overhead, the air buzzed with hornets; it was no time to initiate new long positions.

Once we evaluate the market environment for GO and STOP signals, then we can decide where to allocate funds. If we choose to move into sector funds, we can consider the following Select Sector SPDRs:

- Strong markets, offensive sectors
  - Materials (XLB)
  - Energy (XLE)
  - Financials (XLF) (can also be somewhat "defensive")
  - Industrials (XLI)
  - Technology (XLK)
  - Consumer Discretionary (XLP)

- Uncertain markets, defensive sectors
  - Consumer Staples (XLP)
  - Health Care (XLV)
  - Utilities (XLU)

Figure 8.2 shows a monthly chart of the Select Sector Energy ETF (XLE). When the economy is moving forward on all cylinders, the energy sector can provide robust profits.

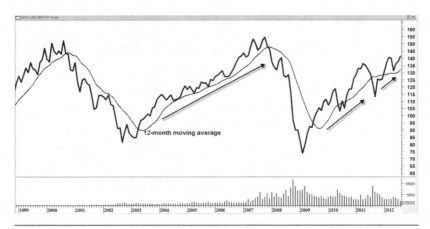

FIGURE 8.1   A monthly line chart of the S&P 500 SPDR (SPY) with a 12-month moving average.

You can see how the SPY rose from its 2002–2003 lows and stayed in a bull market until the end of 2007. This span of time, until we neared the price top, was a good time to be long the market and most sectors. Chart courtesy Metastock.

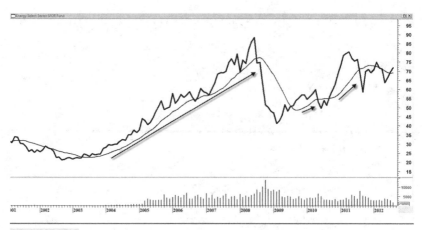

FIGURE 8.2   **A monthly line chart of the XLE with its 12-month moving average.**

You can see how the XLE trended higher from 2003 through the middle months of 2008, then fell with the SPY until March 2009. Since then, the XLE has trended higher, but has dipped below its 12-month moving average during times of global economic weakness.

Chart courtesy of Metastock.

That said, we have to remember that the XLE consists of energy-related equities—and energy (oil, natural gas, heating oil) is a commodity. Since we know from Fred's experience that commodities can be volatile, we accept the risk with the potential reward. Just so, if we own shares of the XLE and we see it close below its 12-month moving average in a STOP signal, we can consider paring our position.

Figure 8.3 displays a chart of the SPDR Consumer Staples ETF (XLP). When the market is climbing a wall of worry, the XLP can provide investors with an opportunity to stay in the market—minus the sleepless nights. Of course, like any position, risk must be managed.

We can see how the staples fund, which can be a wallflower and rarely finds itself in the media spotlight, gained about 56 percent during the uptrend from our entry in April 2009 to current times. (Those who exited and re-entered lost very little of that percent gain.)

Figure 8.4 shows the SPDR Technology Fund, the XLK. While this sector can offer great returns, the road to profits may be an exciting one. Growth stocks represent a high percentage of the stocks in

HOT TIP

It's the end of the year, and you're preparing your tax forms. You've been carrying shares of Microsoft Inc. (MSFT) in your standard margin account, at a loss. You'd like to take the loss on your taxes, but you think Mister Softee will gain traction and rise in the coming months. (The IRS won't allow you to sell a stock, take the loss, and then immediately buy it back.) Idea: Sell your shares of MSFT, then purchase shares of the iShares S&P North American Technology-Software Fund (IGV). Because of its market cap, Microsoft is usually one of its top components. You take the loss and then effectively replace the position with a very similar one. And you won't miss out on a potential move to the upside.

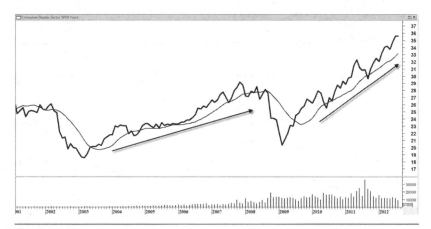

FIGURE 8.3 **A chart of the Consumer Staples SPDR, the XLP.**

Note how the staples ETF took off in the spring of 2009 and trended sharply higher, much of it on the back of worries about the eurozone economy. While the staples ETF can do well in a bull market economy, it represents a defensive strategy in worried markets.

Chart courtesy Metastock.

this sector. And when muscular growth stocks take the spotlight, they can really boogie. That's the good news.

Here's the less-than-charming news: statistics tell us that when the broad market falls, growth stocks fall one and one-half to two and one-half times faster than value stocks. When using the XLK or a similar technology fund in your tactical approach, you'll want to manage it appropriately.

Finally, let's take a look at the SPDR Utilities Fund, the XLU, as charted with its 12-month moving average in Figure 8.5. Long considered more mild-mannered than some of its wilder sector siblings, the dividend-paying utilities sector represents a safe haven when investors are worried. In fact, as Gordon discusses in Chapter Four, when anxiety comes into an uptrending market, you will many times see the XLU pop higher.

While the XLU can offer a sweet spot in the context of a tactical approach, please be aware that during times of extreme market duress, the XLU and its underlying components will tumble south with the other sectors. So, as with all of your positions, manage the XLU wisely.

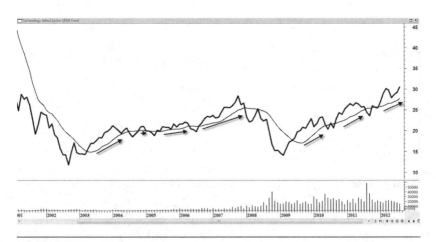

FIGURE 8.4 **A line chart of the SPDR Technology fund with its 12-month moving average.**

Note how the technology sector can give investors a bumpy ride as it jostles along on its 12-month moving average. Still, except for two summer retracements, since the XLK broke above its 12-month average from April 2009 to August 2012, the fund has grown 72 percent. Chart courtesy Metastock.

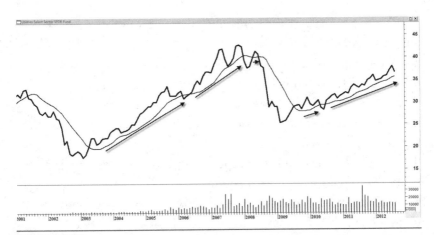

FIGURE 8.5 A monthly line chart of the XLU utilities fund with its 12-month moving average.

We know that this sector tends to do well when energy prices are low (utilities use a lot of energy) and interest rates are low. We can see that by using our GO and STOP signals during the time period shown, we could have reaped nice gains, while avoiding the downturns. Remember too, many time utilities pay an annual dividend that exceeds the interest on a ten-year Treasury bond. Chart courtesy Metastock.

I trust that this chapter has offered you insights into ETFs that will benefit your investing journey and help you reach your goals.

In Chapter Nine, Gordon is going to expand our discussion of asset allocation. I know you will enjoy it.

Key Points to Remember

→ An exchange traded fund (ETF) contains a basket of stocks or other securities that track a particular index, or theme.

→ ETFs trade on the exchanges throughout each trading day, like a single stock.

→ ETFs represent every major asset class, including equities, bonds, commodities and currencies.

→ ETFs provide diversity within each share.

→ In comparing the fees of index-tracking mutual funds to index-tracking ETFs, most times the ETFs sustain lower expense ratios.

➤ Because of the way they are constructed, ETFs can have tax advantages over mutual funds.

➤ Before you purchase shares of ETFs, make sure they fit into your overall investing strategy and meet your risk requirements.

➤ For updated information on an ETF's current holdings and index, go to the fund family or sponsor website and bring up your target ETF's page(s).

➤ In weighting the equity components in their underlying indexes, ETFs can be cap-weighted or equal-weighted.

➤ Fundamental-weighted ETFs focus on one or more fundamental factors, such as book value, cash flow, revenue, sales, or dividends.

➤ ETNs are debt securities (notes) designed to exist for a limited period of time (normally ten to thirty years).

➤ ETFs fit nicely into the two standard approaches to asset allocation, strategic and tactical.

➤ When researching ETFs, evaluating a monthly line chart plotted with a 12-month moving average can offer added guidance for buying and selling decisions.

PERSONAL GAINS

— Toni —

What's Your Emotional IQ?

What lies behind us and what lies before us are tiny matters compared to what lies within us.

—RALPH WALDO EMERSON

In past decades, we measured a person's intelligence by means of a score, or an "IQ," meaning "Intelligence Quotient." Those with high IQs were revered; those with average scores, or lower, were shrugged off.

A few years ago, however, researchers discovered that the greater percentage of people with the highest intelligence levels underperformed those with average brainpower. In other words, the saying "The 'A' students usually find themselves working for the 'C' students" emerged as more than theory. Now it was fact.

What do the C students embody that propels them to greater success in life? Studies now reveal that they exhibit enhanced levels of emotional intelligence, or EQ.

In *Emotional Intelligence 2.0,* authors Travis Bradberry and Jean Greaves explain, "We enter the workforce knowing how to read, write, and report on bodies of knowledge, but too often, we lack the skills to manage our emotions in the heat of the challenging problems that we face. Good decisions require far more than factual knowledge. They are made using self-knowledge and emotional mastery when they're needed most."(Travis Bradberry and Jean Greaves, *Emotional Intelligence 2.0*, San Diego: Talent Smart, 2009, p. 14.)

The authors go on to say that our brains are "hardwired to give our emotions the upper hand."

Were we to examine the actual, physical process, we would see that our senses constantly send messages through our bodies in the form of electric signals. When these signals arrive at our brain, they travel from the base of the brain to the upper front. Along the way, though, they must pass through the limbic system, where emotions are produced. Once the feeling gets tagged with an emotional "label," your reasoning or "rational brain" takes over. Bradberry and Greaves tell us, "The communication between your emotional and rational 'brains" is the physical source of emotional intelligence."

In order to raise our levels of EQ so that we enjoy our lives more fully, we first need to identify our personal emotional patterns and establish a mindset of awareness. Can we feel emotions as they begin to bud deep inside? Further, can we learn how to manage negative emotions and diffuse them before they become actions? Can we instill feelings of calm, confidence and caring into everything we do?

Studies in emotional intelligence show us how we can leverage our established storehouses of knowledge, education, and material successes by understanding our emotional patterns and how they play an integral part in our lives. When we introduce high levels of emotional intelligence into our intellectual intelligence, we employ a full-circle dynamism that leads to a more fulfilling life.

CHAPTER NINE

Two Simple Strategies for Investing to Win

— Gordon —

INVESTORS NEED strategies for investing before they can have any hope for success in growing or keeping their money. Imagine that you jump in a car with a loved one and take off driving. After a few uncertain directional changes, your passenger furtively asks where you are going. At that moment you realize you don't know precisely. "I'm not sure," you reply with candid honesty. Hoping to reassure your partner, you optimistically point out that "wherever it is, it will surely be better than where we are now!"

Though this might sound like *Alice in Wonderland* revisited, it is actually a scene played out every day in the investing world. While most investors know they want to grow their hard-earned money, or at least not lose it, they have no idea how to go about it. Without identifying a specific approach, an investor may simply dive right in, placing money in a fund or buying a stock without having any particular plan for when to take the money back.

The GainsMaster approach is intended to help you identify a strategy that is suitable for your circumstances and your personality. Experts point out that using a strategy that fits your personality has a major impact on your ability to successfully navigate the markets. (See Jack D. Schwager, *Hedge Fund Market Wizards*, Hoboken, NJ: John

Wiley and Sons, 2012, pp. 449–450. See also Van K. Tharp, *Trade Your Way to Financial Freedom*, New York: McGraw-Hill, 2007, p. 1.)

The information in this chapter is designed to provide you with two strategies that can be adapted to your circumstances and your personality.

The overriding characteristic of the strategies in this chapter is simplicity, but each of these strategies is also adaptable. The strategies are meant to be easy to understand and simple to implement. The strategies also have the ability to be adjusted to fit your particular goals for investing.

I have been amazed to discover that no two investors ever make money in exactly the same way. The four keys of the GainsMaster approach, once turned, open a door to the simple but powerful strategies I will share with you in Chapters Nine and Ten. The strategies in this chapter are low-maintenance approaches that can be adapted to even the most lethargic investor. From these you may find something you can easily modify to fit your circumstances.

Switching between Opportunity and Safety

The core concept in these strategies is to use the market-mood signals (the GO signs and STOP signs discussed in Chapter Four) to move your money to where it will find safety or to where it will find opportunity for growth. The strategy assumes that the bond market represents a place where investors go when they are seeking safety and the stock market is the best place to look for growth and opportunity

Many may debate that statement as an oversimplification. Others may insist that there are other alternatives where your money can grow better or even be safer. I will not argue that matter. The point of these strategies is to offer a simple yet effective way for you to reach your investing goals. The strategies I am about to share with you don't require you to sweat the details.

These strategies give you a structured way to move your money from stocks to bonds and back again, depending on the prevailing market conditions. In the previous chapter, Toni explained that certain exchange traded funds (ETFs) concentrate on either stocks or bonds. The same is also true of many mutual funds. That means you can move your money from stocks to bonds by switching from one fund to another in your tax-deferred (401k or 403b) savings account in the same way you can buy and sell ETFs in an IRA account.

Being able to move your money around in deliberate fashion between bond and stock funds is all you need to be able to do in order to follow these strategies. As a result, if you can identify how to move your money from stocks to bonds and back again in your own investing account, this chapter will help you know when to do so.

The two strategies are very similar. Both are easy to understand and are designed to be quite simple to implement. Both of them can be adjusted, depending on your personal tolerance for risk and your time horizon until retirement. The strategies differ in the amount of effort you will trade to seek better gains. The first strategy allows you to keep things as simple as possible. The second strategy allows you to take on an added layer of decision making to help improve your gains—while still keeping things quite simple.

Strategy One: Keep It in the Fridge

A cool and calculated strategy for balancing money between stock and bond mutual funds, this strategy is suitable for use with a tax-deferred savings account (such as a 401k or 403b). It also attempts to minimize losses and create opportunity, so as to keep pace with and even outperform the market during turbulent decades.

GainsMaster Key 1. Your risk-tolerance number can be used to limit your exposure to risk with this strategy.

GainsMaster Key 2. GO-sign and STOP-sign indicators will tell you when to move your money from one type of fund to another with your retirement account.

GainsMaster Key 3. Your choices are limited to the mutual funds you have available in your retirement savings account. They will be divided primarily into growth funds (stocks) and income funds (bonds). You won't need any more choices than those.

GainsMaster Key 4. Risk management happens by using a unique allocation technique developed by a highly skilled investment advisor.

The first strategy is intended to help you follow the simplest way I know of to protect your investing account balance and still help it grow during market fluctuations. It is a low-maintenance strategy, well suited for those who have a low risk tolerance and don't like to experience losses. It is also well suited to those who consider themselves to be very patient investors. You don't even have to pick individual stocks. You can make strategy changes in as little as fifteen minutes, and you won't need to spend more than about thirty minutes each month.

The basics of the first strategy were first articulated to me by William Chin, a Registered Portfolio Manager who expertly provides services through e3m Investments Incorporated, a Toronto-based investment firm. William has been working for over twenty years with high-net-worth individuals to manage their portfolios or help them to do so themselves. He explained to me that after beginning to manage investments for his clientele for a short time, he began to notice a common attitude among them. "These people have a different mindset from most investors," he noted. "They don't focus on growth. Their main focus is . . . *don't lose my money!*" Over the years, William has worked out a way to best help them accomplish their goal.

When I first heard William explain his work, I was so impressed that I began to study its feasibility as an investing strategy. After finding that it was both simple and effective, I interviewed him to learn a bit more about how William works to manage his clients' accounts. With his permission, I have used his methods to form the foundation for this strategy. To help you better understand how it all works, I want to explain how William consults with his clients to help them create a customized approach for each of them. This will help you better understand both the power and flexibility of this strategy.

The first thing that William does when working with his clients is to help them identify their tolerance for risk. This is something that any investor should do. But most investors don't know what to do next. William helps them understand how they might translate their risk tolerance into an acceptable range of exposure to the stock market. Figure 9.1 depicts what William explains to his clients.

The opposite ends of this spectrum represent the two extreme possibilities of allocation in his clients' accounts. William recognizes that different market conditions call for allocating money differently. If he had a client that wanted maximum opportunity when times were good, then that client would likely want to move all of available money into a collection of stocks, or into stock-index mutual funds as a simpler solution. Stock-index mutual funds are those that automatically invest in a wide variety of stocks based on an index like the S&P 500.

If times were precarious for investors, William would advise the client to move some or perhaps all of their money into bonds or bond funds. But his method isn't simply to put all of your investing money into either stocks or bonds. There is more to it than that.

For the next step, he works with his clients to determine a range within this spectrum that defines the limits of their risk tolerance in either direction. The range can be smaller or larger, according to their preferences. The greater the risk tolerance for the client, the wider the range; the more the client wants to focus on not losing money, the narrower the range will become. The range of risk tolerance that his client selects will be a function of how much the client cares about fluctuation in prices.

William recognizes that there are times when the conditions are favorable for stock market prices to move higher. In such times his

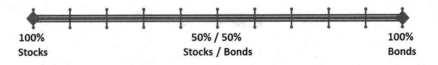

100% Stocks   50% / 50% Stocks / Bonds   100% Bonds

FIGURE 9.1 The investment allocation spectrum or range between the two extreme possibilities of allocation of an investor's account.

clients will need to have some of their money in stocks if they want to win from that circumstance; however, as he and they both know, there is no guarantee stocks will actually go higher in price. Stock prices could go down. They may only go down just a little, but even so, that could cause their holdings to fluctuate in value. How can his clients protect their investments from too much exposure to fluctuation? William's idea for a range of exposure is the answer to that question.

"Think of your risk tolerance limits as bookends on a shelf. If you don't want so much risk, you simply move the bookends closer to each other." William explained to me that he has used the approach for many years, and his clients have found it quite acceptable for their needs. He says this idea helps people think about their risk exposure as flexible to meet their circumstances.

Consider the example in Figure 9.2. This diagram depicts a range defined on the spectrum by two limits. The purpose of this range would be to reduce the overall volatility of the investment account in comparison to regular market price action. The left-side limit designates the maximum amount of allocation to stocks that one client may allow. As you can imagine, these are the allocation percentages that an investor would feel more comfortable with when conditions are favorable for investing in stocks. The right side of the range is a limit for the allocation percentages an investor may use if conditions in the market were becoming too risky.

Adjusting limits gives the investor a measure of control. As investors move the range of these limits they also adjust the flavor of the results they get from their investments. For example, the pair of limits depicted in Figure 9.2 moves the allocation extremes in from the

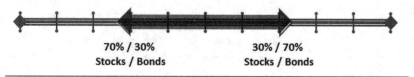

70% / 30%   30% / 70%
Stocks / Bonds   Stocks / Bonds

FIGURE 9.2 **A narrower range of risk tolerance for those who want to reduce their exposure to price fluctuation.**

edges. The intended benefit from doing so is to reduce the impact of the fluctuating price changes in the market. This may be important to some investors who feel as though they don't care if they gain all they possibly can—so long as they make a reasonable gain. While the prices are changing they prefer to be able to sleep at night, not having to think about their investments. This example shows you how investors control the amount of fluctuation they subject themselves to as the market moves along. By limiting the extremes of their mix between stocks and bonds, investors can pay less attention to the markets and more attention to other parts of their lives.

There is another factor investors might consider when deciding how to adjust the extremes of their range. That factor is time. Naturally, investors' goals differ based on the amount of time they have until they reach retirement or some other life event for which they are planning.

Conventional wisdom among investment advisors is that the more time an investor has, the greater the risk tolerance should be. Younger investors with presumably many years before retirement would do better to allow the prices of their assets to fluctuate more, and therefore they could capture more gains. On the other hand, investors closer to retirement would be less tolerant of market swings and may prefer less volatility—even if it means milder gains.

HOT TIP

Every 401(k) or 403(b) savings plan has a few choices available for you to allocate your money. These choices represent mutual funds of one kind or another. The funds will usually feature a couple of key words to help you understand what each fund is designed to do. For example, if the fund has the word "Growth" in its title, then you can be certain that the fund invests primarily in stocks. If the fund has the word "Income" in its title, then you can be certain that the fund invests primarily in bonds. If the fund has both words in its title, then the fund invests money in both stocks and bonds.

Moving money based on the market's mood. In Chapter Four I described the GO and STOP signs that appear as the mood of the market significantly changes. For this strategy you can use these indicators as your decision-support tool for how to allocate money. To accomplish this you simply move your money from a stock-index mutual fund to a bond-index mutual fund.

Turning Key 4: Managing risk with Strategy One. The final key in the GainsMaster approach includes identifying how you will manage risk. Because this strategy is designed to be extremely simple, risk management is simple as well. Following this strategy, all you do is arrange the allocation of your money from one edge of your spectrum to the other, based on the GO and STOP signs. When the market mood is showing a GO sign, then consider allocating your money as specified on the left edge of your limit, wherever you have set it. If the market mood shows a STOP sign, then consider allocating based on the right-edge of your limit. As previously mentioned, those limits will depend on your circumstances and risk tolerance.

For example, younger investors like Rita can put up with greater fluctuation over time, and may trade that tolerance in for greater gains. To accomplish this they will use the entire range of the spectrum and have a strategy based on maximum exposure to help build their investment value most rapidly over time. Their strategic spectrum might look something like Figure 9.3.

This depiction means that when the market mood favors opportunity over safety, this kind of investor would move money into stocks.

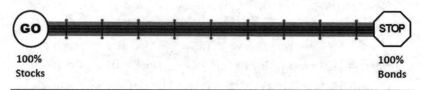

FIGURE 9.3 Using the full spectrum in an aggressive allocation strategy means that your money will be either entirely in stocks or entirely in bonds, depending on what the market signals.

When conditions are favorable for investing in stocks (when the market shows a GO sign), then this younger investor would move 100 percent of her money into stocks. That can be done by simply choosing to allocate all available money into a growth mutual fund. A growth-stock mutual fund is usually the main choice for stocks in a tax-deferred savings account.

When the market mood prefers safety instead of opportunity, this same kind of investor would move money into bonds. That means that when conditions are unfavorable for investing in stocks (when the market shows a STOP sign), then this younger investor would now move 100 percent of his money into bonds. Likewise, this can also be done by simply moving all of the investment money into an income mutual fund that invests primarily in bonds.

Risk control for investors who prefer less fluctuation. Here is where the value of the GainsMaster approach comes to play. If you have already turned Key 1 and determined the percentage of fluctuation that you can tolerate, you can make use of that decision at this point in your strategy. We can even apply it to your allocation percentage.

For example, a younger investor with high risk tolerance might agree that she could tolerate a 50 percent change in the value of her account. The market has made nearly 50 percent drops twice since the year 2000. This implies that a young investor could tolerate the full swings of the market. If so, then she should be comfortable setting her STOP sign and GO sign markers at the extreme ends of the risk spectrum.

On the other hand, investors with less time before retirement might consider choosing a different spectrum of risk. As an example, suppose an investor like Charlie decided that he could tolerate 20 percent fluctuation in the markets. For this strategy he could simply apply that number beginning at the middle of the spectrum—and moving in both directions—to establish his range of risk tolerance.

A 20 percent risk tolerance would designate a narrower range of tolerance between the GO and STOP signs. They would bring the ends of the spectrum into 70 and 30 percent allocation. This will reduce the risk of fluctuation. In that case, the strategy could be as shown in Figure 9.4.

For those approaching or already in retirement, much narrower limits are appropriate. It may also be appropriate to shift the limits to the right to limit exposure to the stock market altogether and stick with the more stable, though lower, returns offered by the bond market. For example, an investor who may have just reached retirement age but has decided to continue working for a year or two more may be more comfortable with a strategic range of risk that looks like that shown in Figure 9.5.

Where you choose to set your limits must depend on how much time you have before retirement and how much tolerance for fluctuating prices you may have.

This is the core information for this investment strategy. With these descriptions in mind, here are the steps to implement the first invest-to-win strategy.

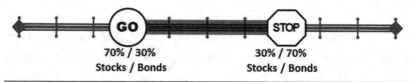

GO
70% / 30%
Stocks / Bonds

STOP
30% / 70%
Stocks / Bonds

FIGURE 9.4 Using a smaller portion of the spectrum, a more conservative investor can choose to be either mostly in stocks or mostly in bonds instead of all or nothing.

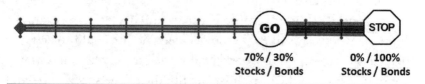

GO
70% / 30%
Stocks / Bonds

STOP
0% / 100%
Stocks / Bonds

FIGURE 9.5 Investors already in retirement (or getting close to it) may prefer safety over opportunity and therefore prefer a range of risk tolerance that looks like this.

Steps to implementing Strategy One. Now that you know the basic concepts behind this strategy, you are ready to hear the steps you'll need to take to implement it. Because this strategy aims to be very low on maintenance and doesn't require that you choose individual stocks, all you need to do is follow these four steps:

1. First, select your range of risk tolerance. Specify the limits that you will use to determine your allocation of stocks and bonds. The more time you have until retirement, the wider your range can be. The less time you have, the narrower you may want your range. If you are already in retirement, you may want your entire range to be no more than 20 or 30 percent wide and centered entirely on the right side of the spectrum.

2. Second, check the market's mood. Based on the criteria I gave in Chapter Four, look for whether the market has most recently given a GO sign or a STOP sign.

3. Allocate your funds depending on the market's mood. If the market is currently under a GO sign, then allocate your investment money to the left-side limit of your risk-tolerance range on the spectrum. If the market is currently under a STOP sign, allocate your money based on the right-side limit.

4. Check the market's mood once a month. Each month spend a few minutes checking to see if market conditions have changed. Follow the procedure for doing so mentioned in Chapter Four. If conditions are the same, then you don't have to take further actions. If conditions have changed, repeat step number three, based on the new conditions. This step puts your money into the market most likely to be of interest to other investors and therefore the market most likely to increase in value.

Strategy One summary. This strategy is extremely simple. It is so simple that the reluctant investor need not do anything other than follow this strategy, and it will give him a reasonably good chance of beating the market or protecting his investments against unwanted volatility while still reaching his objectives. An investor only has to move money from stocks to bonds and back again based on the conditions of the market. Using this strategy requires that you define your range along the spectrum to make sure you feel comfortable with the fluctuation of prices you may experience. Remember that the wider the range, the greater the fluctuation, but also the greater opportunity to win.

Now if this strategy sounds mildly interesting, but you are looking for something with a bit more opportunity, then Strategy Two might be more appealing to you. But keep in mind, the next strategy will take some additional time. If you don't mind taking a quick look at six charts each month, then you will find that you can likely spot more opportunity when it is available. If that sounds attractive to you, I think you'll find it easy to warm up to the next strategy.

Strategy Two: Making Some Dough

A strategy designed to help investment accounts rise faster when market conditions warm up and investors get in the mood to find opportunity. The strategy still looks to move investments between stocks and bonds, but it does so using ETFs. This strategy is best suited for a tax-advantaged account (such as an IRA or Roth IRA).

HOT TIP

Many investing experts tout the benefits of diversification. According to this thinking, investors should have their money spread out over a wide variety of stocks so that they get a smoother kind of return. Strategy One and Strategy Two might seem to have a serious weakness, because these strategies advocate putting all of your money into a single fund. But that is not the case, because each of the funds referenced in these strategies is already a diverse collection of instruments. So the strategies have diversification build right in!

GainsMaster Key 1. Your Risk Tolerance number can be used to limit your exposure to risk in this strategy, the same as in Strategy One. But if you intend to use this strategy, you would likely feel more satisfied with it if you simply increase your risk tolerance by about five percent.

GainsMaster Key 2. GO-sign and STOP-sign indicators will tell you when to move your money from one type of fund to another with your IRA or other retirement account.

GainsMaster Key 3. Your choices should be limited to the six ETFs mentioned at the end of this strategy. You can replace them with your own preferences, but if you do so, be certain that your replacements have comparable performance.

GainsMaster Key 4. As with Strategy One, you set your limits on the spectrum to control risk and adjust them based on your own risk tolerance.

The second strategy builds on the first and simply adds another dimension to the selections. This added dimension is intended to improve prospects for growth. The extra step will provide a way for investors to increase opportunity and capture valuable trends using more powerful tools than simple stock and bond mutual funds. But to make use of this strategy, an investor must be able to use exchange traded funds (ETFs). Toni explained these instruments in the previous chapter. They are excellent tools for the modern investor, and this strategy puts them to work in very constructive ways.

Strategy Two is a medium-to-low-maintenance strategy. This means it will take a bit more work than checking the market conditions once a month. In addition to watching the market's mood, investors will watch for trend changes in a specialized group of six ETFs that include stock and bond funds. This additional step need not take much extra time, but it will take one extra decision, namely: how much opportunity (and with it, price volatility) to add to the portfolio. To understand all that is involved in this decision, you need to learn about three concepts: (1) the benefits of opportunity, (2) the benefits of boring stocks, and (3) the benefits of bargain shopping.

The benefits of opportunity: When risk equals opportunity.
Strategy Two adds a new dimension to the decision making involved in Strategy One. I call it the opportunity factor. The first concept you need to understand is that it is possible to increase your opportunity. Once you have determined what kind of mood the market is in, then you must determine just how much opportunity or safety you personally want to seek under the current conditions. You should also remember that additional opportunity usually comes with one string attached: volatility.

This idea comes from a theory of finance called Modern Portfolio Theory (MPT). This theory has been the most popular collection of market beliefs among professional money managers over the past half century. Among other things, the theory explains that the more opportunity investors seek, the greater the fluctuation they will have to endure. It is a time-honored theory and has offered an excellent model for investing over the years.

The premise of this book is that, as an individual investor, you can outperform MPT by paying attention to the actions of other investors (market mood signals). If you switch your investing based on a market mood that alternatively prefers safety or opportunity, then you are likely to find prices trending in your favor more often. Strategy One is intended to help you capture those trends in the simplest way possible.

Strategy Two is designed to help you expend a bit more effort to enhance your results. The method for doing so simply follows MPT's assumption about risk, namely: that more risk equals more opportunity. If MPT is correct that the more opportunity you seek, the more fluctuation you must endure, then shouldn't it also be true that the more fluctuation you endure, the more opportunity you provide for yourself? If that is true, then simply increasing risk should create the best opportunity for increased returns. That sounds simple right?

Not so fast. It turns out that reality is a bit more complicated than theory. Now it's time to explore the second concept that discusses why boring stocks can actually become... well... exciting!

The benefits of boring stocks: When boring becomes exciting. There is an interesting anomaly that goes against the grain of this MPT reasoning. A report produced by S&P Dow Jones Indices detailed this anomaly dubbed "the low-volatility effect" (Aye M. Soe, *The Low-Volatility Effect: A Comprehensive Look,* New York: McGraw-Hill, 2012). The conclusion of the report is that, simply put, boring stocks do better over the long run. The study cited research into methods of investing that seek out low volatility and simply compared how slow-moving stocks performed over time compared with stocks that move up and down at least as much as the rest of the market.

The researchers were specifically trying to test the MPT-promoted notion that more volatility equated to better returns. What they found surprised them. It turns out that there are periods of time where these turtle-like stocks actually gain better ground than their more hare-like cohorts. This is especially true since the year 2000—a period of time during which the stock market has had major fluctuations.

The studies will tout that the low-volatility investing methods do better than the market averages over 80 percent of the time when markets are in a downward trend. No surprise there. Boring stocks don't drop as far as the others when the market crashes. However, when they rebound from their relatively better low points, they do a more effective job of gaining ground than the higher-flying stocks. That means that over time, these lower-volatility stocks turn out to be a pretty good deal.

The researchers who have studied this anomaly haven't been able to prove conclusively *why* this happens or even theorize about why it *should* happen. Their studies only yield conclusive proof that it *does* happen.

Perhaps the answer to why it happens can be found in the realization that people don't always pay the most rational prices for things.

As the saying goes, one person's trash is another person's treasure. It might be the case that people pay too much for stocks that they think are certain to go up in the future merely because they have gone up so much in the past year. That leaves the exciting stocks overpriced and the boring stocks underpriced.

Regardless of why it works, the findings of these studies have attracted a lot of attention. Up until 2010 the only way to take advantage of this strategy was a pretty complicated set of activities. You would have had to spend some significant time comparing the movements of over 1,000 stocks. Then you would have to sort through some carefully calculated and cleaned up data to arrive at a portfolio of 200 individual stocks. From there you would be burdened with distributing your money evenly across all 200 stocks. Toni and I wrote this book specifically to help you avoid such heavy lifting.

There is good news and bad news about the developments in this new method of investing. First the good news: Investors enamored with this idea don't have to work so hard. As of 2012 this strategy has gotten a whole lot easier to follow. All an investor must do is buy one of half a dozen ETFs that mimic this method. The fund will do all the work for you. Cool, huh?

Now the bad news: The funds have only been around a couple years at most. It's hard to know whether this idea is just another great theory that can't be acted on in the markets or if fund managers will prove that they can demonstrate an ability to exploit the low-volatility effect over time. There is a very real possibility that the mere popularity of this method will be its own undoing—at least in the short term. It is possible that the newfound interest in this method could rapidly increase the demand for those ETFs that implement this strategy.

This increased demand could then translate to unusually high prices for those stocks and the ETFs that track them. But if that turned out to be true, what could be done then? The thing I love the most about the market is that it always has a way of providing opportunities. If one closes, another opens. In this case, we could say that if boring stocks trade for higher prices than they should, it would likely mean that the erstwhile more exciting stocks have become a better value than they once were. That brings us to the third concept.

The benefits of bargain shopping: When exciting becomes boring. During a downward-trending bear market, the stock price of many companies becomes cheap. The ratio of a company's stock price compared to the earnings that company generates each quarter falls to an unusually low number. But many of these companies are running good businesses and are unlikely to shut their doors. Assuming the business cycle carries on the way it has in times past, strong companies with low-priced stocks represent a great value. Looking for such companies in such times is the work of the value investor.

Whether you know it by that name or not, you have probably heard the term value investing. It is a style of investing that seeks to buy low and sell high. In this case, "buying low" refers to buying companies whose fundamental measures, such as their price/earnings ratios, discussed in Chapter Six, are at unusually low levels. Searching for this unusually low level of ratios allows a value investor to compare the business prospects of a company with its current predicament.

If an investor can be patient and not pull his or her money out of the investment for a couple years or more, then an unusually low price on a strong company represents a real bargain. This is the kind of value such investors seek to find. Warren Buffett invests that way. He learned it from the late famed economist Benjamin Graham, who popularized the idea through his book *The Intelligent Investor.* It works well for those who can be patient—but oh, how it can test one's patience!

In September 2008 Warren Buffett announced that he would invest five billion dollars in the company Goldman Sachs. Just sixty days later the value of that investment was estimated to be worth half as much as he paid for it. *Half!* It stayed that way for about two more months before beginning to increase in value. It was eight more months before his investment made it back to break even. The value of the Goldman Sachs investment eventually did reach a point of greater than a 50 percent return within a three-year period.

Now if you think that was a rough ride, consider what he did in the month following the Goldman Sachs deal. In October 2008 he made a three billion dollar investment in General Electric. The value of that investment dropped by over *seventy* percent and had not even made it back to its original value four years later.

If value investing proves to be this difficult for even a seasoned investor like Warren Buffett, you can bet that it could prove challenging for a novice. Despite such challenges, one man by the name of Joel Greenblatt actively promotes the pursuit of value investing. He has written three books on the subject which have made the *New York Times* bestseller list. Being an author is a side endeavor for him, however. In professional circles he is better known as the founder of a hedge fund named Gotham Capital and as an adjunct faculty member at Columbia University. Wherever he goes, he is known as a champion of a modern version of value investing.

Joel has sought for years to make value investing accessible to the average individual investor. He even went so far as to start a fund in which pubic investors can participate along with him in his strategy. In his latest book, *The Big Secret for the Small Investor: A New Route to Long-Term Investment Success* (New York: Random House, 2011, p. 114), Joel explains how to take the idea of value investing a bit further to minimize some of the aforementioned trials that value investors must endure. The approach he explains is quite clever.

It starts with an index of stocks such as the S&P Small Cap 600. The approach is to then spread money across all 600 stocks. That isn't the unique part. Most index-tracking ETFs do the same thing. What is novel about the approach Greenblatt describes is that the money is not distributed evenly. In simple terms this method puts slightly more money in those companies whose prices represent fundamentally good values (based on a comparison of price levels, the company's earnings, and the prices of similar company stocks).

Trying to track 600 stocks and sort them out by value is far too much work for me, and if you are reading this chapter, I'm guessing it's too much work for you too. But fortunately we don't have to do that kind of work. As Greenblatt points out in his book, an investor can simply buy and hold an ETF that does this for you. (One of the ETFs that follow Greenblatt's "value-weighted index" index strategy is the S&P SmallCap 600 Value Index Fund (IJS).)

Such indexes have been shown over time to outperform the regular market indexes. It might just be a little each year, but that small amount adds up. When the market is moving in an upward trend, these indexes and the ETFs that track them tend to offer better returns than the S&P 500; however, when the market turns bearish (downward trend), these indexes fall farther than the S&P 500.

Opportunity in STOP-sign markets. For the purposes of our strategy, an ETF that tracks one of these indexes can be a wonderful tool when the market has shown a GO sign; however, it is not the right tool when the market shows a STOP sign. During the past decade or more, the bond market has been the destination of choice when investors prefer safety over risk. ETFs that mimic the return of various U.S. Government Treasury bonds have shown themselves to be the most frequently selected bastions of safety over the past decade.

But all bonds, even U.S. Government bonds, are not created equal. As I explained to Charlie and Rita in Chapter Two, some bonds are loans that only last a short duration, three years or less. Others will provide interest to the lender for ten to twenty years. The

---

HOT TIP

It is true that there are times when both the stock and the bond markets can go down at the same time. These times occur particularly when interest rates persistently rise. Bond funds do well as safety trades during periods of time when interest rates are low. However, when interest rates significantly outpace inflation and rise above 6 percent, then the kinds of investments investors prefer for safety become something different. For more ideas on how to invest in times of higher interest rates, check out the information at our website www.investtowinthebook.com.

longer the duration, the more desirable that bond is when the market experiences times of uncertainty and investors seek safety.

The safety side of the spectrum does not require as much explanation of how to determine opportunities. Increased opportunity in bonds can be found in a single concept: the duration of the bonds you are investing in.

The more investors demand a certain kind of bond, the greater the degree of change in its prices over time. Like the difference between low-volatility index funds and value-weighted index investing methods, bond-based ETFs have varying levels of risk and opportunity. The bond-based ETFs that track bonds of longer duration generate greater opportunity but also greater price fluctuation. Shorter-term bonds mean less fluctuation, but also less opportunity for gains by the ETFs that track them.

Turning Key 3: Choosing your opportunities. You now understand the three concepts for increasing opportunity in stocks. You also have an idea of how opportunity is found in STOP-sign markets. That means you have what you need to activate the opportunity factor in your investing strategy. This is how we will turn GainsMaster Key 3 in this strategy. What you need to do is select which ETF best matches the amount of opportunity you seek. Table 9.1 will define the circumstances under which each ETF can be used to increase opportunity or control volatility.

Steps to implementing Strategy Two. This strategy begins by having you select your spectrum of risk tolerance, as discussed in the previous chapter, and then specifies that you should choose your opportunity tools to enhance your gains.

1. Select your range of risk tolerance. This step is the same as for Strategy One.

2. Check the market's mood. Also the same as for Strategy One. Look for whether the market has most recently given a GO sign or a STOP sign.

MARKET CONDITIONS		
Opportunity and Volatility Level	STOP Sign	GO Sign
Low	AGG—The lowest volatility bond fund. It provides more income than having your investments in a money-market fund and very little fluctuation in price.	LVOL—The fund that does "Low-Volatility-Effect" investing. It reduces fluctuation and gives respectable returns over time.
Medium	IEF—Medium-range bond fund, based on the 7–10 year government bond. Better returns than AGG, but more fluctuation.	SPY—The fund that tracks the U.S. stock market's primary benchmark. Returns essentially what the market returns, on average.
High	TLT—Long-range bond fund. Greater fluctuation, but the most opportunity for STOP-sign times.	IJS—The fund that does "Value-Weighted-Index" investing. Outperforms the S&P 500 in GO-sign times and over the last ten years, but has the greatest fluctuation of the three.

TABLE 9.1   A post-retirement, conservative allocation strategy, the six ETFs used in Strategy Two.

3. Determine your opportunity factor. Select high, medium, or low as the value of your opportunity factor. Base this decision on the same criteria that you used to determine your risk tolerance. The more time you have before retirement and the more tolerance you have for fluctuation, the higher your opportunity factor should be.

4. Allocate your funds based on the market's mood and on your opportunity factor. If the market is currently under a GO sign, then you can consider moving money towards the left-side limit of the spectrum. If the market is currently under a STOP sign, consider changing your allocations towards the right-side limit on the spectrum. You can set your allocations differently, based on other indicators, if you prefer, but whatever method you use, you should feel comfortable that it is a reliable indicator for adjusting to the market conditions.

5. Check the market's mood once a month. Each month spend a few minutes checking to see if market conditions have changed. If conditions are the same, then you don't have to do anything. If conditions have changed, repeat step number three, based on the new conditions. This step puts your money in the area most likely to be of interest to market participants, and therefore most likely to increase in value.

Strategy Two summary. Strategy Two seeks to help you increase your returns by taking advantage of three well-proven concepts known to professionals in the investment world: Modern Portfolio Theory, the Low-Volatility Effect, and Value-Weighted Investing. The strategy also helps you recognize how to manage opportunity and risk when conditions are unfavorable for investing in stocks. These are the STOP-sign markets, and over the past decade, these times have been much more favorable for bond market investing. Using the three funds, AGG, IEF, and TLT, you can choose to increase or decrease your opportunity and risk based on your individual circumstances.

This strategy, like Strategy One, is built on the idea that you first define your range of risk on the spectrum. The wider the range, the greater the fluctuation you will experience, so the closer to retirement you are, the tighter your range should be in order to reduce volatility. However, with fluctuation comes opportunity, so if you have fifteen years or more until retirement, you will probably want to keep your range of risk as wide as you can tolerate.

Now if this second strategy appeals to you because it offers more opportunity for gain, and you have greater tolerance for risk in your investments for whatever reason, then the strategies in the next chapter will likely be interesting to you as well. If you don't mind reading a few charts so that you can identify where the best opportunities might be coming from next, then I know you'll enjoy the suggestions you'll find there.

To help you better envision how these strategies can be implemented, I'll invite our friends from Chapter Two, Charlie and Rita. As I discuss these strategies with each of them, you will get a clearer picture of how the strategies are applied on a periodic basis. This will further help you identify which strategy might be best for you.

Key Points to Remember

→ The investing strategies in this chapter are for the time-constrained investor who wants the simplest possible strategy that can help him outperform the normal movement of the market.

→ Strategies One and Two are built on the work of William Chin, who has successfully managed money for high-net-worth clients for the last twenty years.

→ William Chin's efforts kept his clients' money safe from the financial crisis in 2008, and if something like that should happen again, these strategies would give you a reasonable chance of avoiding the big drops the market made.

→ Strategy One: *Keeping it in the Fridge* is for tax-deferred savings vehicles like 401(k) and 403(b) accounts.

→ Strategy Two: *Making Some Dough* is for tax-advantaged accounts such as an IRA or Roth IRA.

→ Opportunity selection (GainsMaster Key 3) for Strategy One is limited to growth and income funds within a tax-deferred savings account.

→ Opportunity selection for Strategy Two is limited to the six ETFs handpicked for their varying levels of opportunity.

→ Risk management (GainsMaster Key 4) comes by using your risk tolerance number—defined in Chapter Two—as a measure for where to place the STOP and GO signs on your own risk spectrum.

PERSONAL GAINS

Toni

How Emotions Influence Investing

*You have power over your mind—not outside events.
Realize this, and you will find strength.*

—MARCUS AURELIUS

In Chapter Eight's Personal Gains section, we talked about emotional intelligence. Now let's extend that discussion to discuss how emotions influence our success as an investor.

Indeed, researchers suggest the emotional part of us that thinks, feels, hopes, and aspires has a great deal to do with our portfolio's bottom line. New investors, in particular, fall victim to potent emotions that lead to impulsiveness and gambler-like actions. How can they not? The markets are unpredictable and wide open to interpretation.

Three personal qualities that can help strengthen our mastery of investing include the ability to control impulses, the ability to regulate moods, and the ability to keep anxiety from interfering with decisions during periods of high stress.

First, please know that the ability to control our human impulses lives at the heart of investing success. Each of us needs to be aware of our personal tendencies toward impulsive risk-taking and rein them in, if necessary. Taking uncalculated risks in the market can provide a quick adrenaline rush, but the results can be disastrous. Enter new stock positions only when they align with your risk-management strategy and your investing objectives.

Next, for the sake of making wise decisions, we must avoid allowing the market to dictate our emotions. This syndrome occurs most with those who glue themselves to the market on an everyday basis. When the market moves higher, they are happy. When it moves down, they feel miserable. To add insult to injury... did you know that we humans feel sensations of pleasure when our account balance rises, but in contrast, feel much deeper feelings of pain if it falls by the same amount of money? Result: odds dictate you're going to feel more pain than pleasure if you allow the market's fluctuations to control your emotions. And, by the way, this pain can cause you to make hasty risk-management decisions.

If you find your happiness linked to the market's moods, consider placing automatic stops with your broker. Then take a vacation from watching the market on a daily basis. Remember, it's your overall approach that counts and that will drive your gains/losses success.

Finally, one of the most challenging skills to which we can aspire resides in the ability to keep anxiety from interfering with decisions during periods of high stress.

One of my most vivid memories goes back to September 11, 2001, and the first morning the New York Stock Exchange opened, four days after that horrific event. None of us knew what to expect. Admittedly, we were all scared. Would a wave of uncontrollable selling hit the market? Would we see our portfolio value vanish in front of our eyes?

As an active trader and investor, I *did* know of the thousands of e-mails (we didn't have Facebook or Twitter then) that had circulated among market participants during the past few days.

"When the markets open, don't start selling," the e-mails said. "Let's not give the terrorists the satisfaction of seeing us fearful."

And we didn't. And to a great degree, the market remained calm.

I knew where my protective stops were. And although the market gapped down slightly, my stops were not touched. I kept my positions in place.

I believe that day was a tribute to humankind's ability to think rationally, manage personal emotions, and respond with a heroic approach—all in the face of extreme duress.

To achieve success as investors, we must recognize that our emotions affect the decisions we make. When we approach the market with a calm, well-ordered, anxiety-free mindset, we are most able to make decisions that lead to success.

CHAPTER TEN

Customized Investing
Finding a Strategy That Suits You

Gordon

I F YOU want to get more from your investments than most people get, you need to do more than most people do. The strategies in the previous chapter are intended to help you recognize ways to get excellent returns over many years. Those strategies are also designed for investors who don't have a lot of time to spend. This chapter provides information for those who are willing to spend a bit more time on their investing activities and who are looking for better returns to match.

The cycles of history suggest that investors may be in for turbulent times for several years to come. Investors will need a better understanding of the investment opportunities they have at their disposal if they want to have exceptional returns in such difficult markets. I am convinced that this is possible to do. In fact I'll go one further. I believe well-prepared individual investors are more likely to achieve exceptional returns over the coming decade than a large majority of institutional investors.

Nowadays, professional money managers have more constraints placed on them than do individual investors. Modern investors have greater access to a wider array of investments than ever before. The limits of what an individual can invest in are no longer a competitive advantage for the large investor. The technology and investing instruments available to ordinary investors bring new advantages to the small investor.

Individual investors who use tax-advantaged investing accounts, such as an IRA or a Roth IRA, don't have to limit themselves to investing with strategies designed to avoid the higher tax rates assigned to short-term capital gains. That means they can take advantage of a wide variety of opportunities, some of which may only last for a short while. Investors willing to discipline themselves will find they can achieve the returns they are seeking by simply paying attention to two details: proper self-knowledge and adequate risk management.

Now before going further, I want to point out that it is important for any investor to have a base of security from which to begin. Some people, having scratched together their first twenty thousand dollars in a retirement savings account, immediately want to put it all into high-risk strategies. That isn't wise. One of the strategies in the previous chapter would be more suitable for such an individual. However, if you believe that you have your general retirement needs taken care of and you have additional money that you both want and can afford to put at risk without endangering your retirement status, then the strategies in this chapter may well be worth considering.

That was the case for Charlie and Rita. Let me show you how I worked with both of them to identify strategies suited to their individual personalities and customized for their particular goals. In this chapter I will show how to use the GainsMaster approach with two examples of customized investing strategies. For each of the two strategies I will also show you the amount of time required, the self-knowledge an investor needs, and what the investors must do to manage risk.

The Way of the Sculptor: Charlie's Strategy for Small but Consistent Gains

"Don't get me wrong," Charlie explained, "these ideas you've given us so far are good. That's what we asked you for, but. . ." he trailed off and looked towards Rita.

"Go ahead," she encouraged.

"I'm looking for something more," he said.

I returned his gaze thoughtfully and looked at Rita. She smiled sheepishly.

"Well, I have some ideas," I began, "but you must know they will take extra time."

"Let's hear 'em," Charlie said. "Just give us some picture of what we'd be getting in to."

"We'll be the judges of whether it fits our time frame," assured Rita.

"Fair enough," I said. "But let's start at the beginning. You remember the first key of the GainsMaster approach, to define your objectives, correct?"

Charlie and Rita nodded.

"You can use this approach to create any kind of personal investing strategy you like. Nowadays, investors can choose from a wide variety of strategies and styles. One academic study identified fifty-five distinct, yet successful strategies that could be employed in the markets" (Jennifer Conrad, Gutam Kaul, "An Anatomy of Strategies" *The Review of Financial Studies* Fall 1998, Vol.11, No.3, pp. 489–519).

"Customizing your own investing strategy begins with defining your objectives—because only you can determine what success looks like to you. It also includes knowing what kind of an investor you are—what types of returns you expect, what kinds of losses you can tolerate, and what kinds of expectations you have for your efforts along the way."

"You need to start out with identifying these characteristics about yourself. Determining how much loss you can tolerate and what gains you'd like to achieve is pretty straightforward, but understanding your expectations is a bit more subtle. Let me explain it this way."

I reached for a nearby notepad.

"I believe investing styles can be divided along a spectrum. I label one end of this spectrum 'Winning Small' and the other side of the spectrum 'Winning Big.' The spectrum is a general description of

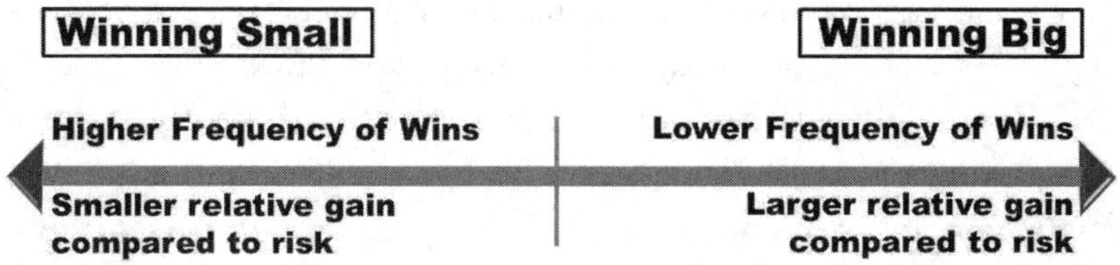

Winning Small	Winning Big
Higher Frequency of Wins	Lower Frequency of Wins
Smaller relative gain compared to risk	Larger relative gain compared to risk

FIGURE 10.1   "Winning Small" and "Winning Big" are two different styles of Investing.

two factors: first, how often your investments should be winners, and second, the relative size of those winners compared to the losers."

"On the left side of this spectrum you have a style of investing that is designed to win more often than it will lose." I pointed to what I had drawn. "Winning Small implies that you seek a higher percentage of winners in your investing."

"You accomplish this by allowing your investment to fluctuate in a generous way until you can take a conservative profit when the opportunity comes along to do so."

"The investing style on this side of the spectrum works well, but it also has a dark side to it," I cautioned. "Once I had a conversation with a professional money manager who explained his investing methodology. Showing me an impressive set of results, he then explained that he had just completed seven years in a row without a single loss in his investing choices. I asked a few questions to learn more. I quickly realized how he accomplished it, but I wasn't certain he understood it himself."

"He thought he had just made shrewd choices. Indeed he had, but he was unwittingly creating the results he wanted just by adopting this Winning Small style."

"Never losing sounds like my kind of style!" Charlie grinned.

"Probably not," I countered. "His big secret was that he never used a stop-loss during those seven years—which incidentally were the years 1993 to 2000. What this individual didn't realize was the amount of risk he was actually taking. By not using any stop losses, he was effectively assuming the market would always keep going higher. That assumption stopped working shortly thereafter."

"When I talked to him three years later he had shuttered his business and moved on to something else. Investing without a stop loss might work in a market that mostly goes up for several years in a row, but when the market trends downward, the results are disastrous."

"I see your point," Charlie conceded.

"Here is something the professional money manager didn't know," I said. "You can achieve a high percentage of winners in your investing without having to risk all, or even most, of your money. It is quite simple to do, and it doesn't depend on investing only in easygoing, GO-sign markets. Applying such a strategy can help investors keep their performances in line with their expectations. If investors naturally have the expectation that their investments should win most of the time, they will become discouraged and give up after a string of losses."

"I have personally witnessed investors who quit just as their strategies were about to pay off." I related the following story to them. "One man in particular showed me his statements of how he was giving up after taking $400,000 in losses in three years. He had started with a one million dollar account, and he began investing in the year 2000. His timing for getting in was poor, because he didn't know how to evaluate market conditions. But his timing for getting out was simply tragic."

"As it turned out, if he had held on just one more month the losses would have begun to reverse. He could have eventually watched those losses turn into gains over the following three years, but he simply couldn't tolerate either the string of losers or the deep losses in his account."

"That's why it is important to help you establish a method for having a high winning percentage." I said. "You need to have the psychological power to keep yourself calm in troubled times."

"Now the basic tactic of this investing style is that you take small, consistent gains when they come along," I explained. "The tradeoff is that you might not get all of the gains that are possible on any one investment. And when you do take a loss, it can set you back more than the gains."

"Some people look at a stock like Apple Computer and remember the days when you could buy it for twenty times less than what it sells for today. They think that investing amounts to being smart or lucky enough to buy a stock like that and hold on until it reaches its peak—somehow knowing to sell it when it stops going higher."

"What they don't realize is that there is another way to grow your money. You can simply take small gains and chip away at your goal. Like a sculptor, you keep your mind focused on the image of what you are trying to create, and you take out small bits at a time. You don't concern yourself with what gains you don't get, only the gains you do capture—preferably on a steady and consistent basis."

"So I just concentrate on making small gains consistently," Charlie confirmed. "Assuming I can do that, what is the risk?"

"The risk is that some unexpected event will come along and make one or more of your investment choices drop rapidly," I explained.

"You mean like what happened in 2008?" Charlie asked.

"No, I'm talking about something different," I replied. "The year 2008 was a STOP-sign market. There's always a risk that could come along, but we've got a plan for that. No, I mean that because the Winning Small style of investing looks for small steady gains, a quick drop in a single day might catch you by surprise and wipe out a lot of the small gains you've been building up—especially if news comes out when the market is closed."

"This sometimes happens to individual stocks when they report worse than expected earnings after market hours. By the time the market is open on the next day, the price is much lower than your tolerance level, and your loss is greater than you planned."

"How do you protect against that?" Charlie said, folding his arms.

"By not investing with individual stocks. You can use ETFs instead," I said.

Charlie thought about that.

"I think I know where you are going with this. Let me see if I understand you," Charlie said as he sat back in his chair and looked out the window.

"ETFs are a bundle of stocks." Charlie paused to consider then looked back at me. "So if one goes bad, it will be averaged out with the other stocks, and that will limit the impact. Is that right?" Charlie queried.

"Correct. An ETF won't often generate such severe overnight drops," I agreed. "Using ETFs you will still likely encounter losses, but you are less likely to make larger losses than you plan for when setting your limits on an investment."

"OK. But how will I know which ETFs to use?" Charlie asked. "Aren't there hundreds of them?"

"You will only need to work with a small number of them," I said. "In fact, I will show you a three-step procedure in this process, so that you don't have to be overwhelmed by a large collection of information to sift through. Once you get used to it, this procedure is something you can complete in thirty minutes or less."

"Sounds just right for me." Charlie grinned. "How do I start?"

"We'll follow the GainsMaster Approach." I made notes on the notepad again. "You'll first define your objectives. Once you are ready to invest, you'll review the market conditions, choose your investments, and manage your risk."

Defining Objectives. "The Winning Big style of investing means you have to put up with having small losses most of the time," I explained. "That plan requires that you have large enough winners to overcome the losers. But it is not easy for most people. It requires that you endure long losing streaks."

"I have a simple indicator for whether or not you can invest using the Winning Big style," I said. "Let me ask you this one question: Are you capable of experiencing fifteen losses in a row?"

I let that sink in for a moment.

"Imagine your investments lose fifteen times in a row, Charlie," I said. "Would you still feel ready to choose the next investment in the same way as you chose the previous fifteen?"

"I can tell you right now, that is not me," Charlie said. "I am not a patient man."

"It's the same for most people," I agreed. "The Winning Small style of investing comes a bit easier for all of us, because we simply prefer being right more often than being wrong."

Charlie slowly nodded in agreement.

"Now if you've decided that you like the idea of working on the left side of the spectrum," I went on, "then the next thing to consider is how much fluctuation you can tolerate in your account. We need to establish what level of loss you want to avoid and what gains you want to target."

"Based on what we talked about before, twelve percent was the number we identified," Charlie recalled. "I'd say that sounds about right for me."

"OK. Now let's look at the amount of gains you'd like to target," I said. "With the Winning Small style, it is appropriate to target gains that are less than your risk tolerance. You may end up making better returns each year, but it is important to keep your expectations appropriate. A simple rule of thumb is that you can target a range of gains beginning with half of what you could tolerate for risk."

"If twelve percent is the amount you are willing to risk, then it would be appropriate to target six to twelve percent growth per year for your investing account. How does that sound to you?"

"Where I am at right now, that would be acceptable," said Charlie. "Obviously I'd love to get more, but if I thought I could get that level of growth consistently, I'd be happy with that."

"That's good," I replied. "That means we have the information we need. In a few minutes, I'll show you how to use this to help you identify your risk-management rules. But before we get there, we need to work through the next two keys of the GainsMaster approach."

Evaluating Market Conditions. "The next key for you to turn," I continued, "is to establish your method for evaluating market conditions. I've explained how you can use the 12-month moving average and the GO signs or STOP signs to confirm the conditions of the market."

"Yep," said Charlie. "If the price is above its 12-month moving average, we look for growth; if it is below, we look for safety—pretty simple."

"And you don't switch between the two unless you see a GO or STOP sign confirming the change," I said.

"Right," Charlie said. "I'll get Rita here to help me identify those."

"Ha," said Rita, "no pressure there!"

"You can handle it," Charlie reassured.

Rita smiled, rolled her eyes, and looked back at Charlie. She started to say something, but changed her mind and went back to writing notes. She didn't look up as she said to me, "You just go on. I'll wait for my turn."

"The key here is that you must do that activity regularly, once a month. Don't let it slip!" I urged them. Rita made more notes.

"Once you have evaluated the market conditions, you will use that evaluation to help you select your investments. We'll create two lists of ETFs for you to choose from: one to use for GO-sign conditions and one to use for STOP-sign conditions. From these lists you'll select opportunities and also keep an eye on the markets."

Choosing opportunities in a GO-sign market. "Investors today can always find something in the world that is going up in value," I reminded Charlie. "You don't have to limit your thinking to the U.S. stock market. In fact, it is important to keep an eye on the bond market, the commodities market, and global markets for non-U.S. stocks and currencies also."

"That sounds like a lot of research," Charlie said with concern.

"Don't worry, we'll keep it simple," I assured. "Once you have determined whether the market is in a GO-sign condition or a STOP-sign condition, then you'll use a two-step procedure to spot opportunities. To carry out this procedure, you set out to answer two questions: 'Which are the strongest two markets right now?' and 'Which are the strongest ETFs in those markets?'"

"The first step is to review what I call your primary list for a GO-sign market—a market that is trending higher. This is a list of five ETFs that represent the different markets."

"These ETFs cover five different classes of assets that people can invest in. When the market first begins trending upward, both stocks and commodities will usually be strongest; however, that won't always be the case. That's why you need to keep an eye on these. Once each

Symbol	Subject
SPY	U.S. stocks
DBC	Commodities
EFA	Non-U.S. stocks, developed
EEM	Non-U.S. stocks, opportunities
LQD	Corporate bonds

TABLE 10.1 ETFs that track five different kinds of investment. Use this list to determine which markets are strongest at a given time.

HOT TIP

You can find out how much prices have changed over the previous three months in a number of different ways, but my favorite way is to use a comparison chart. To make this work, you can use charts from a brokerage or go to almost any website that features charting tools. On such a website you will look in the charting tools for a "comparison" feature. This will allow you to compare all five of the stocks on the primary list. Once you have done so, you can simply look at this chart for the past six months. It will show all five ETFs as lines on the same chart. At the right edge of the chart, the two highest lines represent the two strongest markets of the five.

month you will check these to determine which are the strongest two on this list."

"When you say 'strongest,' what am I looking for?" asked Charlie.

"You want to know which are moving higher, based on percentage of the price," I explained. "You will look for the two that have gone up in price by the highest percentage in the last six months."

"Once you have an idea of which markets are rising the fastest, then you'll move to a secondary list—one for each market. This group of secondary lists is another collection of ETFs. Each ETF on these new lists is related to one of the five ETFs from the primary list. Here are the secondary lists." I showed them my notepad.

"I see," Charlie said as he reviewed the lists. "It's a hierarchy. If stocks are strong, I go to the secondary list for stocks; if commodities are strong I check out the commodities list."

"Correct. In all there are only twenty-five ETFs for GO-sign markets. But you will only have to review those in the lists for the two strongest markets."

"Sounds simple enough," Charlie said as he looked over the lists. "What am I looking for in these secondary lists?"

"The same thing as the primary list, only this time you are looking for the strongest four in the two secondary lists combined," I said.

"What happens during STOP-sign markets?" Charlie asked.

"You use the same procedure to identify the four strongest ETFs—those that have risen by the highest percentage in the past three months," I said.

"What do I do then?" asked Charlie.

"You buy them," I replied.

"Just like that?" Charlie asked further. "Is there a special technique I should use to be sure I get in at the right time?"

"You can use a special technique for entry, but it isn't required. I think you will gain an advantage if you wait for the price to break through its highest price in the previous week, but it is more of a psychological advantage than a statistical advantage," I replied. "You feel more secure in your decision when you watch the price go in your favor from the beginning."

"Now it is important that you do not place a purchase order without completing one more step," I cautioned.

"What's the step?" asked Charlie.

Symbol	U.S. Stocks
SPY	S&P 500
XLB	Basic material production
XLF	Financial
XLI	Industrial
XLK	Technology
XLP	Consumer staples
XLU	Utilities
XLV	Health care
XLY	Consumer discretionary
MDY	Mid-sized companies
IWM	Small-sized companies

TABLE 10.2. Secondary list 1 for GO-sign markets: The ETFs for the major sectors of the U.S. Stock Market (with small- and medium-sized companies). When stocks are the strongest market, look for the strongest sectors in this market.

Symbol	Commodities
DBC	Top-traded commodities
DBA	Agricultural commodities
DBB	Materials commodities
GDX	Precious-metals mining companies

TABLE 10.3 Secondary list 2 for GO-sign markets: The ETFs for the major classes of investments in the commodities market. When commodities are the strongest market, look to use the strongest ETFs on this list.

Symbol	Non-U.S., Developed Markets	Risk and Opportunity (Volatility)
EFA	All developed markets	High
EWA	Australia	High
EWG	Germany	High
EWJ	Japan	High
EWS	Singapore	High
EWU	Great Britain	High
EWP	Spain	High
EWH	Hong Kong	High

TABLE 10.4   Secondary list 3 for GO-sign markets: The ETFs for the major classes of investments in the non-U.S., developed markets. This is primarily Europe, Australia, and Japan.

Symbol	Non-U.S., Emerging Markets	Risk and Opportunity (Volatility)
EEM	All emerging markets	High
EWZ	Brazil	High
PIN	Russia	High
RSX	India	High
FXI	China	High
EWM	Malaysia	High
EPP	Pacific Rim (not Japan)	High
ILF	Latin America	High

TABLE 10.5   Secondary list 4 for GO-sign markets: The ETFs for the major classes of investments in the non-U.S., emerging markets.

"You need to know precisely how many shares to buy," I said. "That's the biggest part of how you control your risk, no matter what you are investing in. But we're not there just yet. Before we get there I need to show you what to do about a STOP-sign market."

Symbol	Corporate Bonds	Risk and Opportunity (Volatility)
LGD	Investment-grade, long-term corporate bonds (safer, lower returns)	Medium
HYG	High-yield, long-term corporate bonds (riskier, higher returns)	Medium
CIU	Medium-term corporate bonds	Medium
CSJ	Short-term corporate bonds	Medium

TABLE 10.6 Secondary list 5 for GO-sign markets: The ETFs for the major classes of investments in corporate bonds. These tend to trade more like stocks than bonds, but future conditions could potentially create circumstances where this class could outperform most others.

HOT TIP

Here's my favorite answer to a question like Charlie's: use what is called a "buy-stop" order. Set it just five cents above the highest price in the last week. The buy-stop order may not be familiar to you, but if you are investing with the use of an IRA, like Charlie, then you'll want to find out about it. What it does is useful. Simply put, the buy-stop order triggers your entry into the position at a specified price—a price higher than the current price. The benefits of using a buy-stop order in this case are twofold. First, you open your position when the price is going up, so there is a reasonable chance the price will continue higher. Investors feel more comfortable when their investment choice quickly becomes profitable right from the beginning. Second, if the price goes down, you will not open your position. If for some reason the price starts going down and keeps going down, then this was a position you would be glad to avoid. The buy-stop order, set just above the highest price in the last week, is an effective tool for catching the next upward move in the price trend.

Choosing opportunities in a STOP-sign market. "You will switch to a different ETF list when the market has moved below its 12-month moving average and has confirmed that movement with STOP signals." I explained to Charlie. "Once you are in a STOP-sign market, then you will look at a different set of ETFs to compare. Here are the lists."

I showed him what I had just written on the notepad

"This is just one large list instead of five small ones, but how do I select?" asked Charlie.

"This list allows you to first identify how much risk and opportunity you will tolerate," I explained. "If your goal for a STOP-sign market is to simply hunker down and protect your investments, then you'll want to select from among the items at the top half of this list. If you want to look for things that will likely show substantial growth

Ticker	STOP-Sign Investing Instrument	Risk and Opportunity (Volatility)
Government Bonds		
AGG	All U.S. government bonds	Low
SHY	U.S. government bonds 1–3 years	Low
UUP	U.S. dollar, leveraged two times	Low
IEF	U.S. government bonds 7–10 years	Medium
TLT	U.S. government bonds, 20-year note	Medium
MUB	U.S. municipal bonds	Medium
EU	Eurozone bonds	Medium
EMB	Emerging-market bonds	Medium
Interest Rates and Inflation		
TBT	Inverse U.S. government bonds, 20-year note, poised for rising interest rates	Medium
TIP	Inflation-Protected Treasury Bonds	Medium

Ticker	STOP-Sign Investing Instrument	Risk and Opportunity (Volatility)
Currencies		
EUO	Inverse euro (very similar to UUP, but more leveraged)	Medium
FXA	Australian dollar	Medium
FXF	Swiss franc	Medium
Precious Metals		
GLD	Gold	High
SLV	Silver	High
Inverse Funds		
SH	Goes opposite to the S&P 500	High
SCO	Goes opposite to the price of oil, leveraged two times	Very High
DZZ	Goes opposite to the price of gold, leveraged two times	Very High
DXD	Goes opposite to the Dow, leveraged two times	Very High
QID	Goes opposite to the NASDAQ 100, leveraged two times	Very High
TWM	Goes opposite to the Russell 2000, leveraged two times	Very High

TABLE 10.7 Selection list for STOP-sign markets: The complete ETF list for the ETFs to consider in STOP-sign markets. Not all of these will rise in a STOP-sign market, but it is almost certain that no matter what kind of STOP-sign market the future brings, something on this list will be going up during those times.

during a time when stock prices are in a prolonged downward trend, then you'll move further down the list."

"Now it's important to understand something here," I cautioned. "I've structured the list in this way for an important reason. STOP-sign markets don't always work the same. Over long periods of history the market dynamics change around. For example, in most STOP-sign markets, bond markets do well as stocks fall, but there are also times where both bonds and stocks fall together, as interest rates rise."

Charlie frowned. "Am I going to have to know how to watch interest rates and international currencies and . . . whatever? Because I know myself well enough to know that that is something I won't do for very long."

"I don't blame you for being concerned about that," I told him. "This method is meant to be simple, but that is exactly why this list contains what it does. The list is designed to help you be prepared for uncertain times. It has in it components from a wide variety of markets, and that variety is the key. You won't have to know all of the reasons why one of these ETFs is going up in price. All you care about is which ones seem to be increasing in price over the past six months.

"No matter what happens or how it happens, it is a good bet that at least a few of the ETFs on this list will be going up during a STOP-sign market. If you check all of the low-risk and medium-risk ETFs, or if you check all of the high-risk ETFs and very-high-risk ETFs, you will likely find something that is a suitable selection for your investing during those market conditions."

"What if I just go to cash and not invest in anything at all during those markets?" Charlie asked.

"You could do that, but if inflation accompanies a bear-market move, your savings could lose their purchasing power while you wait it out," I said. "However, if that were happening, don't forget that you would be watching the interest-rate ETF rise higher."

I pointed near the middle of the list to the heading that read "Interest Rates and Inflation."

"If inflation is happening, then either one of these two funds, TBT or TIP, should start to rise."

Charlie looked over the lists and slowly nodded his approval.

"This is excellent," he told me. "I think I can work with this."

"Glad you like it," I replied. "But we're not done yet. You will still need to know how to control how your investment account will fluctuate. You need to know how to control risk."

Managing Risk. "When you say 'control risk,'" asked Charlie, "Do you mean that I will have to do some hedging? I mean buying one fund to offset the risk of a different fund—or stuff like that."

"What I am talking about is simpler than that," I said. "In a nutshell, you are going to manage your risk by not buying too much of one thing."

"How will I know how much is too much?" Charlie questioned.

"By establishing a rule that you will risk more than one percent but no more than two percent of your account on any single investment," I replied. "Let me explain how you accomplish that. Every time you open a new position, you will have two targets: one target that designates when to take a profit—we'll call this your profit price—and one target that tells you when to get out of the position with a loss—which we will call your loss price."

"For example, let's suppose you decided you want to purchase the ETF that is an average of all government bonds; the ticker symbol is AGG. This fund is currently available at a price of $100 per share. The next step you follow is to identify your profit price and your loss price. A simple rule of thumb for establishing the profit price and the Loss Price is to use this table."

I drew for Charlie Table 10.8.

"As you can see in this table, AGG has a 'Risk and Opportunity Level' of 'Low,'" I pointed out. "According to this table, that means your profit price will be set at a 5 percent increase of the original purchase price. For example if AGG were currently priced at $100, then after you bought it, your profit price would be $105."

"So you mean if it rises to $105 I just sell it?" asked Charlie.

"That's right," I said.

Risk and Opportunity Level	Profit Price Equals Entry Price Plus...	Loss Price Equals Entry Price Minus...
Low	5%	10%
Medium	7.5%	15%
High	10%	20%
Very High	12.5%	25%

TABLE 10.8 Profit and loss guidelines: Charlie's profit and loss guidelines for the different volatility levels he may select from.

Charlie followed on with, "What if it keeps going up after I sell it?"

"You don't care," I replied. "You make a profit; you move on and get ready to do it again."

Charlie looked at his paper for a moment, then shrugged, "And my loss price would be $90, 10 percent lower, right?"

"Yes that's correct," I replied. "But on the high volatility and very high volatility funds, you can also consider nudging the profit and loss orders higher. A good strategy is to move them both higher by one percent after each month if your investment has increased in value but has not reached the profit price yet."

"So I just take whatever profit comes and then start over and do it again, taking a managed risk each time," Charlie restated, "and if I think the investment might keep going, I can just move my orders higher like brackets, one percent each month, until either the top or the bottom takes me out."

"That's right," I said, "though it won't be the usual pattern; you might find that you end up making a profit on the same ETF multiple times in one year."

Charlie nodded. "I like it."

"Now the most important idea about managing risk is purchasing the right number of shares," I continued. "It might take some pondering to understand why, but the simple explanation is that selecting the right number of shares is the most effective way you can limit your exposure to any one investment. Let me show you how to arrive at the correct number. Use this three-step procedure:

Step 1: Determine your account balance at the time and multiply it by two percent (.02). This value will be called the risk amount.
Step 2: Subtract your loss price from your order price. This value will be called the risk size.
Step 3: Divide the risk amount by risk size. This number is the proper number of shares to buy.

"Using these three steps ensures that you buy the proper number of shares. This keeps your loss from being too large and your gain from being too insignificant."

"Why would I risk twice as much as the profit I take?" asked Charlie.

"You do that so that you can win more often. Typically you will win about 66 percent of the time when you invest this way, maybe more if you correctly identify the market conditions," I explained. "Last of all, you should not hold any more than five positions at once."

"Why is that?" asked Charlie.

"So that you can limit your losses to 10 percent if all of your choices go wrong at the same time. It is doubtful they will, but if they do, you have still met your objective of not losing more than 12 percent in your account for a calendar year, because if necessary, you could stop at that time until the year is up."

"I understand. That makes sense," Charlie agreed.

Charlie, Rita, and I then worked together to capture his customized investing plan on a single page. Once we had it completed, it looked like Table 10.9.

"Now this style of investing can be tricky," I cautioned. "Though you will get to win more often than not, you must resist the tempta-

Objectives	Avoid losing more than 12 percent of my investing capital annually, targeting gains of 6 to 12 percent per year.
Market evaluation	Determine whether the market is above or below the 12-month methods moving average.
	■ If price is above the moving average, assume market participants are in a mood for seeking opportunity. Invest using the GO-sign ETF list.
	■ If price is below the moving average, assume market participants are in a mood for seeking safety. Invest using the STOP-sign ETF list.
	At the end of each month, check to see if the price of the S&P 500 has just crossed above or below its 12-month moving average.
	■ If price has recently crossed the moving average, then check volatility and risk preference to see if the market has given a new GO or STOP sign.
	■ If the sign persists for two months, then switch my assumptions about the market.

Continued…

Investment selection	**For GO-sign markets:**

Step 1. Review the five primary ETFs for the current market mood and see which two have performed the best in the last six months.

Step 2. Review secondary list of ETFs corresponding to the two selections from Step 1.

Step 3. Select the four best-performing ETFs from the secondary list and prepare entry orders for each of them.

For STOP-sign markets:

Step 1. Review the ETF list and determine the level of risk and opportunity desired.

Step 2. Select the two best-performing ETFs at my level of risk tolerance by identifying which are going up in value over the previous six months.

Special Entry Order procedure:

Identify the highest price of the last twenty trading days and add five cents. This is the order price. Be prepared to place a buy-stop purchase order just above that price. Do not place a purchase order until completing the risk-management activity (below). Repeat this procedure every month if I have fewer than the maximum of six positions going at once.

Risk management

Get out of the investment if the price rises to profit price or drops to loss price.

- Set a stop-loss order at a loss price level, based on degree of volatility.
- Set a take-profit order at a profit price (half as much as loss price).

Consider nudging these orders both higher by one percent after each month if my investment has increased in value but has not reached the profit price yet.

Risk less than 2 percent on each investment. Accomplish this by identifying the correct number of shares to buy, based on the following formula:

Step 1. Account balance (at time of trade) times .02 (risk amount).

Step 2. Subtract the loss price, from the order price (risk size).

Step 3. Divide risk amount by risk size. This gives me the number of shares to buy.

TABLE 10.9 **Charlie's complete customized investing plan—Starting balance $950,000.00**

tion to let your investment move beyond the limits you've established. You must allow yourself to take losses according to your plan—otherwise you end up like my friend who had to close his business."

Charlie took in all that I had explained, then nodded once and turning to me said, "Got it! I think this will work for me." Charlie beamed. "Now what about Rita?"

The Way of the Gardener: Rita's Strategy for a Big Harvest

"Are you sure about this?" I asked Rita.

My question hung in the air as Rita considered what she had just explained previously. Though I asked her the same question that I had asked of Charlie earlier—whether or not she could endure a losing streak of fifteen in a row—she answered the question differently from Charlie.

"Yes," she replied. But I didn't think she sounded fully confident.

Charlie looked at Rita as I prepared to question further. He spoke before I could.

"I can tell you this. If anyone I know possesses the patience and determination to endure that kind of a losing streak and keep on going, it is Rita here," he said. "This gal is a tough cookie! She doesn't get thrown off track, and she doesn't quit."

Rita smiled at him. "Thanks, Charlie."

I don't usually recommend the strategy I had in mind for Rita, because most people are not naturally suited for it; however, those who are capable of actually investing in this manner have the potential to outperform the markets very well. This particular strategy—investing for big gains but enduring a lot of losses—is a favorite among some of the very best investors in the world. Most people won't do it. It is hard.

"Unless," I said out loud. I didn't mean to.

Charlie and Rita waited with puzzled expressions.

"I have to tell you," I started over. "This strategy is almost too difficult for most individual investors to accomplish . . . unless . . . you know what to expect before you start. Even then it's—" I hesitated. "Well, it's not complicated; it just takes resolve. You've got to stick with it. Since Charlie seems to think you've got that talent, perhaps this is right for you."

Rita took a deep breath and let it out. "Well. What do I do?"

I grinned. "You plant a lot of seeds and you pull a lot of weeds."

Rita gave me a funny look.

"It's a bit like gardening," I explained. "For this strategy, you will do as the gardener does: you'll plant more seeds than you expect to grow; you'll pull out weeds and unwanted plants; you'll cultivate the strongest ones to help them become as productive as possible; ultimately, about the time you are sick of doing that, you'll reap a bountiful harvest. You see, in your investing you will expect that most of your investments will be small losses. The trick is that when they aren't, some of them produce very big gains."

Rita chuckled a bit. "Sounds a lot like the marketing campaigns I used to run in my former job," she said.

"That's a good comparison," I said. "Sales professionals know it's all about the numbers. The more times you attempt a sale, the more times you can make money. As long as each attempt doesn't cost you too much in money, time, or sanity, you can keep going until you get rewarded for your efforts. This strategy follows that same philosophy."

"I can relate to that," said Rita, leaning forward with interest. Charlie made a subtle grin. He took his turn to work with the pen and the notepad.

"OK, Rita, let's walk through the GainsMaster approach and define your strategy."

Defining Objectives. "We determined before that you were willing to take on a significant amount of risk in your portfolio. That's the first key to turn," I reminded Rita. "Thirty-five percent is a bit more than $10,000 from your $30,000 account. Is that accurate? Do you think you could keep going even if you lost that much in a year?"

"Yes," she said. "Joe has been building our retirement savings, being very conservative with it. My money is what we decided to invest with. If I lose it, our lifestyle won't be affected."

"Good. That's an excellent place to start from," I said. "All the same, we certainly don't want you to lose any more than necessary."

"For this strategy you'll use what I call a five-position method," I explained. "You'll seek to have five positions going, that is to say, five stocks you are working with, on any given week. You will buy up to five stocks for your portfolio—only five—and if one of the stocks gets sold out in a week, you'll attempt to replace it the next week."

"Why only five? Don't I want diversification?" asked Rita.

Charlie looked up from the notepad. She shrugged back at him.

"What? That's what our broker friend is always saying," Rita explained. "Don't I have to have a couple dozen stocks to build out a robust portfolio?"

"It's a fair question," I replied. "People trained to invest money on behalf of others usually have a lot of money they have to put to work. They need to find an investment for several million or maybe even billions of dollars. In that kind of investing it makes a lot of sense to diversify assets by choosing lots of different stocks."

"However, for someone with a small account, having a lot of positions is dead weight. You can get some benefit from diversifying, but in a small account you have to be certain that your diversification doesn't wipe out its own potential benefits. Every investment costs a commission, and each one takes your time and attention. The more you choose, the busier you are, and the more expensive it gets. Which brings us to our next point: how much time are you willing to spend on this?"

"Well I don't have a lot of time, but I was thinking—hoping really—that I could do this in maybe one hour each weekend. Is that realistic?"

"Actually, yes," I said, "if you use this strategy I show you. Once you get used to it, you might find you can do it in even less time than that!"

Evaluating Market Conditions. "Don't forget," I reminded Rita, "your investment selection will change, depending on market conditions. To turn the second key you'll have to be prepared to evaluate the market. Since you and Charlie will both be watching for the same GO and STOP signs, you really will be able to help each other in that area. Do you feel comfortable that you know how to observe those signals?"

HOT TIP

Be sure to check out the website Toni and I created. Here you will find a section with chart examples that will help you get practice on this topic: www .investtowinbook.com.

"I understand it the way you've explained it," she said tentatively, "but I'd like to get some practice recognizing the symbols. Do you have any suggestions for that?"

"I do have some resources you can use to do just that," I replied.

"Once you feel comfortable that you can identify the difference in market conditions, you will be able to switch between the different filters for finding the stocks you choose from."

"How do I know what to buy anyway?" asked Rita.

Choosing Opportunities. "The next key is selection. It is important to remember that you are seeking stocks that can produce significant growth," I explained. "You'll want to find stocks that show evidence of growth now and opportunity for future growth. I'll give you an idea of what kind of search filter you can use to find this."

HOT TIP

The search filter criteria I explained in Chapter Six are an excellent resource you can use to find both growth stocks and safer stocks. These criteria can be used in one of the stock screeners available through a broker or a website like www.finviz.com.

"Each week you'll sit down to run your search filter and be presented with a list of stocks," I explained. "The next step is that you will compare them."

"What am I looking for? Do I have to read the financial statements?" asked Rita.

"Nothing so complicated," I said. "Once the stocks have made it through your filter, all you will need to do is compare the previous month's closing price of each stock with the current price for the same stocks."

"In GO-sign markets you will use the Growth-and-Opportunity search filter only. In STOP-Sign markets you will use the Growth-and-Opportunity search filter as well as the search filter for safer stocks, but you'll divide your choices up: three from one list and two from the other."

"Which list is the three and which is the two?" Rita asked.

"It doesn't matter," I pointed out, "so long as you have a mix between the two during STOP-sign markets. This is your version of diversification."

"All right," nodded Rita, "that's good to know. So I simply pick out five stocks to begin with and then keep replacing each one as it sells out of my portfolio, correct?"

"That's right," I said.

"And how do I know when to sell them?"

Managing Risk. "That brings us to the fourth key. The first part of this key is that you will use something called a trailing stop," I explained.

"What is that and how does it work?" Rita asked.

"A stop order is an order you set based on a trigger price. If the stock's price drops to your trigger price, then you are automatically sold out of the stock. A trailing stop is an order that moves higher as the stock price moves higher. Eventually, if the stock price goes high enough, the trailing stop will have moved up so that it is higher than the original entry price. This action allows you to lock in profit, so to speak."

"So does the trailing stop move upwards automatically, or do I have to change its price each month?" asked Rita.

"If your broker has an automatic trailing stop, you should just use that," I said, "If not, you would have to move it higher yourself."

"How do I know where to put the stop order?" asked Rita.

"That's the easy part," I told her. "For all of your investments you will put the stop order 25 percent lower than the purchase price."

"So..." Rita looked out the window, then back at me, "if I buy a stock at $40, then I set my stop order at $30?"

"That's right," I said.

"And if the stock goes up to $60, the stop loss will go to... $45, right?" Rita asked.

"Correct," I said. "Do you see how the stop order can automatically move up?"

"I think so," she said, "but what happens if the price goes down? Does the order go down also? If so, how would it protect my profit?"

"No, it doesn't go down," I corrected. "The stop order only moves up."

"OK," she said. "Now I understand."

"Great," I continued. "The last part of turning this key in the GainsMaster approach is to determine the number of shares to buy."

"OK," said Rita. "I took notes for Charlie's strategy. Is mine going to be the same?"

"Yes, but with one small difference," I cautioned. "You will only be risking one percent per investment choice."

"If I can tolerate more risk than Charlie can, shouldn't I be risking more than he, not less?" asked Rita.

"Charlie's strategy is likely to experience a lower percentage of losses than yours," I explained. "Your style of investing will, statistically speaking, generate losing streaks. It will also generate some spectacular gains that will offset and outpace those losses, but those will come along less frequently. You need to be able to endure the losses."

"This part of your strategy is crucial," I reiterated. "Imagine losing on fifteen investments in a row. This losing streak might take place over six months or more. Though you don't know it at the time, you might be only a few choices away from you next big winner. A winner so large it will put you well into in positive territory for the year. All you need to do is stay clear headed and execute your strategy the same way you've been doing it. Now do you think you'll be more clearheaded if, on that day, Joe looks over your shoulder and sees your account is down 15 percent as opposed to 30 percent?"

"Ah!" Rita said pointing at me, "you make a good point. Joe's an understanding guy, but I admit that could rattle me."

"Over time you'll figure out whether one percent, or two percent, or somewhere in between is the right amount of risk for you," I said. "While you are getting started, I recommend you do stick with one percent risk per investment choice."

"That makes sense!" she agreed.

"Well, that's the basics of the strategy. Any questions?" I asked.

"Just one," she said. "Will this really work?"

I smiled. It was the obvious question.

"I can't see into the future, and I can't perfectly predict how you will choose to make the strategy work for you," I cautioned. "Here's why I believe that if you are careful and patient, this strategy actually will work. First off, before suggesting this strategy to any of the people I work with, I ran a quick test of all the stocks in the Nasdaq 100. I applied this strategy to them to see if, individually, these stocks could yield gains. Of course the strategy showed gains during the good years."

"I also ran a test that began in the year 2000 and ended in the year 2009. That was a tough test, because during those years the vast majority of investors lost money on average, year after year. I also made it tougher by taking out stocks that weren't household names in the year 2000. I did that to try to avoid a thing called survivorship bias—the skewed effect that happens when testing stocks that are good merely because they have stuck around a long time."

"What did you find?" asked Charlie.

"I found that about 60 percent of those stocks, which were bought and sold in the manner described by your strategy, showed gains during those years. In fact, the average outcome of this investing style across all those stocks seemed to indicate that the stocks could return an average of 30 percent gains or better during that stretch of time."

"That's good performance for those years!" said Rita.

"That seems hard to believe," said Charlie. "If I remember right, the Nasdaq 100 never has gotten back to its highs of 2000. Not anywhere close."

"You're right," I said. "At the end of the year 2009, it was trading at only half of its peak level from its high in the year 2000. But remember that Rita's strategy is not a buy-and-hold style of investing. The average length of time Rita's strategy will keep her in a stock is only about four months."

"Some of the investments will last much longer, some much shorter, but I think you get the idea. With this strategy, you don't hang on and ride a stock down to the bitter end. You get out, and you move on to something else that's moving up."

Charlie, Rita, and I continued to work through her strategy to capture it into writing. When we were done, the one-page result was Rita's customized investing plan, shown in Table 10.10.

Objectives	Avoid losing more than 35 percent of my investing capital annually, targeting gains of 35 percent or more each year.
Market evaluation	Determine whether the market is above or below the 12-month methods moving average. ■ If price is above the moving average, assume market participants are in a mood for seeking opportunity. Invest using the GO-sign ETF list. ■ If price is below the moving average, assume market participants are in a mood for seeking safety. Invest using the STOP-sign ETF list. At the end of each month, check to see if the price of the S&P 500 has just crossed above or below its 12-month moving average. ■ If the price has recently crossed the moving average, then check volatility and risk preference to see if the market has given a new GO or STOP sign. ■ If the sign persists for two months, then switch my assumptions about the market.

Continued...

TABLE 10.10   **Rita's complete customized investing plan—Starting balance $30,000**

Investment selection	Use a five-slot method. For GO-sign markets:

If I already have five stocks in my portfolio, I have nothing to do for that week. Each week that I do not have five stocks in my portfolio, I follow these three steps.

Step 1. Search for growth and opportunity companies each week.

Step 2. Identify the companies found in Step 1 that have increased in price the most over the last one month.

Step 3. Place one entry order for the number of stocks needed to fill the five slots.

For STOP-sign markets:

Step 1. Search for both growth and opportunity companies, but also SAFE companies each week.

Step 2. Identify the companies found in Step 1 that have increased in price the most over the last one month.

Step 3. Place one entry order each of the stocks needed to fill the five slots. Be certain that no more than two of my stocks are from the growth and opportunity search and that no more than four of my stocks are from the SAFE search.

Special Entry Order procedure:

Identify the highest price of the last twenty trading days and add 5 cents. (This part works the same way as Charlie's strategy.) Be prepared to place a buy-stop purchase order just above that price. That way if prices don't go up, I don't get in. Do not place a purchase order until completing the risk-management activity (below). Repeat this procedure every month if you have less than the maximum of five positions going at once.

Risk management	Get out of the investment if the price drops more than 25 percent from the initial entry or its highest point thereafter.

- Set a stop-loss order at a price level that is 25 percent lower than the order price. This is your loss price.
- Move the stop price up automatically, if possible, or manually each week to 25 percent below the highest price in the last week.

Risk less than one percent on each investment. Accomplish this by identifying the correct number of shares to buy based on the following formula:

Step 1. Account balance (at time of trade) times .01 (risk amount).

Step 2. Subtract the loss price from the order price (risk size).

Step 3. Divide risk amount by risk size. This gives me the number of shares to buy.

Key Points to Remember

➜ The GainsMaster approach guides you to apply the four keys by defining your objectives (including your investing style), evaluating market conditions, choosing your investments, and managing your risk.

➜ An investor adopting a customized investing plan should select his investing style and set his expectations to match that style.

➜ Investors should match their risk management rules to the characteristics of the investing style.

➜ Charlie's style of investing was designed to take small gains and chip away with consistent gains over time, keeping his risk at less than 12 percent.

➜ Charlie limits his investing to twenty-five ETFs in GO-sign markets that he selects from and twenty ETFs in STOP-sign markets that he selects from.

➜ Charlie sets his profit price and loss price based on the volatility of his investment choices.

➜ Charlie also limits risk by planning for no more than 2 percent risk on any one position.

➜ Rita limits risk by using the five-position method and planning for no more than 1 percent risk to each position.

➜ Rita selects stocks using the Growth and Opportunity filter criteria discussed in Chapter Six.

➜ Rita uses a tactic called a trailing stop to help minimize losses and capture gains on her individual stock investments.

➜ Rita risks only 1 percent on any single investment choice—this helps her endure losing streaks.

PERSONAL GAINS

— Toni —

Think Less, Decide Better!

Always bear in mind that your own resolution to succeed
is more important than any other one thing.

—ABRAHAM LINCOLN

Have you ever spent the morning accomplishing multiple small tasks, with the goal of preparing for a big, important project? Maybe you answer e-mails, pay bills, return phone calls, and even grab a sandwich for lunch. Once you clear your desk, though, and face the big project, your brain revolts. You can't focus, and your creativity has dried up. It's as though your brain is signaling to you, *I'm done for the day. I don't want to think anymore. I especially don't want to think any "big" thoughts.*

Guess what? Studies have shown that our mental energy is a limited resource. Simple decision making draws on our energy reserves, tires our minds, and reduces our mental resolve.

In the late 1990s, Roy Baumeister (a professor at Florida State University) and colleagues performed several experiments showing that certain types of conscious mental actions appeared to draw from the same "energy source"— gradually diminishing our ability to make smart decisions throughout the day.*

We now know that a tired brain makes us more likely to eat junk food, tell fibs, procrastinate, or otherwise exhibit poor self-management actions. Even making common, everyday choices—deciding what to wear, what to eat for breakfast, which freeway to take—takes a toll on our mental energy.

No wonder time specialists tell us to avoid opening our e-mails first thing in the morning when we arrive at work. After all, we must decide how to answer many of them and what to reply. Then we

---

* http://psycnet.apa.org/journals/psp/74/5/1252/.

choose which messages to delete, locate the folders to file the e-mails we keep, select which ones to share, and finally, decide which ones to print. All of these seemingly simple choices deplete our mental energy. Consequently, when we tackle top-priority tasks, we have already drained our energy and lost our mental edge.

The wiser choice would be to leave energy-depleting chores until later. I know CEOs of large corporations who—to protect their mental energy—rotate a selection of suits that they automatically wear with certain shirts and ties. This mechanical dressing cuts down on first-thing-in-the-morning decision making. Some have the same food for breakfast and have structured their morning routines so perfectly that decision making is not a factor. They guard their minds for the far more important decisions they will have to make later in the day.

To work and play (!) at your highest levels, decide which projects are important to you in the day ahead. Then target routine tasks and put them on autopilot. Strive to keep your mind serene and free of action item details until you encounter the priorities that count. That way, your mind will be clear and energetic, and you can complete your work—or enjoy your golf game—with ease and effectiveness.

CHAPTER ELEVEN

What's Your Style...
Growth or Value?

Toni

W E LIVE in a world of dichotomies... north and south, black and white, up and down, good and bad, yin and yang.

So it makes perfect sense that when we explore the world of equities, we find two traditional "styles" of investing: growth and value. Indeed, Wall Street tends to assign individual stocks to either one "team" or the other. Both growth stocks and value stocks bring benefits to investors, yet each style has its own characteristics.

Definition-wise, we find no hard and fast rules, although we do draw on certain criteria to describe each style. Basically, with growth stocks (think Google Inc. (GOOG) or Bidu Inc. (BIDU)), we may happily buy high and sell higher. With value stocks (like Walt Disney Co. (DIS) or AT&T Inc. (T)), we look for *value*, so we revert back to the old market adage, "buy low and sell high."

In raging bull markets, many investors turn to muscle-bound growth stocks to earn the biggest gains. In uncertain or even down markets, more sedate, dividend-paying value stocks can outperform. If you plan to include stocks in your portfolio, you will want to diversify by holding both styles. You can simplify your research by investing in high-quality equity exchange traded funds that target growth- or value-oriented companies. (I'll give you a list of these later in the chapter.) Value- or growth-focused mutual funds may also work for you.

Mainly, however, this chapter builds on the information Gordon shared with you, Rita, and Charlie, in Chapter Six, which relates to choosing stocks. Rita has a longer time horizon before retirement than Charlie does. She also has a larger risk tolerance. Rita can benefit from discovering more about growth and value stocks and learn the best methods to select those with the best capital gains appreciation potential.

Gordon's client Charlie may choose to avoid stocks altogether. With his relatively short time horizon before retirement, Charlie's portfolio holds only relatively non-volatile ETFs. Still, were Charlie to venture into equities, he would do best to choose from mild-mannered, dividend-paying, value-oriented issues.

This chapter is devoted to the growth and value equity styles... their advantages, their differences, and how to invest in them for the best possible gains. Enjoy!

Investing in Growth Stocks— Earnings, Earnings, Earnings

When you invest in growth stocks, you concentrate on companies that you believe will deliver the biggest bang for your investing buck in the form of rising stock price. You want to target a company developing innovative new products, market positioning, or plans for expanding overseas. If you recognize a budding new industry just

HOT TIP

Coined by famed Fidelity Magellan Fund manager Peter Lynch, in the financial context, a "ten bagger" refers to a financial investment that grows to ten times its original purchase price. The term is derived from baseball, where the number of "bags" or "bases" reached by a runner measures the success of a play.

dancing into the spotlight—currently cloud computing and social media come to mind—*and* pinpoint early on a leading issue blazing the trail, you may hit a "ten bagger."

We label stocks "growth" when they outperform the stock market. Growth stocks are the party animals. Also called "glamour stocks," during bull markets, they often bask in the media spotlight and commentators talk endlessly about their sales and earnings.

Of course, like most party animals, growth stocks can suffer hellish hangovers by falling quickly from their highs when a bull party is over and the revelers go home (market retracements or corrections). That's why, as a wise investor, you'll keep an eye on your growth stocks to manage risk.

Here are common traits of growth stocks:

- Growth companies typically do not pay dividends; rather, they choose to reinvest their profits back into the business.
- Growth stocks can flaunt higher P/E ratios than value stocks, and unless the ratio flies *too* high (say, over 50), no one minds.
- New growth stocks tend to shoot for price expansion in the near future (one to four years).
- With growth stocks, it's not where they've been that's important (price-wise), it's where they're going; thus, with this style, you can "buy high and sell higher" successfully.
- Many (but certainly not all) growth stocks reside in the technology sector.
- The NASDAQ stock market lists the great majority of growth stocks.

HOT TIP

If a company earns a profit, it can decide to pay that profit out to shareholders as a dividend, reinvest it back into the business for research and development and expansion, use it for debt reduction, or repurchase its own shares.

Meet the Masters of Growth Investing— Philip Fisher and William O'Neil

Let me introduce you to two masters of growth investing, Philip Fisher and William O'Neil. Each of these gentlemen, in his own way, developed highly successful methods of this style.

Philip Fisher. Philip Fisher was a true pioneer of growth investing. He began his career in finance in 1928, when he dropped out of Stanford Business School to work as a securities analyst with the Anglo-London Bank in San Francisco. In 1931, he started his own money-management business, Fisher & Co. He managed the company's affairs until he retired in 1999 at the age of 91. Fisher is known for making extraordinary gains for his clients. Indeed, Morningstar has called him "one of the great investors of all time" (http://news.morningstar.com/classroom2/course.asp?docId=145662&CN=COM&page=1).

Fisher began his career long before "tech" stocks from Silicon Valley took the market by storm. Fisher recognized early on the value of growth orientation and specialized in innovative companies driven by research and development. In his seventy-plus years of managing money, he insisted on investing only in well-managed, high-growth companies, which he held for the long term. Indeed, Mr. Fisher bought shares of Motorola stock in 1955—and didn't sell them until his death in 2004.

Fisher's investment classic, *Common Stocks and Uncommon Profit*, details his investment philosophies, which are still relevant today. As a matter of fact, it was the first book on investing to make the *New York Times* bestseller list.

In *Common Stocks*, Fisher's famous "Fifteen Points to Look for in a Common Stock" cover two overall categories: 1. management's qualities and 2. the characteristics of the business. When Fisher examined a company, he looked for management qualities such as integrity, conservative accounting, accessibility, good long-term outlook, openness to change, excellent financial controls, and sound personnel policies.

If management scored passing points on those requirements, Fisher then turned to the company's business qualifications. He looked for high profit margins, high return on capital, commitment to research and development, leading industry position, above-average sales organization, and proprietary products or services.

In *Common Stocks,* Fifteen Points, Fisher asks intriguing questions, such as, "Does the company have products or services with sufficient market potential to make possible a sizeable increase in sales for at least several years?" "What is the company doing to maintain or improve profit margins?" And "Does the company have outstanding labor and personnel relations?" Indeed, if you read *Common Stocks* and consider Fisher's Fifteen Points, you may agree with me that these points could well act as a short list of guidelines for any CEO who wants to run a prosperous and productive company.

In his regular column published in the March 11, 2004, edition of *Forbes* magazine, Fisher's son, Kenneth L. Fisher (currently a market professional in his own right), wrote a eulogy for his father, saying, "Among the pioneering, formative thinkers in the growth-stock school of investing, he may have been the last professional witnessing the 1929 crash to go on to become a big name. His career spanned seventy-four years, but was more diverse than growth stock picking. He did early venture capital and private equity, advised chief executives, wrote and taught. He had an impact. For decades, big names in investing claimed Dad as a mentor, role model, and inspiration."

William O'Neil. A later colleague of Fisher's, William O'Neil has dedicated his career to bringing computerized investing information to private and institutional investors. Also a growth investor, O'Neil started his career in 1958, becoming a stockbroker at Hayden, Stone & Company, and he developed an investment technique that used early computers. In 1960, O'Neil was accepted to Harvard Business School's first Program for Management Development. He went on to create his now-famous CAN SLIM investment strategy. At age thirty, he became the youngest member to buy a seat on the NYSE.

In 1972, O'Neil created *Daily Graphs*, a printed book of stock charts that was delivered weekly to subscribers. By 1998, O'Neil launched Daily Graphs Online, an online equity research tool. Those who were still drawing moving averages on their printed *Daily Graphs* turned to their computers and retired their pencils permanently.

Of course, most of us know William O'Neil best as the founder of his newspaper, *Investor's Business Daily*, which I mentioned as a top investing resource in Chapter Seven.

In his book *24 Essential Lessons for Investment Success* (New York: McGraw-Hill, 2000, p. 18), William O'Neil says, "From our study of the most successful stocks in the past, coupled with years of experience, we found that three out of four of the biggest winners were growth stocks, companies with annual earnings per share growth rates up an average of 30% or more—for each of the past three years—before they made their biggest price gains. Therefore, concentrate on stocks with annual earnings growth rates of 30% or more for the past three years. In my own stock selection, this is one of the most significant rules."

Mr. O'Neil goes on to say that companies that have gone public in the last eight or ten years may not exhibit three years of earnings growth. IPOs (initial public offerings) fall into the same category. In these situations, the famed growth investor continues, "I want to see earnings in each of the last six quarters up a material amount (50% or more) compared to the same quarter the year before."

Mr. O'Neil is not interested in promises that mediocre earnings will improve. He insists that the "vast majority" of his historical models had strong, accelerating earnings "*before* their huge price earnings increases began."

Takeaway Points from Philip Fisher and William O'Neil

Both Philip Fisher and William O'Neil identified criteria important to successful growth-oriented companies. ROE and earnings growth or earnings per share (EPS) represent two key metrics we can use from their criteria to spot high-potential growth stocks.

Return on Equity, also known as ROE. A strong ROE can give us clues as to how well a company's management runs the business. That was very important to Philip Fisher, and it should be important to us as investors. After all, we don't want to invest in a company that just makes ends meet. That's not good enough. In our growth stocks, we want a strong ROE, plus we want it to rise percentage-wise from year to year.

ROE is a simple metric. To simplify it more and to understand its importance, we can apply it to our own finances. When we calculate our own ROE, we quickly discover how proficient we are with our own money.

The ROE shows the amount of profit a company earns in comparison to the total amount of shareholder equity listed on the company's balance sheet. Here's the most basic formula:

Net Profit / Average Shareholder Equity for Period =
  Return on Equity

Let's take this example to home base. Imagine that this year, you earned $10,000 in "net profits" (the amount you earned in salary and other income, minus your expenses). Then, let's say your net worth (assets minus liabilities) comes in at $100,000. Here's the math: we

---

HOT TIP

An ROE of at least 10 percent shows that a company's business management is solid. Just so, you can use 10 percent as a good general measure of management effectiveness. While you're at it, you may want to calculate your personal ROE to assess your money management effectiveness on an annual basis, just as companies do. The exercise makes for an insightful reality check and can help you plan for future goals.

take your net profit of $10,000 and divide it by your net worth of $100,000. That equals a .1000 return on equity, or 10 percent ROE. *Very nice!*

Now, let's apply ROE to a company. We'll say that Shiny Semiconductors earned $1 million in net profits this year (sales minus expenses). Shiny's net worth (assets minus liabilities) is $5 million; this is also called "shareholder equity." We take Shiny's net profit of $1 million and divide it by its shareholder equity of $5 million, and *voila*! Shiny boasts an ROE of 20 percent... shiny in any industry!

If a company has a strong ROE, we can assume it can generate cash more easily than a company with a low ROE. Also, the higher a company's ROE compared to its competitors, the better it is for us, the investor. That makes sense. After all, if you and your neighbor Fred both earn the same paycheck each year and have the same expenses, and your ROE is 10 percent, but Fred's is 5 percent, the numbers indicate that you manage your money more effectively than Fred. And if Shiny's ROE is 20 percent and its competitor, Slinky Semis, shows an ROE of four percent, we can expect Shiny to grow faster than Slinky in the near future.

Where to find ROE. You can find a company's ROE by going to http://finance.yahoo.com, bringing up the stock's summary page, clicking on "Key Statistics," and then checking under "Management Effectiveness." You should also be able to find the ROE on your broker's website, following similar steps. *Investor's Business Daily* also lists the ROE of each company in its stock tables.

Earnings per share, or EPS. Earnings per share, or EPS, growth rates lay the basic foundation for William O'Neil's methodology. As you remember, we define "earnings per share" by dividing the amount of money earned that quarter by the number of shares outstanding (number of shares traded publicly). (If you want to review EPS more thoroughly, please turn back to Chapter Six.) As Gordon stated in Chapter Six, when you're reviewing a stock, you'll look for EPS that expands or gains value over time. Some companies, because of the nature of their businesses, may show heightened earnings in certain quarters of each year. For example, retailers generally show the fourth quarter of the year as the biggest earnings quarter. Just so, you are wise to compare the *EPS for the same quarter*, year over year (or yoy); naturally, you'll want those EPSs to show sequential growth, or at least a general trend to the upside.

Where to Find EPS. Again, you can find EPS graphs at http:// finance.yahoo.com, on each stock's summary page, or your stock's summary page on your broker's website.

Investor's Business Daily's stock tables also display EPS. You will find terrific proprietary rankings for each stock, including *IBD's* Composite Rating (ranks stocks on scale from zero to 100, with 100 representing the highest value) and the Earnings Per Share Growth Rating, which compares a stock's last two quarters, along with three years' profit growth, to all other stocks. I appreciate that IBD crunches the numbers for me, compares them to other companies, and then serves up the results. *Nifty.*

Where to Find High-Potential Growth Stocks

Investor's Business Daily features various indexes that list high-quality growth stocks. For example, the "IBD 50" is a computer-generated watch list of the market's leading growth stocks, along with their charts and thumbnail company information. I recommend those of you who want to investigate growth stocks to pick up a copy of *IBD* at your newsstand or subscribe to the print or electronic version (www.investors.com).

Here's another method to target high-possibility, good-growth contenders: check out the growth-focused exchange traded funds listed in Table 11.1. Funds one through eleven are iShares (iShares. com). Funds twelve, thirteen, and fourteen are SPDRs (SPDRS.com). As you can see by their names, some of the funds represent large-cap equity indexes (S&P 500 and Russell 1000); others represent mid-cap and small-cap issues.

You can use these ETFs for two purposes: 1. to go into their holdings and choose the top five, ten, or more equities to form a watch list or 2. to select one to three funds as tactical additions to your core portfolio.

Let's look at the first purpose. To create a growth-oriented watch list, let's say you went online to iShares.com and clicked on the holdings of the S&P 500 Growth Index Fund (IVW), a large-cap growth index ETF. Currently, Apple Inc. (AAPL), Exxon Mobil Corp. (XOM), International Business Machines (IBM), Google Inc. (GOOG), and Johnson & Johnson (JNJ) hold the top five slots.

Maybe you like Exxon Mobil, because it's one of the world's largest companies, and you think energy prices will soar in the near future as well as the coming years. You move to that stock's page on your broker's website, finance.yahoo.com, or a similar resource. A glance

Name	Symbol
1. Russell 3000 Growth Index Fund	IWW
2. S&P 500 Growth Index Fund	IVW
3. Russell 1000 Growth Index Fund	IWF
4. Morningstar Large Growth Index Fund	JKE
5. Russell Top 200 Growth Index Fund	IWY
6. S&P Mid-Cap 400 Growth Index Fund	IJK
7. Russell Midcap Growth Index Fund	IWP
8. Morningstar Mid-Growth Index Fund	JKH
9. Russell 2000 Growth Index Fund	IWO
10. S&P Small-Cap 600 Growth Index Fund	IJT
11. Morningstar Small Growth Index Fund	JKK
12. SPDR S&P 500 Growth ETF	SPYG
13. SPDR S&P 400 Mid-Cap Growth ETF	MDYG
14. S&P 600 Small-Cap Growth ETF	SLYG

TABLE 11.1 **Growth-focused equity ETFs**

at Exxon's earnings summary shows that for the past two and a half years, the huge integrated energy company has grown its EPS in most quarters. That's acceptable, considering that Europe is currently suffering from a recession. Now you click on Exxon's "Key Statistics" tab and check out the ROE, which is 28.33 percent. *That works.*

Next, you bring up a monthly chart of Exxon and see that it is uptrending nicely above its 12-month moving average at 92.68. When you look left on the chart, back to 2008, you see that the stock approached its all-time highs of about $96 several times in 2007 and 2008. You deduce that if it rises through those prior highs at $96, then it has "blue sky" above. "Blue sky" is market jargon for "brand new price territory." In this case, Exxon will explore blue skies over $96, so it has no old technical resistance above that price. When market conditions are favorable, that can result in nice moves for the stock.

Now, though, let's say that a glance at the S&P 500 tells you that the benchmark is also trading near all-time highs; it looks "toppy." Plus, you're smack-dab in the middle of earnings season, and a presidential election is less than a month away. That's a lot of uncertainty for the market to absorb.

You decide to wait until the election and earnings season come to a close before purchasing Exxon shares. You want to see which way the S&P 500 moves after those two events. You also want to wait until Exxon stock closes above $96, which will confirm willing new buyers (demand) above that price, to buy shares. What you don't want to do is buy Exxon (or any other stock), only to see its price tumble if the election and earning season pound the market south. Keeping "some powder dry" right now seems the wisest risk management. (Gordon and I will talk more about how to look at the economic and political climate in Chapter Thirteen.)

Of course, the situation above could be different. You could be looking at Exxon and other growth stocks in the midst of a bull market and no nearby election or earning season to consider. In that case, you'll decide if you want to purchase shares of Exxon for your portfolio and how much capital you want to commit.

Risk Management for Growth Stocks and ETFs—The Best Insurance for Your Profits

For the best results, you'll purchase shares of growth stocks during times when the S&P 500 displays a GainsMaster GO signal. The S&P should be uptrending nicely above the 12-month moving average, as should your stock candidate.

Since we're savvy investors, once we've purchased shares, we limit risk by placing stop-loss orders—be they static or trailing—with our brokers. Think of it this way: You wouldn't think of driving down the street without car insurance. Chances are you also pay for home insurance, health insurance, and maybe even life insurance. It makes perfect sense, then, that you would use stop-loss orders as a safety net, or insurance, for your stock and ETF positions.

> **HOT TIP**
>
> As a general rule, during market downturns, growth stocks sell off faster than their value counterparts. Many investors don't want to give up the dividends they receive from their value stocks.

In Chapter Ten, Gordon recommended to Rita that she establish a 25 percent (25 percent of a single share price) trailing stop on each of her equity positions. If you find that stop too loose (too far away from your purchase price), you can tighten (make smaller) that percentage. Ten or fifteen percent trailing stops also work well.

Also, as Gordon explained in Chapter Ten, keep in mind that an automatic trailing stop will follow your stock's price higher. Should that price make a U-turn and dive, your stop will turn into a market

> **HOT TIP**
>
> Remember to click on the "GTC" or "good-till-cancelled" option when placing your stop order; otherwise your order will remain good only for the day you place it. Also check with your broker. Some brokers keep a GTC order in place for sixty days only; then you have to reset it.

order when it touches the price that is 25 percent (or whatever percentage you designate) lower than the highest price recorded. For example, say you bought a stock at $40 per share and set a 25 percent trailing stop. The stock moved generally higher for several months, never falling 25 percent during any one pullback. When the stock reached $60 per share, the market turned south... and your stock followed. Your automatic stop-loss order was triggered when your stock's price reached $45, which is a 25 percent drop from $60. ($60 x .25=$15 and $60 - $15 = $45)

Alternatively, you can establish a stop order that you adjust yourself every week or two, at a price just below the 12-month moving average on a monthly chart (or below the 14-week moving average on a weekly chart), as your position's stop-loss point. Remember, the tighter (smaller percentage) the trailing stop, the shorter period of time you will potentially hold that position.

Investing in Value Stocks— Bargains and Dividends

If growth stocks are the powerhouses of style investing, then value stocks represent the "slow and steady Eddies." New investors, conservative investors, and retirees who want to own equities find value stocks to be their best bet. If Gordon's client Charlie decided to add stocks to his portfolio, he would choose value stocks for their slow approach to growing profits while paying regular dividend checks.

Your primary goal when investing in value stocks is to buy stocks whose shares appear to be underpriced (undervalued) when compared to fundamental values we'll discuss in the section that follows.

We *could* say hunting for the perfect value stock is like finding an unrecognized treasure at a garage sale. You arrive early in the morning and forage through the owner's cast-offs. And then you see it—a perfect figurine that *you* know is a fine antique and worth hundreds of dollars—yet the owner has stuck a $2 label on it. *Now, that's a value.*

Here are common traits of value stocks and characteristics you want to identify:

- Value investors look for companies with strong fundamentals.
- Sought-after value stocks typically exhibit low P/E ratios, under 15.
- Value investors also seek stocks with low price-to-book ratios (explained later).
- Value-oriented companies usually pay quarterly dividends to their shareholders.
- In market downturns, value stocks usually sell off more slowly than growth stocks (investors are reluctant to part with the dividends).
- Value stocks may take longer to rise in price, and most investors intend to hold them for the long term.
- Many value stocks reside on the Dow Jones Industrial Average and the New York Stock Exchange; the utilities sector also contains a large portion of value stocks.

Meet the Masters of Value Investing— Benjamin Graham, Warren Buffett, and Peter Lynch

Benjamin Graham. Benjamin Graham, known as "The Father of Value Investing," began teaching at Columbia Business School in 1928. Along with David Dodd (who also taught at Columbia), Graham wrote the "textbook" for value investing, *Security Analysis*, in 1934. In 1949, Graham penned the 1949 investing classic *The Intelligent Investor,* which remains the value classic until this day.

Graham's main focus and gift to investors was his *margin of safety* concept. Graham defines the margin of safety as the difference between a company's business valuation and its market valuation. (Business valuation = book value + earnings. Book value = the stock price divided by the value of a company's assets. The market value is, of course, the stock's current value per share.) While the exact valuation related to the margin of safety can be difficult to pinpoint, the bottom line for you, as a value investor, is to remember your goal: to buy a high-quality value stock at the best price possible.

Graham maintained that to be successful, you, as a smart investor, should pay a low price for a stock no matter how dazzling its future looks. That way, if the market slides south, you will have paid such a bargain price, the stock will remain a good value even if it trades at lower prices.

Warren Buffett. America's favorite mega-investor, Warren Buffett is one of Graham's biggest fans. As a student of Benjamin Graham's at Columbia University, Buffett read Graham's *The Intelligent Investor* and called it "the greatest book on investing ever written."

Buffett himself has been described as one of the ultimate value investors of all time. This early story shows how the "Oracle of Omaha" thinks: At only six years old, Buffett purchased a six-pack of Coca Cola from his grandfather's grocery store for 25 cents. Then he resold each of the bottles to his friends for five cents each, pocketing a five-cent profit. Now, there's a forward-thinking six-year-old!

When he turned eleven, Buffett purchased his first equities for his older sister Doris and himself, buying three shares of Cities Service Preferred at $38 per share. The stock soon fell to $27, frightening Buffett, but he gritted his teeth and held on. When the shares rebounded to $40, he sold them—a mistake he later regretted. Cities Service went on to rocket to $200 per share. That experience taught Buffett the "buy-and-hold patience" that he has used ever since.

As the Chairman of Berkshire Hathaway Inc. (BRK.A and BRK.B) for the past forty-eight years, Buffett told his shareholders in his 2011 letter to shareholders, "Over the last 47 years (that is, since present management took over), book value has grown from $19 to $99,860, a rate of 19.8% compounded annually."

Known for his affable yet straight-shooting personality, Buffett freely admits his mistakes in his letters to shareholders. In the 2011 letter just mentioned, Buffett writes, "Last year, I told you that 'a housing recovery will probably begin within a year or so.' I was dead wrong."

As he continues that subject's discussion (Berkshire Hathaway owns five housing-related companies), he reveals his sense of humor: "Every day we are creating more households than housing units. People may postpone hitching up during uncertain times, but eventually hormones take over. And while 'doubling-up' may be the initial reaction of some during a recession, living with in-laws can quickly lose its allure."

In 2012, Buffett's worth was listed at $46 billion, ranking him as one of the wealthiest men on earth. In 2012, *Time* magazine named Buffett one of the most influential people in the world. He is a notable philanthropist and has pledged to give away 99 percent of his fortune to philanthropic causes via the Gates Foundation (owned by Microsoft's Bill and Melinda Gates).

Unlike most investors, Buffett doesn't pay much attention to stock price. But we must realize, he doesn't buy shares of stock to participate in a company's growth. He buys the entire company!

In terms you and I can use, Buffett advises value investors to focus on finding outstanding companies at sensible prices (rather than generic companies trading at bargain prices). Indeed, we can use that guidance nicely when we approach *any* stock as an investment vehicle.

Peter Lynch. Although we will not refer to the legendary Peter Lynch as a strict value investor, he did take a fundamental and "bottoms up" approach to investing.

Lynch graduated from Boston College in 1965 with a degree in finance. He served two years in the military before attending and graduating from the Wharton School at the University of Pennsylvania with a Master of Business Administration in 1968.

Lynch joined Fidelity Investments as an investment analyst, eventually becoming the firm's director of research, a position he held from 1974 to 1977. In 1977, Fidelity named Lynch the manager of the little known Magellan Fund. At the time, the fund's assets totaled less than $20 million. When he retired from the fund in 1990, Magellan's assets totaled $14 billion, and it was the largest mutual fund in the world. More important, Lynch beat the S&P 500 Index in 11 of those 13 years, achieving an annual average return of 29 percent. If you had invested $10,000 with Magellan when Lynch took the helm, by the time he retired from the fund your investment would have grown to $190,000.

How did Lynch gain such profits? First, Lynch was often described as a "chameleon," because he used the investment style that worked at the time. As for his work ethic, Lynch routinely worked six to seven days a week. With two assistant researchers, he invested successfully in some 1,400 stocks at one time(!). Like Fisher, Lynch personally met with company management, investment managers, and analysts to gain firsthand information about companies and the stock market. As you see, his persistence and long hours paid off, with Magellan's gaining an annual return of 29.2 percent during the 13 years he served as its portfolio manager.

Lynch wrote three books, *One Up on Wall Street*, *Beating the Street*, and *Learn to Earn* (written for beginning investors, mainly teenagers). In all three of his texts, he insisted investors should "invest in what you know."

Now Peter Lynch devotes much of his time to philanthropy. The Lynch Foundation supports education, religious organizations, cultural and historical organizations, hospitals, and medical research.

Takeaway Points from Graham, Buffett, and Lynch

Invest in what you know. In picking stocks, both Warren Buffett and Peter Lynch focused on companies that produced products and services that they were familiar with or could easily understand.

Lynch declared "local knowledge" as the "Lynch" pin to successful investing. He insists that we can find great companies when we are on road trips or shopping at the mall. In so doing, we dig up possible investing targets one by one and become familiar with the companies' business. Next, he suggests, we conduct the fundamental analysis to verify growth potential and profit expectations.

My husband Mike took this advice to heart. A big fan of the "big box" store Costco (Costco Wholesale Corp. (COST)), Mike decided he wanted to investigate the company and possibly invest in its shares. His plan was to visit several of the Costco stores in our area and gather information about their business.

Now, Mike is an engaging guy and can start a conversation with anyone. He traveled to six or seven Costco stores within the space of a month. In each store (armed with a shopping cart full of paper towels and beer), he struck up a conversation with the manager and several employees. After each trip, he returned home with stories of the conversations... the employees genuinely liked working for Costco... many had worked there for years... the company treated them very well... the managers were excited about the new stores opening all over the country. Plus, Mike noted the aisles crammed with shoppers and full carts in every store.

At home, Mike watched a documentary on CNBC that showed how Costco chooses products. Another documentary showed the warehouse company—already known for its large selection of wine—developing its own brand of Kirkland fine wines that Costco is confident will compete with the best. Mike researched the company's business model and, as a businessman himself, recognized its potential for growth.

Finally, we checked out Costco's company fundamentals and chart. Currently, the specialty retailer pays a quarterly dividend of 28 cents. Its earnings have grown over the last three years. Since it's more of a growth stock than a value stock, I checked its ROE, which came in at 14.03 percent—very nice. When I brought up the chart, the S&P 500 issued a GO signal, and Costco was trending higher above its 12-month moving average.

You know the end of this story. Mike invested in Costco (COST) shares, and they have been very happy together ever since. Plus, we have enough paper towels in our attic to stretch around the world.

P/E Ratio. Value investors Benjamin Graham and Warren Buffett believed in purchasing outstanding companies for sensible prices. One way you can ensure the price is "sensible" is to look at a stock's price-to-earnings, or P/E, ratio.

As you remember from Chapter Four, the P/E ratio is calculated by dividing the stock's share price by the current quarter's earnings. (You don't have to do the math. P/E ratios are usually listed on a stock's summary page.) Investors use the P/E ratio to determine how "expensive" a stock is compared to the amount of money the company brings in. As a general rule, you'll look for value stocks with P/E ratios of 15 or less. You can consider them "cheap."

Which leads me to explain this: When you tune in to CNBC or another financial network or peruse the financial newspapers, you'll often hear an analyst refer to stocks they promote as "cheap." Please know, they are not talking about the stock's price. They are usually referring to the stock's P/E ratio.

For example, at present International Business Machines (IBM) is trading near its 2012 highs at $210 per share. I don't know about you... but to me, that's a hefty price to pay for a share of stock! It's a "high" price for IBM, too. As a matter of fact, "Big Blue" currently trades near its all-time high.

Talk to an analyst, though, and she will tell you it's still relatively "cheap," with a current P/E ratio of only 15.31. On the other hand, GE currently trades for about $23 per share. So far, its all-time high is 60.50, in August of 2000. So it's down 62 percent from those highs. Still, our analyst would tell us that

> **HOT TIP**
>
> Peter Lynch said, "In this business if you're good [choosing stocks], you're right six times out of ten. You're never going to be right nine times out of ten."

GE is more "expensive" than IBM, because GE's current P/E ratio is 18.63. If analysts' jargon confused you before (as it did me for a long time), now you know how to translate "cheap" and "expensive."

Price-to-Book (P/B) Ratio. Warren Buffett, especially, advises investors to seek companies with low price-to-book ratios. This straightforward ratio indicates whether or not a company's asset value is comparable to the market price of its stock. It acts as a helpful tool for locating value stocks, especially in the financial arena in banks, brokerages, and insurance companies.

Caveat: The PB ratio is not a good indicator for growth companies, especially those that spend a lot on research and development. Nor does it work well for companies that hold large properties or other fixed assets—those asset prices can spike or fall dramatically. Many technology companies show high PB ratios.

What you need to know: The price-to-book ratio = the value of a company's assets divided by the stock price. A P/B ratio of less than 1.0 suggests a stock is undervalued, while a ratio greater than 1.0 can indicate a stock is overvalued.

Where to find P/E and P/B ratios. Because these two ratios are referred to often by individual and institutional investors, you will find them prominently posted on your stock's summary page or under the tab "Key Statistics" on your broker's website or other financial websites.

Where to Find High-Potential Value Stocks

One easy way to locate value stocks is to zero in on the industrial icons in the Dow Jones Industrial Average. Personally, I like investing in Dow stocks. They are chosen with great care. Each represents a sector or industry group representing a part of the U.S. economy.

> **HOT TIP**
>
> Check out the health care, utilities, telecom, and defense and aerospace sectors for good value stocks.

Although the Dow represents only thirty stocks, as we mentioned in Chapter Three, it is the most watched economic benchmark in the world. And it trades in close lockstep to the S&P 500, although the S&P measure is about one tenth of the Dow value. When you look at the two on charts side by side, you see a very close similarity.

A glance at the Dow's components gives you a snapshot of the leaders in U.S. industry. I'll bet my duck slippers that you conduct business with—or purchase products or services from—several of these companies. Do you have a credit card or account with American Express Co. (AXP), Bank of America (BAC), or J.P. Morgan Chase & Co. (JPM)? Do you have insurance with the Travelers Companies, Inc. (TRV)? Ever fly on a Boeing Co. (BA) aircraft? Bought gasoline from The Chevron Corp. (CVX) or Exxon Mobil Corp. (XOM)? Used Johnson & Johnson (JNJ) shampoo or taken medications manufactured by Merck & Co. (MRK) or Pfizer Inc. (PFE)? When was the last time you enjoyed a Coke made by Coca Cola Co. (KO)? Took your kids to McDonald's (MCD)? Worked on Microsoft (MSFT) software? Or paid a phone bill from AT&T Inc. (T) or Verizon Communications (VZ)? And most all of us can say we have been touched by the "We bring good things to light" folks at the General Electric Co. (GE). I consider this conglomerate to be analogous to a diversified mutual fund. You can find GE in financials, aerospace and defense, energy infrastructure, mining, water processing, healthcare, transportation, and financial services. It's hard to find a place in industry where GE isn't!

The editors of the *Wall Street Journal* periodically weed out laggards and replace them with more timely U.S. market icons. For example, in June of 2009, Cisco and Travelers replaced two casualties of the 2008 bear market and recession (although their respective falls from grace were certainly *not* casual), Citigroup (C) and General Motors (GM). In September 2012, Kraft Foods (KFT) was replaced by health care giant United Health Group, Inc. (UNH). As you can see, the Dow stocks are multi-billion-dollar, multinational corporations and leaders in the global economy. While they can get creamed—we all remember with a wince GM's fall from October 2007 to December 2008, when the stock lost 91 percent of its value and the company was forced into bankruptcy. Financial giant AIG, tangled up in the housing bubble and subsequently delisted from the Dow in September 2008, lost 78 percent of its value in that month alone.

Dow stocks are not impervious to negative market shocks. Most of the time, though, their sheer size and financial strength contribute to their resiliency in market downturns.

Many Dow stocks meet the basic criteria of value stocks. They display P/E ratios at or below 15, acceptable P/B ratios, plus they pay dandy dividends. Even when their stocks reach high prices, historically, the Dow stocks can still be considered "cheap."

If you like the Dow for its value stocks, you can consider purchasing the SPDR Dow Jones Industrial Average ETF (DIA). You will receive the annual dividend yield in monthly installments. That's the easiest way to buy the all the Dow components and profit from them.

Another popular tactic entails investing in the "Dogs of the Dow." Back-testing of the Dogs of the Dow methodology shows that, especially during times of declining interest rates, this strategy can earn rates of return that exceed comparative returns of owning all thirty Dow stocks.

What you do: You create a portfolio of the ten stocks in the Dow that currently pay the highest dividends, dividing capital equally among them. Once a year, you spend an hour or less to rebalance the portfolio. You sell the stocks that have risen in price and thus pay a smaller yield by percentage. (You should see some nice capital gains with the positions you sell.) Then you replace your sells with Dow stocks that now pay the highest yields.

Want to limit your Dow doggies to five? That's works well, too. Choose the five lowest-priced stocks that show the ten highest yields in the Dow and then use the same yearly rebalancing process.

HOT TIP

Don't get caught in a "value trap." Just because a value stock shows low P/E and P/B ratios and perhaps even pays a dividend, it is not automatically a value winner. Continue your research by checking its earnings growth and price chart. "Cheap" is no guarantee of a good investing vehicle.

If you want to investigate these Dogs further—and even better, let someone else to do the price and dividend analysis for you—go to www.dogsofthedow.com and check out the reigning "dogs." You can learn all about the tactic, plus you can check out "Current Doggishness" and learn more about "Dog Steps." Sounds like fun to me!

Dow stocks are not the only value game in town. One way I target strong value candidates is to check out the ETFs designated as "value funds." You can simplify your research by simply purchasing shares of these funds or high-quality value-oriented mutual funds.

Alternatively, as we did with the growth ETFs earlier in this chapter, we can go online to the fund's holdings to see which stocks they've chosen as their top value candidates. Their selections may confirm value stocks you've had in mind.

Table 11.2 shows a list of value ETFs. You'll note large-cap, mid-cap, and small-cap value ETFs. Additional "style" ETFs reside in the fund universe; I pulled those shown in the table from iShares.com and SPDRS.com. For the first 11 funds on the list, go to iShares.com to check them out. For the final three funds starting with "SPDR," go to SPDRS.com.

Size Matters

When you look at Table 11.2, you'll see large-cap value stocks represented in the first four funds. Beneath those you will find mid-cap value funds and then small-cap value funds.

I could load you down with tables of data here, but instead I'll give you a valuable investing nugget in a nutshell: over time, mid-cap value stocks and small-cap value stocks tend to return more than large-cap stocks. Maybe it's because the smaller stocks have more room to grow. Maybe it's because the management of small and mid-cap companies can act faster and adapt to changing market environments more quickly. And of course, many of the giant behemoths that form the large-cap indexes were once small- or mid-caps, themselves and were real winners while they grew from outstanding small-cap companies to outstanding large-cap companies!

Name	Symbol
1. Russell 3000 Value Index Fund	IWZ
2. S&P 500 Value Index Fund	IVE
3. Russell 1000 Value Index Fund	IWD
4. Morningstar Large Value Index Fund	JKF
5. Russell Top 200 Value Index Fund	IWX
6. S&P Mid-Cap 400 Value Index Fund	IJJ
7. Russell Mid-Cap Value Index Fund	IWS
8. Morningstar Mid-Value Index Fund	JKI
9. Russell 2000 Value Index Fund	IWN
10. S&P Small-Cap 600 Value Index Fund	IJS
11. Morningstar Small-Value Index Fund	JKL
12. SPDR S&P Value ETF SPYV	SPYV
13. SPDR S&P 400 Mid-Cap Value ETF	MDYV
14. SPDR S&P Small-Cap Value ETF	SLYV

TABLE 11.2 **Value-focused equity ETFs.**

You can see proof of this point on your charts. Simply take the ETFs in Table 11.2, and evaluate each of them on a monthly chart. You will see how the small- and mid-cap value ETFs outperformed the large-caps over time.

If you'd rather check out individual mid-cap and small-cap stocks, one method is to go to the funds' websites (ishares.com or SPDR. com), bring up the ETF's page, and click on "Holdings." Here are the ETF's symbols from Table 11.2 to help streamline your process: IJJ, IWS, JKI, and IJS are iShares mid-cap value ETFs; the MDYV is the SPDR mid-cap ETF. IWX and IWN represent small-cap iShares ETFs; SLYV is the SPDR small-cap fund. Jot down the top five to twenty holdings in each fund to create a mid- and small-cap value stocks watch list.

HOT TIP

When you are evaluating a value stock that pays a dividend, remember to check out its earnings graphs. Good earnings = good dividends. A company that experiences deteriorating earnings may have to cut its dividend or stop paying it altogether.

Another valuable resource that you will want to consider is Value Line (www.valueline.com). An independent investment research and financial publishing firm based in New York, the company is best known for publishing *The Value Line Investment Survey* newsletter. The newsletter features Value Line's Ranking Systems for Timeliness, which ranks approximately 1,700 stocks relative to each other for price performance during the next six to twelve months. The newer Value Line Technical Ranking System predicts stock price movements over a three- to six-month time period. In both, stocks are ranked from 1 to 5, with 1 being the highest ranking. They also show a Safety ranking, using the same levels.

ValueLine.com displays both free and subscription content on their site. Currently, their website features a Value Line complimentary report, "Dow 30 Profile." The report shows the Dow 30 stocks, lengthy research and profile reports, along with the Timeliness and Safety Rank for each. Bottom line: if you want access to the legendary *Investment Survey* and its rankings, along with a host of valuable website content, you'll pony up the subscription amount and dive into the data to start learning.

What You Need to Know about Dividends

As you know, when a company pays a percentage of its quarterly profits to its investors, it is called a *dividend*. Early in the twentieth century, investors purchased stocks primarily for the dividends.

On a stock's summary page or in newspaper stock tables, you will see the stock's current price (on that day), plus the dividend yield and the quarterly or annual dividend. Please keep in mind, the stock price and yield posted are good for that day only. You know that stock prices change constantly throughout the trading day. That means the yield changes too. (The actual dividend amount changes quarterly or annually—more about that below.)

Yield = the percentage rate of return paid on a stock in the form of dividends

Dividend yield = dividend amount/stock price per share

Keep These Points in Mind about Dividend Yields

■ If you already own a dividend-paying stock, the yield you see listed for the stock in today's financial pages may not be the yield you currently receive. Say you bought shares of Dilly Drugstore four months ago at $30 per share. The annual dividend is $1 per share, so your dividend at that time = 3 percent. Now, though, Dilly sells for $40 per share. So the current yield quoted on your broker's site or financial pages is 2.5 percent. Don't panic. Your dividend did not get cut by a half percentage point, because you purchased your Dilly shares when the stock still traded at $30 per share. Investors purchasing Dilly's shares now, though, will receive a smaller percentage of yield, because the actual dividend amount ($1 per share annually, probably paid quarterly at $.25 per share) hasn't changed.

■ The previous point leads us to one of the main goals to strive for as value investors. You want to find high-quality value stocks trading at bargain prices. That way youreceive the highest dividends *and* the stock's price has room to grow. For you, this means optimum capital appreciation!

Dividend Dates You Need to Know

■ **Declaration Date:** Before a dividend is paid to stockholders, the company's Board of Directors must declare the payment. This is called the declaration date. On this date, the Board creates a liability on its books, because it owes that money to the stockholders. It also announces a date of record and payment date.

- **Date of Record:** The date of record is also known as the "ex-dividend" date. On this day the stockholders of record become entitled to the upcoming dividend payment. Those who buy shares of the stock after this date will not receive the dividend for the current quarter (most companies pay quarterly, although some pay annually). A stock will begin to trade ex-dividend about the fourth business day before the payment date. During this time, the stock's share price will reflect (have subtracted from) the dividend payment.

- **Payment Date:** On the payment date the dividend is awarded to company shareholders. If you receive a dividend payment, you will see it appear in your brokerage account.

Risk Management for Value Stocks

Gordon and I suggest you apply the same risk management and stop-loss strategies to your value stocks and ETFs that we discussed in this chapter for growth stocks and ETFs. While in the event of a market downturn value stocks may not tumble as fast as growth stocks, please know that if the downturn is severe enough, stocks of all stripes get thrown overboard. Our goal for you is that you participate in the market when it's giving out gains, and stand aside or become highly conservative when it starts taking those gains back. That is the best way to earn and keep profits in bull and bear markets!

The Best of Both Worlds

If you have been researching growth and value stocks, in some cases you've probably found the dichotomy to be unclear. You've probably seen stocks that have qualities of both sides ... maybe the stock pays a dividend like a value stock, yet it shows elevated P/E and P/B ratios and has earnings rising upwards of 25 percent annually. We can call these value-oriented growth stocks. There are lots of them out there

(think Apple Inc. (AAPL)), and the good ones present golden investing opportunities.

Although you may get an argument on Wall Street, growth
and value criteria do not have to be mutually exclusive. In fact, in
our opinion, your best bet (in GO-signal markets) is to find strong
growth stocks in promising industries. Then check their fundamentals, just as you would for a value stock, and of course evaluate their
price charts for strong uptrends.

You may remember the earlier section in this chapter that referred
to Peter Lynch. We said he was often described as a "chameleon,"
because he used the investment style that worked at the time. Lynch
is a great example of a value-oriented growth investor. Graham and
Buffett may have had different approaches, but they too applied the
concepts of value-oriented growth investing throughout their legendary careers.

Bottom line: If you apply each of the principles you've learned
in this chapter to each stock you evaluate, you should be able to
discover high-potential, value-oriented growth stocks that turn into
real winners!

Key Points to Remember

→ We label stocks "growth" when they outperform the stock market.
→ In raging bull markets, many investors turn to muscle-bound
growth stocks to earn the biggest gains.
→ When looking for growth stocks, target companies developing
innovative new products, market positioning, or plans for expanding overseas.
→ Most growth stocks do not pay dividends and show P/E ratios
above 15.
→ Many growth stocks reside in the technology sector.
→ Philip Fisher and William O'Neil are two well-known growth
investors.

➡ Solid return on equity (ROE) and rising earnings per share (EPS) are two metrics that can help us spot high-potential growth stocks.

➡ To create a growth-oriented equity watch list, find candidates in *Investor's Business Daily* and pull the top components from growth-focused ETFs.

➡ Value stocks represent the "slow and steady Eddies."

➡ New investors, conservative investors, and retirees who want to own equities find value stocks to be their best bet.

➡ Value investors look for companies with strong fundamentals, low price-to-book ratios, and low P/E ratios.

➡ Value-oriented companies usually pay quarterly dividends to their shareholders.

➡ Many value stocks reside on the Dow Jones Industrial Average and the New York Stock Exchange; the utilities sector also contains a large portion of value stocks.

➡ Benjamin Graham, Warren Buffett, and Peter Lynch were legendary value investors.

➡ Lynch maintains that we should invest in companies that produce products we understand and then conduct our analysis to verify growth potential and profit expectations.

➡ The Dow lists many fine value stocks; we can also check the components of value-focused ETFs to create a value-oriented equities watch list.

➡ Value companies that show good earnings typically issue quarterly dividends to their shareholders.

➡ We highly recommend buying both growth and value stocks in GO-signal markets only.

➡ We also recommend placing trailing stops on all equity positions.

➡ Are growth and value mutually exclusive? Maybe not. Value-oriented growth stocks can earn substantial profits.

PERSONAL GAINS

Toni

Overwhelmed? Delegate It!

*I am rather like a mosquito in a nudist camp; I know
what I want to do, but I don't know where to begin.*

—STEPHEN BAYNE, ANGLICAN BISHOP

You feel buried in work, overwhelmed, actually, and you see no way
to *ever* "get it all done." What's more, the stress of it all is getting
you down and wearing you out. How do you take a break from this
hamster wheel? Answer: delegate.

Oh, that. Your face falls. You know that delegating a task can save
you time. Plus, turning over jobs to others can help them develop
new skills. So . . . why the hesitation?

In his book *Getting Things Done: The Art of Stress-Free Productivity* (New York: Penguin Group, 2001, p. 131), author David Allen
offers a terrific rule to take care of an action item: do it, delegate it,
defer it, or drop it. From my experience and in discussing the topic
with others, the second choice is one of the most difficult actions to
take. From moms to corporate managers, most of us put shoulder to
the wheel and push on, unable or unwilling to hand over duties that
others could accomplish nicely.

If this describes you, let's reframe what delegation can accomplish: Delegation is a vital skill that leaders in all walks of life need to
cultivate in order to be effective. If you teach those around you how
to think when they approach a certain task and what questions to ask
if they need to, then you should be able to move on to projects with
bigger ROIs or even escape for a day or two without a problem.

If you're not sure that delegating is the right thing to do, observe
the people around you. Are you the only one in your family folding
clean clothes from the laundry basket at midnight? Is your assistant
at work leaving at 5 p.m. every day while you work into the wee
hours? Are people around you asking, "Can I help you with that?"

Finally, ask yourself, "Am I the best person to be doing this job?" Your answers to those questions may tell you that you're missing an opportunities to delegate.

Of course, card-carrying non-delegators have many reasons for not sharing tasks with others. Some are perfectionists who either believe they do things better than anyone else or that it's easier to do it themselves than take the time to teach someone else the ropes. Others think—perhaps subconsciously—that giving out work will diminish their own significance. Still others don't want to take the chance of being outdone by subordinates.

If you have trouble delegating even the simplest tasks, first accept the realization that you can't do everything yourself. Then seek out the proper people to help you. Target those who will benefit from the added skills associated with the task and who will take ownership of them. Again, help them understand critical thinking skills associated with the job. Then observe and support them without micromanaging or dictating their actions.

Once you learn to delegate, the payoff is immensely satisfying. Not only will you be able to dedicate more time to projects that bring in the biggest ROI, you will have shared your valuable skill sets with those around you, who will benefit from that knowledge. Best of all, you will have more time to spend with people you love, doing things you want to do, and for a little while escape the hamster wheel.

CHAPTER TWELVE

Anticipating Market Opportunities

How Investors Can Make Gains from Sector Rotation

— Gordon —

AN INDIVIDUAL investor can improve his returns year after year by knowing how to watch money move around in the investing world. Following the flow of investments from one sector of the economy to another isn't difficult, but it takes some understanding to see the movement clearly. This chapter will provide you with details and perspective to help you identify the ebb and flow of investment money. It will also show how you can integrate this knowledge into the Gains-Master approach to increase profits from your investment selection.

The world moves in cycles. The rhythms of the seasons, weather, astronomy, agriculture, human physiology, and even generational psychology have been documented in ways thought to be relevant to investing. Financial markets experience cyclical influences, and investors sense this, but few know how to follow the money around its circular path. Once you understand the key forces that drive investment market cycles, it isn't too difficult to anticipate the movements of investor money as it chases around the market.

Toni described in Chapter Two how investment money moves from one kind of business opportunity to another, based on the normal flow of a business cycle. In this chapter I will build on that theme and fill in a few key details that investors need to know when considering market movements. I want to introduce you to a concept called sector rotation. It isn't a new idea, but only in the past few years have individual investors been able to use it so effectively. It is a powerful concept that can transform the efforts of investors like Charlie and Rita into a highly successful and profitable investing.

If you understand how investment professionals create—sometimes unwittingly—the rotating cycles of movement in the markets, then you are better able to read them. I will share with you some investing insights I have gained about how this rotation occurs, and more important, how it can be easily spotted. By the end of this chapter I guarantee that you will see the market with a whole new perspective that will leave you better prepared to profit from the concept of sector rotation.

To help you see these cycles more clearly, I want to explain to you my perspective on how the investing world's three primary components interrelate. I think of these components as the parts of a larger mechanism—one that processes the money given to it by investors. I call these three components simply inputs, operating rules, and outputs. Let me explain to you how I think about each one of these components to show you what I consider to be some of the most valuable insights available to modern-day investors.

Where Does It Come From? Identifying the Inputs of the Investment Mechanism

In the late 1980s an important shift began to take place. Investment savings began to shift from the defined contribution plans to the 401(k)-style plans and individual retirement accounts that are much more common today. The result of this shift was a subtle change in the way investment money found its way into the stock market. This shift effectively increased the rate of input from individual investors into mutual funds from around 1988 to the year 2000. Eventually money allocated to mutual funds would become the largest single category of invested money in the markets.

During this period, technology advances in computing and software and ultimately the advent of a widely accessible Internet gave rise to rapid growth in jobs and hiring. In turn the higher-paying jobs provided by the technology industry also brought a greater level of disposable and investable income. A large number of Americans were able to find better paying jobs with better working conditions than they had ever experienced before.

During the 1990s the supply of good jobs grew faster than the supply of skilled workers. This created competition for good talent among technology companies. Employers in these industries had a great deal of incentive to attract capable workers with a package of attractive benefits. After a while these benefits became expensive to maintain. Employers quickly found a creative alternative that allowed them to pay money to employees that they could save on taxes. They came up with the matching donation to a retirement fund.

This practice of matching a percentage of the employee's contribution to a savings account gave incentive for employees to save more. It was a good idea, but it also had an important consequence. It dramatically increased the input to the U.S. stock market. When employers began to match a percentage of the savings employees put away, the practice unwittingly pushed more money into the markets. That happened because these accounts grew incrementally when both employee and employer dollars were automatically added with each paycheck.

These retirement savings accounts had a variety of options for the employees to allocate their money to different types of investments. The investment choices were usually a collection of carefully selected mutual funds. The selections most often included several stock market funds, an occasional bond fund, and a money market fund. Though most employees did not fully understand how these funds worked, they did comprehend the salient facts of where the money went—even if only in a vague way. They knew the money was going to the stock market.

What most investors did not realize at the time was just how much impact this shift had on the stock market in general. Every month, as new paychecks put new dollars into savings, and subsequently into the mutual funds that employees chose, fund managers were swamped with new money that they had to put to work. This constant input of money into the markets drove stock prices higher for over a decade.

Naturally, under such conditions investors sought opportunity wherever it could be found. The markets were in a prolonged state of GO-sign conditions. During these times professional money managers' primary struggle was simply finding enough quality places to put the money that came under their management. The stock prices of many companies began to reach levels considered much too high when compared with the standards most professional investors used.

Even so, the experience and training these investment managers possessed did not stop these professionals from continuing to buy comparatively high-priced stocks. In overly simple terms, they had to buy them. They had no other choice. The rules by which these managers operate required that they keep buying those stocks even if their own standards of valuation told them that doing so was a bad idea.

What Is It Doing Here? Recognizing the Operating Rules of Institutional Investors

Professional managers of mutual funds are commonly referred to as institutional investors. Institutional investors also include those who manage pension funds and other kinds of money collections. All institutional investors have three major influences on their decisions: (1) the need to invest according to the identity and objectives of their fund, (2) the attempt to outperform a benchmark index the fund is compared with, and (3) the goal of minimizing the impact of taxes on the performance of the fund.

Investing According to Fund Objectives—Staying Invested and Being Clever about It. Institutional investors manage funds that are identified by their stated objectives. These objectives may be specific to a particular level of performance, but most often the objective is connected to a particular class of investing asset. Mutual funds often identify themselves by a combination of the kinds of returns they seek and the kinds of investing assets they use to accomplish these returns. The fund may specify whether it seeks growth, income, or both. The fund may also designate that it will pursue its returns within the scope of large-, medium-, or small-sized companies or by investing in a certain class of bonds. Often a fund will specify that it is a "blend" of one or more characteristics.

The key point here is that an investing fund must stick with its stated objectives. A fund that calls itself a "Total Return Income" fund communicates that the fund manager will be investing in an array of various bonds. Its fund manager, by law, cannot go investing its money into the coolest new small-cap stock, no matter how certain the fund manager may feel about that stock's potential. The fund manager has to invest in a way that is consistent with the stated objectives of the fund.

That single fact has a major influence on a mutual-fund manager's choices—especially when you consider that cash is merely another investing choice. What it means is that even if a fund manager somehow *knew* that the market was about to start a profoundly downward trend, he or she could not simply sell all the stocks and just hold on to cash while waiting for the market to rebound. It might seem like a good idea to have all available investing money out of stocks when the market is going down, but it is not considered legal or ethical for the fund manager to do that.

This point frustrates investors in rising markets and infuriates them in falling markets. Investors imagine that the ultimate objective ought to be to make more money for investors no matter what the market does. They may wonder why fund managers don't operate according to *that* objective. The answer is that the law prohibits them from operating that way.

After the stock market crashed from 1929 to 1932, legislators made efforts to put protections in place for the individual investors. The mutual-fund industry was heavily regulated, beginning in 1934. Those laws strongly influence how mutual funds operate today. Many of those regulations come down to keeping the mutual fund from investing irresponsibly. To protect investors from rogue fund managers, the laws designate that a fund must stick with its own stated objectives.

If the fund states that its objectives include investing in stocks, then that's what it must do. Most fund managers therefore do not attempt to maximize returns by trying to anticipate market downturns and moving to cash when things look bad. According to the laws put in place in the 1930s, making that kind of decision would mean that the fund manager misrepresented the fund and did not follow its stated objectives.

Ironically this kind of rule means that a fund must remain invested even if it means standing by while those same stocks plummet lower. In the aftermath of a downward-trending market, this behavior looks terrible to an investor. When markets experience prolonged periods of poor performance, investors pull their money out of mutual funds—as they have done in recent years.

If you think about it, you realize that institutional investors have to have a way to find good returns in a down market. They cannot move all of the fund's money out of stocks and into plain old cash. Instead they move the money into what they perceive to be safer stocks—stocks that have lower volatility than the market. This may not guarantee that the fund will grow in value, but there is a good

HOT TIP

Bad Markets Attract Money into Boring Stocks. Institutional investors have a dual mandate: don't leave investors' money in cash, and beat the benchmark. Taken together these mandates imply that when the market begins a downward-trending move, institutional investors need to find stocks that won't go down as far. While this certainly includes utility companies, it also might include stocks of large companies in well-established businesses. Companies like General Electric (GE), Microsoft (MSFT), Disney (DIS), and Wal-mart Stores (WMT). These stocks don't move fast, and they also pay a dividend.

chance this tactic will help keep the fund from losing as much as it might otherwise. The result that occurs when many fund managers employ this tactic is that money moves towards stocks with low volatility—the boring stocks.

Outperforming a Benchmark—Chasing Opportunity around the Sectors. Mutual-fund managers, individually, are rewarded based on whether they can help the fund have better investing returns than a benchmark standard. That standard is often, though not always, the S&P 500. Rather than focus on growing five, ten, or fifteen percent every year, the institutional investors concentrate on merely outperforming their relevant benchmarks.

For example, suppose that the S&P 500 increased by just two percent in one year. If the mutual fund increases by three percent in that same year, the mutual fund manager may be rewarded with bonus pay. The bonus is the manager's incentive to help the fund perform better than the benchmark—in this example the S&P 500.

This incentive is no small matter. The manager's bonus can amount to millions of dollars. It doesn't take much imagination to recognize that when this is their incentive, the manager will focus more on beating the benchmark than on attaining a specific percentage of growth each year.

Fund managers will often attempt to outperform their benchmark by identifying which stocks within their benchmark are likely to perform exceptionally well over time. To accomplish this task, they pay close attention to the business cycle—the progression of economic development that Toni made reference to in Chapter Two. Rather than try to make a lucky guess by investing in a single stock, fund managers analyze which sector of the economy is likely to benefit from the natural turn of the business cycle. If they can discern that business conditions favor one sector over another, they may choose to spread their money across several similar stocks in that sector.

The business cycle moves through three general phases that accompany a GO-sign, upward-trending market and three general phases that accompany a STOP-sign, downward-trending market. You can think of the phases as simply the early, middle, and late parts of each market as depicted in Figure 12.1.

Institutional investors know that each part of the business cycle creates conditions in which certain of the stock-market sectors are likely to show better profits than the rest. Armed with that knowledge, they try to invest more heavily in companies that provide the most needed goods and services associated with the current part of the business cycle.

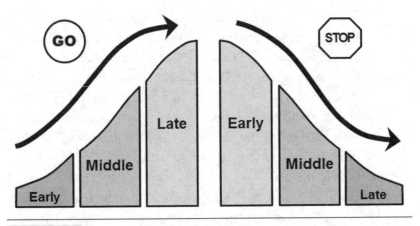

FIGURE 12.1 GO and STOP markets often show three phases, each with an emphasis on different market sectors.

As an individual investor, you can attempt to anticipate the movement of investment money from one sector to another. To do so, you must understand the characteristics of each of the three parts in GO-sign and STOP-sign markets. If you think about these movements as if they were happening to a small business, it makes them a little easier to comprehend and remember.

Early GO: Imagine a small business getting started on its way to success. The owners have a great idea for marketing, making, and delivering products, and the business has already gotten a lot of interest from potential customers. The owners are worried that the company may not be able to make enough of its product to fill customer demand. What does the company need? It needs to borrow some money, but it also needs to be efficient—especially at first. So the business seeks three things: a small amount of raw materials, some computer systems to help them extend their work, and a loan to pay for what they purchase.

Now consider what just happened to that small business. It went to the financial and technology sector for help. In the first part of the business cycle, as businesses begin to grow, these are the sectors that do well. That's what happens when stocks first start to rise after having been down for a bit: institutional investors often select financial and technology companies for investment.

Middle GO: Imagine further that the small business begins to grow as overwhelming customer demand drives them to increase production and ship more products. The company grows rapidly and in turn buys more raw materials. They may also buy some heavy machinery to increase production by orders of magnitude and ship out more products to many more customers, perhaps thousands of them. It's not hard to see the effects on the economy if you multiply this circumstance by a large number of businesses.

The middle part of the GO-sign market sees an increase of demand for basic raw materials, an increase in demand for industrial equipment, and an increase in transportation activity. This part of the GO-sign market also sees a continuation of the demand for financial and technology services. Institutional investors target these industries when they perceive that they are in the middle part of a GO-sign market.

Late GO: Imagine that the small business isn't as small as it once was—it is now in its heyday. It has been shipping products and using raw materials at a previously unimaginable rate. And something expected happens. Prices go up. The cost of shipping and the cost of raw materials increase. The company wasn't expecting costs to rise, but they notice that the prices of oil and gasoline have risen dramatically and assume that this is the primary cause. They adjust to these circumstances by cutting back on some expenses and trying to streamline their operations. The company focuses its spending on strategic initiatives designed to increase profit margins.

During this part of the GO-sign market energy costs commonly increase to some degree. This happens as a natural effect of consumer demand and companies of all sizes striving to meet that demand. The more success these companies have, the more that success drives a demand for fuel to run machines and transport finished goods. Producers increase demand for fuel and drive up energy prices of all kinds. This in turn leads them to be choosy about what they purchase. Fund managers know that under these circumstances, the energy sector and the consumer discretionary sector are likely places to look for growth and opportunity.

Early STOP: Our growing company has, in a very short time, come a long way from the small business days. It has grown into a far-flung enterprise. The company faces a new mix of challenges. Energy costs remain high, but competition from other companies has cropped up. The company adopts complex business processes to ensure product quality, but these processes have come at a high cost and have cut into the company's earnings. Salaries and benefits to employees have risen rapidly over the years and are also crowding the profit margins. Though the company appears to still be earning money, it seems to struggle with maintaining growth prospects. Rumors begin to spread about possible layoffs in less essential functions.

During this period, fund managers recognize that growth is hard to find. Though they are content to hold on to their energy costs, they begin looking among stocks in the utility sector, which seem to be doing well amidst higher energy costs. They also consider the consumer staples sector and the health-care sector for opportunity. This is mostly the boring stuff that doesn't move with as much volatility as the rest of the market and will also pay a dividend, although within the health-care sector some pharmaceutical companies can still offer growth prospects. Pharmaceutical companies are known for sporadic growth spurts; however, when corporations look to lower expenses by providing efficient health-care benefits to employees, the pharmaceutical companies are the innovators to whom everyone turns.

Middle STOP: The once small company is now having big problems. Demand for product has dropped amidst weak economic conditions, and sales have fallen off. A new marketing campaign was attempted, but it failed to produce significant improvement. Revenues are unable to outpace expenses. Product development contracts, and the company retrenches around its most profitable offerings. Despite all their best efforts, they are losing money. Layoffs occur, and the severance pay gets smaller with each round. If new employees are hired, it is on a temporary basis. Rumors circulate that the company may merge with or be bought out by a competitor.

Fund managers recognize that in times of crisis, the main goal is to not lose as much as the market. When the market is down, say 25 percent or more, a fund manager may still get paid a good bonus if his fund is only down 20 percent. Therefore, investing in safety stocks is a primary strategy. During this period, temporary workforce companies may begin to show a mild uptrend. Utility and consumer staples companies may begin to trend downward but will not fall as far as the rest of the market. The bond market improves during this time. Some activity in the financial sector may begin to occur as a result of merger and acquisition activity.

Late STOP: Our hypothetical company has been humbled from its heyday and has sought to restructure some of its financing so that it can keep the talented employees it needs to survive and rebuild. It has begun to look at relocating operation centers to locations that require less expense. It has retooled its product line and developed new offerings that seem to have traction but will require new technology and training to produce.

Fund managers know that during these times they must be patient and wait for signs of opportunity. They cannot put all of their money in cash, but they can put a greater percentage of it into cash now than at other times. They hold money back from investing to wait for the best opportunities. During this period, education companies may show signs of growth, as well as some kinds of real-estate companies. Financial activity begins to pick up as new loans occur and more are planned to take advantage of lower interest rates.

This final phase of the business cycle returns to an earlier state of the markets where companies are poised for growth as they more effectively produce goods and services that consumers want. Astute fund managers recognize the characteristics of this cycle and attempt to invest accordingly so that they can outperform their benchmarks.

Along the way, however, there is an important dynamic that shapes the operating activity of fund managers and helps explain the timing with which institutional investors transition from one phase of the market cycle into another. That dynamic is the strategies institutional investors employ to reduce the impact of taxes on their returns.

HOT TIP

Compare ten ETFs to see the sector rotation. To recognize the movement of investment money from one sector to another, you will need to compare the performance of the various sectors. This is surprisingly easy to do if you can create a comparison chart of eleven ticker symbols: XLB (for basic materials), XLE (for Energy), XLF (for Financials), XLI (for Industrials), XLK (for technology), XLP (for Consumer Staples), XLU (for Utilities), XLV (for Healthcare), XLY (for Consumer Discretionary, IYT (for Transportation), and IYR (for Real Estate). Place all eleven of these in a comparison chart and view them on a six-month time frame. The top performers will tell you what part of the business cycle the market is in right now.

Minimizing the Impact of Taxes—The Timing for When Investors Rotate to the Next Sector. The third major influence on institutional investor decisions is a prevalent but rarely considered principle that shapes how the stock market moves. That principle is tax avoidance. I'm not talking about illegal tax evasion; I'm talking about investing in a way that the government encourages through its tax policy.

The U.S. government's tax policy specifies that profits made from the sale of stock held longer than one year are subject to the long-term capital gains tax rate rather than the ordinary rate of income tax. For most people and corporations, the long-term capital gains tax rate is lower than the ordinary income rate—often by half. Investors have significant incentive to avoid these higher taxes, and all they have to do is hold on to their stock for at least one year.

Most institutional investors adopt that tactic as part of the investing rules. Unless they absolutely, positively, unavoidably, undeniably MUST sell the stock sooner, they will not sell that stock in any less than 366 calendar days later than the time they bought the stock. The cost of selling earlier is just too high.

Once you understand that tax avoidance is a prevalent tactic in the markets, it is no stretch of the imagination to expect that you might see evidence of its effects; after all, the majority of money in the stock market is managed by institutional investors. In fact, if you look closely at the S&P 500 index chart going back to 1995, you can see evidence of this tactic in use. See for yourself in Figure 12.2.

HOT TIP

Watch out for selling activity as measured every fifty-six weeks (13 months) from the start of a GO-sign market. When institutional investors take profits, they buy and sell a much larger number of shares than a single individual investor would. This actually makes prices in the stock market move lower for about four to eight weeks at a time.

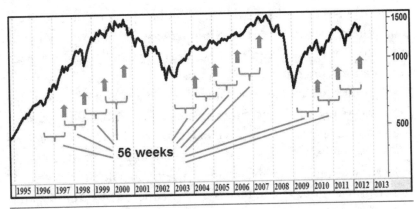

FIGURE 12.2   **Various degrees of selling occur at 56-week intervals in a GO-sign market.**

A quick glance at this chart shows you where the price drops to some degree after every fifty-six-week period in a bullish market. Here, I am measuring based on a fifty-six-week length. I add in the extra four weeks to take into account the necessary time for institutional investors to close out old positions, research and select new ones, and implement new trades. I believe that each of these intervals through the bullish markets marks a period where institutional investors make a concerted effort to take profits from those trades that show profit and then move money into new sectors, based on the progression through the business cycle.

Where Is It Going? Identifying Opportunities by Seeing the Outputs of Investor Decisions

If you understand what I have explained in this chapter so far, then you now have a significant advantage in the market. Individual investors equipped with the knowledge of the inputs and operating rules of institutional investors can anticipate the output of their decisions. As an individual investor you can nimbly anticipate both when and where a market move may occur and be prepared to profit from it.

If you can look back in recent history and see when the market made its most significant low price in the past year, then you can count fifty-six weeks forward in time and be prepared to anticipate some selling activity. Once the selling activity is complete (it will usually take about four to eight weeks), then you can look for evidence of a rotation from one sector to another.

Finding such evidence will allow you to research the most significantly rising sector and either invest in that sector's ETF or select individual stocks within that sector. If you track the progression of sectors through a GO-sign market, you may also be able to recognize what sectors you can use to anticipate where you will find opportunities. This technique would fit as a nice enhancement within Charlie or Rita's strategies.

Charlie would have a good idea which ETFs to anticipate as potential investments by following the sector progression. Rita would be able to use that same information to identify individual stocks within those sectors that might be poised to go higher. Both of them would also know when to be patient and wait for the next significant upward move in a GO-sign market.

To anticipate market moves in your own trading strategy, you must keep an eye on the expected progression of investment money through a GO-sign market and track it based on 56-week increments. Table 12.1 will help you do that.

	Phase	Sectors to Watch for Growth
GO	Early	Financial, Technology
	Middle	Technology, Basic materials, Transportation, Industrials
	Late	Energy, Consumer discretionary, Healthcare
STOP	Early	Healthcare, Staples, Utilities
	Middle	Utilities, Bonds
	Late	Bonds, Real estate, Financial

TABLE 12.1 Investors move through a progression of sectors as the business cycle progresses.

HOT TIP

The 2010 Flash Crash occurred fifty-seven weeks from the previous market bottom. On May 6, 2010, the Dow Jones Industrial Index fell nearly 1000 points in a single day, only to dramatically rise right back up within a matter of minutes. Many have speculated about what caused this event and have even suggested that the event represents a tremendous weakness in the way the modern market works. Many want to blame high-frequency trading computers that handle orders in an automated way. Others point to a large order made early on that day that may have created panic on the trading floors. However, the explanation for the events of that day may be much simpler, and far less sinister, than so many have made it out to be. When you consider that the swift and steep STOP-sign market of 2008 ended on March 9, 2009, then an interesting fact emerges. If we assume that the rapid downward movement of the markets in 2009 represents everyone's investing clock, then that day in the market marks the beginning of the new 56-week window count. The first week at which a significant number of institutional investors were likely to be able to take profits began on April 27, 2010; that day marks 56 weeks from March 9, 2009. Now not all institutional investors bought and sold at the same time; however, by the first week into the selling period, it is possible that so many institutional investors had collectively decided to take profits that the market simply began a selling spree with a highly dramatic effect. That the market rose back upward dramatically is evidence that the selling was not the result of bad news or panic but merely an opportunity to take profits at a lower tax rate—as well as to prepare to move from one sector to another. From this point of view, the flash crash may have occurred simply because of an unusually well-synchronized moment of tax-avoidance behaviors and sector rotation by institutional investors.

Key Points to Remember

→ The majority of the money in the market is managed by institutional investors who manage money on behalf of a mutual fund, pension fund, or other collection of money.

→ Money often enters the market as an input from retirement savings. The more money in, the greater likelihood that market prices will go up.

→ Institutional investors' operating rules require them to invest according to the stated objectives of their funds.

→ Funds must keep money invested in order to follow the fund objectives.

→ Fund managers establish a benchmark to determine the value of their performance and receive a significant bonus for beating their benchmark.

→ A common tactic for beating a benchmark includes moving money to the strongest components within the benchmark index.

→ A commonly used tax-avoidance tactic among fund managers includes holding on to a stock for more than 366 days.

→ Tax-avoidance tactics often mark the shift from one sector to another during GO-sign markets.

→ Individual investors can be alert to periods when the market may drop in price by counting fifty-six-week intervals during a GO-sign market.

→ Individual investors can watch for the output of institutional investor decisions by anticipating the shift from one sector to another after a 56-week interval.

047

PERSONAL GAINS

Toni

Make Your Circle Bigger

Unless you try to do something beyond what you have already mastered, you will never grow.

—RALPH WALDO EMERSON

I first heard the title of this Personal Gains at church one morning, about ten years ago. Our minister, Reverend David, used it as the title of his sermon. "Make your circle bigger, make your circle *bigger*," he said, pacing back and forth in front of the podium, gesturing in expansive circles with his arms. "You each have a circle of knowledge and familiarity that you live within. That is your circle of comfort. When was the last time you stepped out of that circle and learned something new or experienced something new?"

I pondered his words. Indeed, I had a comfortable life, great family, wonderful friends, and I was secure in every way. In other words, I pondered, staring at the church program I held in my lap, I lived in a cushy *rut*.

"If you're not making your circle bigger, you are not growing," David continued. "Think of each area of your life, your family relationships, your career, your social life, your mental, physical, and spiritual health. You need to *plan how you can grow* and *how you will proceed to grow* in all of these areas."

Hmm. I bit my lip. I looked around and noticed my fellow parishioners shift in their seats. For most of us, change is uncomfortable. Taken far enough, it can be downright scary.

As if he read our minds, the good reverend called out, "It's *good* to go beyond your comfort zone. When you are expanding your consciousness and experience a totally new situation that you've created, you may be scared. Really scared. *Good!* If you're uncomfortable, it means you are growing, learning, and becoming a better, more competent person. People who don't grow are never scared and so never experience new worlds outside their own circles that could provide them with great joy, prosperity, and happiness."

David's words that day truly inspired me. I decided to take on his ministerial "dare." I walked out of church that day with a new mantra, indeed a new mandate. *I would make my circle bigger.*

And I did. I looked for new skills to acquire, new places to visit, new people to know. At times, I have taken on new "circle stretchers" that scared my socks off (public speaking was one of them). But I've stayed the course. And the rewards have been tremendous.

Will you take my "make your circle bigger" challenge? Perhaps you start small by reading a book on a subject outside of your knowledge base. Then maybe you take a class you've always wanted to sign up for, join a new hobby club or special interest group, volunteer at a hospital or charity organization. Maybe you take a trip to a foreign country and take a crash course in their language before you go. Perhaps you learn how to scuba dive or snow ski or join a health club (and go!).

Please know that we humans are created to expand and grow and achieve good things in each area of our lives. It's an inherent part of our being.

And so I promise you this... if you experience fresh worlds outside of your own circle and continue to keep making your circle bigger, the new people, places, and things you encounter will provide you with great joy, prosperity, and happiness.

CHAPTER THIRTEEN

Invest with a Winning Mindset

Toni and Gordon

Toni

Congratulations! We're nearing the end of our journey. We've traveled a long way together, and Gordon and I trust you've enjoyed the trip.

Now let's turn our discussion to macro issues and most important—how we approach them with our hearts as well as our heads.

I am a realistic person. I am fully aware that many of you believe that your emotions haven't anything to do with your investing choices. While you may agree that short-term traders who immerse themselves in the minute-to-minute gyrations of the market ricochet between pain and pleasure, those of you who check in with your portfolios occasionally may declare that when it comes to your investing choices, your emotions hold no sway.

I respectfully—and cheerfully!—disagree with that notion. We're talking about *your money*, for gosh sakes! All of us feel strongly about our money. If we don't have enough money, we worry how we will get more of it. If we have excess money, we worry about how we can keep it. Just so, most of the emotions we feel around our money involve hope and fear.

We invest with the happy expectations that our investments will increase in value over time and we will ultimately profit. That's the "hope" part. On the flip side, until our global leaders solve issues like war and world hunger—and until we see them smiling, singing, and holding hands around the campfire—I suspect economic monsters will continue to lurk in the shadows. These "monsters" can cause worry and fear to creep into our imaginations.

Gordon

It is clear to me that investors are worried, Toni. They are worried not only about what could happen in the near future, but they are also worried that the stock market may not provide the long-term returns that it has at certain times in the past. I often have people ask me about what the future could bring. And many times they ask about hyperinflation—the idea that the value of our money could rapidly decline while prices shoot upward until everything is unaffordable. What investors often overlook is that their "worry mindset" inflicts more influence on their investing returns than the actual influence of inflation.

Worry is a powerful motivator, partly because people assume their worries are natural and logical responses to observable facts. But by holding themselves in that state of worry, investors close themselves off to the opportunities that might occur around them.

Some make a case for why hyperinflation is inevitable. On the other hand, I see equally plausible arguments for why it will *not* occur in our lifetimes. Who is right? To this question I say, "It doesn't matter. Either path represents opportunity, if only you are prepared to see it."

The definition of inflation is simply that the purchasing power of a currency declines. That means it takes more dollars to buy the same stuff. It is useful to focus on that definition, because it is easy to think of a dollar as a constant—as if it had a fixed amount of value. It doesn't. The value of the U.S. dollar shifts, like the value of a stock. If you adopt this view, then you can look at its changing value as opportunity. If the value of the dollar declines (if we have rapid inflation), then the things you buy with dollars go up in price—things like oil and gold.

As an investor, your opportunity is simply to look for what is going up when the dollar is going down. That's what the GO-sign and STOP-sign ETF lists are all about. You couldn't put together such a list five years ago, but in today's market you can. You simply look down those lists, and you will find what is going up.

When you think about investing with this mindset, you are focused on finding the opportunity rather than hiding from what you fear. One of those responses can make you money, but the other one cannot.

No matter what happens in the future, the winning investors will assume there is opportunity to be found and go looking for it. That attitude will allow them to release their worries and to profit in bull and bear markets.

Toni

When I talk to investors, Gordon, another worry I encounter is the concern over policies emanating from Washington D.C.. After all, politics highly influences the economic environment. And the economic environment dictates the direction of our portfolios.

Here's the political policies' domino effect: politics creates policy, which influences the economy, which has an impact on a certain sector or industry group, which affects companies within that group, which helps or hinders the price of the companies' stocks, which sways your portfolio's bottom line.

Government directives result in laws, regulations, taxes, price controls, and capital controls that sometimes deal "belly punches" to an industry and thus the companies that compose it. Currently, for example, one of our federal agencies has the coal industry in its sights and has burdened this energy-producing industry with new regulations. In fact, you may have seen the headlines that read, "War on Coal." Result? We can attribute a portion of the current decline in the price of coal stocks to these policies. In another example, cash-strapped Europe has scaled back what once were generous subsidies to solar power firms. In turn, many European solar stock prices have shrunk.

While you need not worry about politics, as a wise investor, you will keep an eye on the policies coming out of Washington and determine the potential impact they could have on your investments. We advise you to pick up a copy of (or go online to read) the *Wall Street Journal, Barron's,* or other major financial newspaper bi-monthly and at least check out the headlines. That way you will see if policies dictated from Washington target any of your positions for better or worse. (Regulations usually have a negative effect on industries.) If they do, manage your risk accordingly.

Caveat: please don't react to a headline the instant it comes out. Wait for the market to absorb it. She may feel *very* different about the news than you imagine she would. Just so, if you see a headline that you believe will influence your holdings, be patient and observe how the market absorbs the news before you act. Once you confirm the market's opinion, then you can make an informed decision.

Gordon

Speaking of investor worries, Toni, let's talk about interest rates. This subject is really hard to ignore, because interest rates represent the cost of borrowing money. Borrowing costs in a modern, debt-based society are a ubiquitous influence. Every purchase you buy on credit is influenced by these numbers. How can you *not* worry about interest rates?

In reality interest rates fluctuate like everything else, and wherever there is fluctuation, there is opportunity. Winning investors need to be able to see interest rates for what they are, and then they can see where the opportunity lies.

Here's my favorite way to see interest rates: as a gauge for the demand for borrowed money. The idea is that if interest rates are high, then there must be more demand for borrowed money than the supply of available money to lend out. Now, it is easy to get lost in the fog of political and economic headlines about interest rates. But if you ignore all of those and focus on this one idea about what interest rates represent, I think your perspective on interest rates can more easily shift from one of worry to one of seeking opportunity.

For example, if we think back to the days of double-digit interest rates, particularly to the years 1979 to 1984, then you can recall that this was an era when the baby-boom generation in the United States was entering their home-buying years. This was a time when a lot of people had a need to borrow money all at the same time, and the banking sector wasn't prepared to lend out as much as people wanted to borrow. When competition among borrowers heated up, the only way the market could decide who got to borrow the money was to ascertain who was willing to pay the highest interest rates. And those rates soared to double digits.

If you contrast that period of time to more recent years, say from 2007 until 2013, you see a different story. That same generation has passed its peak home-buying years, and they are beginning to down-size their living arrangements. They don't need big-family homes, and they don't always need to borrow as much money. Add to that the fact that in the year 2007, more new banks were *created* than at any time in history. So you have this combination of excess supply of money to borrow and declining demand for borrowing it. The only way the market has of responding to that situation is to try to attract borrowers with the lowest rates possible.

When you look at these fluctuations in this way, you can see where the opportunity lies. You can see that before interest rates will rise again, we will have to see either a smaller supply of money or a greater demand for borrowing. Winning investors know they can simply watch those ETFs associated with interest rates to see which one is thriving in the current marketplace to determine where the opportunity for gains might be.

Toni

Your viewpoint certainly takes the "worry" out of rising interest rates, Gordon. And you just used one of my favorite words, *opportunities!*

We have a virtual smorgasbord of them waiting for us in the future by way of mega-trends.

The first mega-trend that I think many of our readers will profit mightily from is the health-care industry. As you know, the baby-boomers are those of us born between 1946 and 1964. At present, we (yes, I'm one of them) are 78 million strong.

Boomers are such a big bunch, the Congressional Budget Office (CBO) reports that spending for Medicare, Medicaid programs, and total health spending in 2009 alone each accounted for 3 percent of the Gross Domestic Product. By 2035, in absence of any dramatic change, the CBO says the spending for Medicare alone will more than double in growth to 8 percent; by 2080 it will have grown to 15 percent.

Why the big percentage moves? The post-war boomer generation, which is on the cusp of retiring, simply spends more on health care than their parents did. Of course, we know health-care costs are rising; no mystery there. But I will personally admit that I want to be healthy and enjoy my retirement years to the maximum. My friends feel the same way. And most of us will do just about anything to achieve that goal.

So, this is where the opportunities emerge. Baby Boomers visit the doctor more, consume more services, and aren't afraid to use their $7 trillion in collective wealth to improve their quality of life. Think of all the companies (and investors) that will benefit! A massive amount of new technology will arrive on the market for people willing to pay for it. Look around your local drugstore or on the Internet. Adds pop up everywhere advertising "anti-aging" products. The husband of one of my friends is a neuroscientist assigned to the "successful anti-aging" department in a local, prestigious university.

Because of the new health care plans, a lot of the new technology will come by way of government-sponsored services. From physical therapy, to plastic surgery, to the latest in life saving technology, boomers are refusing to grow old gracefully, and the bill is going to be hefty.

Just so, each of the industry groups in health care will surely profit—as will the investors who spot the opportunities. While many stocks in this sector will profit, ETFs also present good "one-size-fits-all" choices. iShares and SPDRs ETFs sponsor health-care sector funds, such as the iShares DJ US Health Care ETF (IYH) and the Health Care Select Sector SPDR (XLV), respectively. If we look at the various industry groups within the health-care sector, we find pharmaceuticals, medical equipment, biotechnology, and health-care providers. Each of these groups is represented by ETFs that you can explore. When chosen appropriately, these funds should offer wonderful opportunities for you now and in the future.

Gordon

I am always struck by how many opportunities do exist in the future of investing. As a society now, though, we seem to be going through a time of less optimism in general. We hear a lot of people telling us how dire and bleak our future might be. While there are undoubtedly challenges ahead, what strikes me is the reality that markets will tend to rise. They might rise because of inflation, or technological innovation, or the end of a war, or the beginning of an energy boom, but sooner or later, they tend to rise. So long as people are free to invest, they will seek out and find value, or create it themselves. History suggests that is what people naturally do.

Forty years ago many economists predicted that by now we would run out of certain resources. It hasn't happened. I don't believe it will. People instinctively move towards value when they can, and that means better efficiency, greater innovation, and brighter prospects for the collection of people in a society where that can happen naturally.

No matter what reasons are thrown at us to the contrary, I don't see anything in the future that will stop the market from doing what it's done for over a century—move higher. If you back up and look at a 100-year history of the Dow Jones Industrial Index, something that jumps out at you is a repeating pattern. For about 17 and a half years, the market will fluctuate in a sideways fashion. Then it starts a remarkable upward trend for about the same amount of time. The one big exception to this was the severe bear market from 1930 to

1932. Outside of this short chunk of time, though, the pattern seems consistent.

We began a sideways movement in this Dow Jones pattern around the year 2000. So then, is it possible that as early as 2016 we may be standing on the edge of the best investing opportunity we have seen in our lifetimes? Even if that turns out to be true, there will be some who won't believe it until long after it is history. They won't know to watch for it, and they won't believe it could possibly happen.

Winning investors know that there is always opportunity some-place in the market if they are prepared to identify it. They know that just about the time everyone around them is certain stocks will never be a good investment again, that's the precise time that they are the best investment of all!

Toni

You are exactly right, Gordon. And that 100-year pattern of the Dow is reassuring.

Furthermore, as investors, if we look at the world around us, even now, we can see new, or relatively new, industries cropping up. Just a few years ago, Big Data and cloud computing, tablet computing, smartphones, and social media were all just a twinkle in the eye of technology. Now they are commonplace and, naturally, still evolving. We can all think of different companies in those particular niches that have taken off and skyrocketed. And as you say, investors who make it their business to become aware of the opportunities and go hunting for them are those who profit nicely. For those who prefer ETFs, funds have quickly sprouted up around those specialized tech groups and more are arriving on the scene.

When I gaze into the future now, and in doing so take into account recent world events, I ask myself questions... What opportunities exist in advanced cyber security? As we've witnessed the rise of recent hacking attacks into U.S. organizations, including banks, one would think that industry will have to become even more sophisticated than it is now. And what about water? Much of the world's population doesn't have clean drinking water. In years to come, will water become a commodity, like oil? And more exciting, what will happen with space travel? Private industry is now moving into that other-world realm. Which companies will benefit? And who are their suppliers?

As you can see, if you plan well and manage risk wisely, the stock market is a market of opportunities, indeed, a "field of dreams."

And now we say to you, our readers, *thank you* for joining us on this journey. Gordon and I have enjoyed walking this path with you and trust that you will benefit from it. Take good care and God bless!

Key Points to Remember

➤ Much of the time, our investing decisions are influenced by fear or hope.

➤ Many investors worry about hyperinflation—when the value of our money could rapidly decline while prices shoot upward

➤ Successful investors don't worry about potential economic disasters (that usually never take place); they look for the opportunity in every market environment.

➤ Government directives result in laws, regulations, taxes, price controls, and capital controls that sometimes deal "belly punches" to an industry, and thus the companies that compose it.

➤ Savvy investors watch the headlines, stay aware of policies out of Washington, and manage their positions accordingly; this is a great example of how "knowledge is power."

➤ Avoid reacting to headlines; wait until the market absorbs the news, observe the market's reaction, and then respond if necessary.

➤ Interest rates fluctuate, and wherever there is fluctuation, there is opportunity.

➤ Winning investors need to be able to see interest rates for what they are, and then they can see where the opportunity resides.

➤ Baby boomers will undoubtedly fuel a huge megatrend in the health-care sector for years to come.

➤ If you look at 100-year history of the Dow Jones Industrial Index, you will see a repeating pattern that is very positive.

➜ Even now, new mega-trends are popping up in Big Data and cloud computing, tablet computing, smartphones, and social media, and more are taking shape.

➜ Winning investors know that there is always opportunity someplace in the market if they are prepared to identify it.

PERSONAL GAINS

Toni

Look Forward... Your Compelling Future

"Only those who will risk going too far can possibly find out how far they can go."

—T.S. ELIOT

A very wise man once told me, "In order to be happy, each of us needs to have a compelling future." Be it a material item, a relationship with a loved one, a skill set, or an action we intend to acquire or accomplish, we humans feel the happiest when we have positive expectations of the future.

One of our greatest fears, especially as we advance into our retirement or "empty nest" years, is that we will become obsolete. *Good grief.* Even the word "obsolete" gives me goose bumps. We dread the thought of becoming obsolete to our business associates, our children, or those around us. Being needed, being relevant, being appreciated... these are feelings that make life worthwhile.

To take steps into your compelling future, consider these three steps:

First, take my suggestions in Chapter Twelve's Personal Gains to heart. In other words, plan to make your circle bigger. Don't wait for someone or something to show up and present you with a new opportunity. Create your own opportunity and start today. Read something, make a list, call someone, or go somewhere... do whatever it takes to pull fresh and exciting experiences into your life.

Second, be present in every moment. You may not realize it, but you could be "living in your head." Instead of dwelling in the present moment, you may be sifting through memories or contemplating the future. This kind of non-present thinking can exhaust you and cause stress. Why? Because your body is dealing with the present, but your mind is wading through different situations in different places. Besides, when you are not fully engaged in the present, it robs you of the enjoyment of the moment, and those around you feel left out of your attention.

I have a good friend, Joyce. Whenever I am with her, she is fully present, fully engaged. She gives her complete attention to what we are doing and to our conversation. When I am talking, her gaze doesn't wander. She doesn't interrupt. She asks sincere questions. No wonder Joyce has so many friends and is so successful in business.

Third, to maintain your compelling future, *choose* to be happy. Happiness is feeling content, right now, wherever you are, whatever you are doing. If you think of happiness in those terms, achieving it isn't that difficult, is it?

Let's assume that you have the basic essentials to live—enough to eat, a roof over your head, clothes to wear, and someone who thinks you're OK. If you have the basics for survival, happiness is a choice. After all, you *can* choose your thoughts, right? So, choose good ones!

"Oh, it's not *me*," you exclaim. "It's Grumpy. *He* (or *she*) makes my life miserable!"

Some years ago I learned a nifty way to deal with the "Grumpies" in my life. I discovered that if I mentally "reframed" them—and no matter what they did, I thought of them as kind and loving (whatever positive attributes you choose)—they changed before my very eyes! Truly! Now, I don't know if they changed or if I changed, but it doesn't matter. The reframing trick works. Try it.

To create a compelling future is to create the most fantastic gift you can give to yourself. We could call it "Future Perfect." Stretch yourself, live in the present moment, and choose happiness.

After all, life is meant to be lived to the fullest, to be relished, to be savored. You have within you the ability to make that happen and to have a compelling future. Enjoy!

Index

Abelson, Alan, 154
Accumulation, 102–103
AGG, 160, 173, 203, 225
Allen, David, 270
American Express, 113–115
Analyst ratings, 148–150
Analyzing company performance, 118–140
  earnings growth, 122–131
  EPS, 127, 128
  FINVIZ.com, 134–138
  forward P/E ratio, 131–132
  GO screen, 135, 136
  insider trading, 132–133, 136
  institutional investors, 133–134, 136, 138
  list of stocks, 121, 135–138
  P/E ratio, 127
  pitfalls, 123–125
  quarterly earnings reports, 125–126
  recognizing signs of growth, 121–131
  speed of the market, 124
  STOP screen, 137, 138
  tasks of fundamental research, 120–121
"Anatomy of Strategies, An" (Conrad/
  Kaul), 210
Anticipated annual investment perfor-
  mance, 37, 38
Anticipating market opportunities,
  272–290
Anticipating market trends. *See* Reading
  the market's mood
Apple, 15, 51, 119, 172, 250, 268
Asset allocation, 173–175
ATR, 65–67
AT&T, 50, 105–107, 172, 241
Average true range (ATR), 65–67

Balanced portfolio, 143
Bank of America, 142
Bar chart, 93–95
Barclay iPath ETNs, 168
Barclay iShares, 164, 165
Barron's, 154
Barton, D. R., 23
Baumeister, Roy, 239
Bayne, Stephen, 270
Bear market, 11, 45, 46, 52
Beating the Street (Lynch), 257
Beginner's Guide to Day Trading Online, A
  (Turner), 17
Beginner's Guide to Short-Term Trading, A
  (Turner), 17
Berkshire Hathaway, 170, 255
Bidu Inc., 241
Big Secret for the Small Investor: A New
  Route to Long-Term Investment Success,
  The (Greenblatt), 27, 200
Bill Barrett Corporation, 130–131
Bloomberg, 151, 152
Bond-based ETFs, 160, 202
Bond duration, 201–202
Bond market, 184, 201
Book value, 86, 254
Boom times, 41–42
Boring stocks, 197–199, 278
Bottom-line growth, 122
BP oil spill, 43
Bradberry, Travis, 181
Broker recommendations, 148–150
Brokerage commissions, 142
Buffett, Warren, 16, 199, 200, 255–256, 268
Bull market, 12, 45, 46, 52, 119

Business cycle, 41, 279, 283
Business valuation, 254
Buy-and-hold approach, 2, 3, 24
Buy/sell recommendations, 148–150
Buy-stop order, 221

CAN SLIM investment strategy, 245
Candle charts, 95–97
  benefits of using, 96
  candle formations, 97
  chart time frames, 97–99
  color, 96
  terminology, 96
  website, 95, 96
Candle line (candle), 96
Cap-weighted ETFs, 166
Cash account, 145
Cash-flow statement, 123
Charles Schwab, 142, 143
Chart reading, 82–117
  bar charts, 93–95
  base/accumulation, 102–103
  candle charts, 95–97
  chart time frames, 98
  downtrend/mark-down, 104
  higher highs/lower lows, 107
  line charts, 87–93
  pullbacks/retracements, 107
  review/points to remember, 115–116
  tight/orderly price range, 103
  top reversal/distribution, 103–104
  trend/cycles, 100–107
  types of charts, 87
  uptrend/mark-up, 103
  X/Y axis, 87
Charting software, 57–58, 65, 108, 153
Chevron Corp., 166, 170
Chin, William, 186, 205
Closing prices, 88
CNBC, 151, 152
Coal industry, 293
Coca-Cola, 50, 170
Commodities, 119
Commodities ETFs, 160, 163
Common Stocks and Uncommon Profit
  (Fisher), 244, 245
Conrad, Jennifer, 210
Consumer Discretionary (XLY), 169–170,
  175
Consumer Staples (XLP), 170, 176, 177

Contractions, 42, 43
Corporate bond, 12, 221
Costco, 129, 257–258
Currencies ETFs, 160
CurrencyShares Canadian Dollar (FXC),
  160
CurrencyShares Euro Trust (FXE), 160
Customized investing, 208–240
  customized investing plan, 227–228,
    236–237
  ETFs, 216–224
  number of shares to buy, 226
  review/points to remember, 238
  stop loss, 211–212, 233
  survivorship bias, 235
  trailing stop, 233–234
Cyber security, 298

Daily Graphs Online, 246
Daily line chart, 88, 89
Date of record (dividends), 267
Declaration date (dividends), 266–267
Demand and supply, 47–49
Disagreement between buyers and sellers,
  65–67
Discount brokers, 143–144
Diversification, 23, 194, 241
Dividend, 137, 265–267
Dodd, David, 11, 254
Dot-com bubble, 74
Dow, Charles, 50
Dow 30 Profile, 265
Dow Chemical, 172
Dow Jones Industrial Average, 49–50,
  260–261
Dow Jones Utility Average, 70
Dow stocks, 260–262
Downtrend, 104
Downward trending bear market, 199
Duke Energy, 173

e3m Investments Incorporated, 186
Early GO phase, 280, 286
Early STOP phase, 281–282, 286
Earnings growth, 122–131
Earnings per share (EPS), 127, 128,
  248–249
Earnings-weighted ETFs, 167
Economic contraction and expansion, 42,
  43

Emotional Intelligence 2.0 (Bradberry/
   Greaves), 181
Emotional quotient (EQ), 180–182
Emotions, 206–207, 291
Energy (XLE), 170, 175–176
Energy prices, 281
Enron, 124
EPS, 127, 128, 136, 248–249
Equal-weighted ETFs, 166–167
ETF. *See* Exchange-traded funds (ETFs)
ETN, 168
E*TRADE, 142, 143
Ex-dividend date, 267
Exchange-traded funds (ETFs), 158–182
Exchange traded note (ETN), 168
Exelon Corp., 173
Exogenous shocks, 43, 151
Expanding economy, 41–42
Exxon Mobil, 166, 170, 250

Failures in the financial sector, 86
Falling prices, 11
Fidelity Investments, 142, 143
"Fifteen Points to Look for in a Common
   Stock" (Fisher), 244, 245
Financial consultant, 143. *See also* Invest-
   ment broker
Financial Industry Regulatory Authority
   (FINRA), 142
Financial institutions, 86
Financial publications, 154–155
Financials (XLF), 170, 175
FINRA, 142
FINVIZ.com, 134–138
   filters, 136, 138
   GO screen, 135, 136
   STOP screen, 137, 138
Fisher, Kenneth L., 245
Fisher, Philip, 244–245
Fixed-income ETFs, 160
Fluctuation percentage, 35–37
Forbes, 155
Forex (foreign exchange) market, 160
Forward P/E ratio, 131–132, 136
401(k)/403(b) savings plan, 187. *See also*
   Tax-deferred savings account
Fox Business, 151, 152
FreeStockCharts.com, 153
Full-service broker, 142–143

Fund families, 164–165
Fund manager, 278–279
Future investment opportunities, 298–299

GAAP, 124
GainsMaster approach, 30–32
General Electric, 50, 51, 89–91, 93, 95, 171,
   200, 259, 278
Generally accepted accounting principles
   (GAAP), 124
*Getting Things Done: The Art of Stress-Free
   Productivity* (Allen), 270
GO screen, 135, 136
GO sign, 58, 73–77
GO-sign ETFs, 219–221, 293
GO-sign market, 280–281
Goldman Sachs, 123, 199
Good-til-cancelled (GTC), 252
Google, 15, 51, 132, 241, 250
Gotham Capital, 200
Graham, Benjamin, 11, 167, 199, 254–255,
   268
Greaves, Jean, 181
Greenblatt, Joel, 27, 200, 201
Greenspan, Alan, 67
Growth-and-Opportunity search filter, 135,
   136, 233
Growth-focused equity ETFs, 250
Growth-stock mutual fund, 191
Growth stocks, 177–178, 242–253
GTC, 252
Guggenheim (Rydex), 165

Hansen, Mark Victor, 54
Health-care industry, 171, 175, 296–297
Health Care Select Sector SPDR, 297
Hedge Fund Market Wizards (Schwager),
   183
High-beta ETFs, 167–168
Hill, Napoleon, 19
HLOC, 95
"Hold" rating, 149
Home Depot, 170
Honeywell, 171
Hutchinson Technology Incorporated,
   129–130

IBD, 50, 249
IBM, 50, 99, 101, 172, 250, 259

IEF, 160, 203
IJS, 173, 201, 203
Index investing, 119, 200–201
Index-tracking ETFs, 158, 162
Individual investors, 22–23, 26, 37
  advantages, 21, 121, 208, 209
  anticipate market opportunities, 285
  attitudes towards the market (opportu-
    nity/safety), 56
  investing objective, 27
  risk tolerance, 16, 35, 36
Individual retirement account (IRA), 194.
  See also Tax-advantaged account
Industrials (XLI), 171, 175
Inflation, 30, 42–43, 292
Insider trading, 132–133, 136
Institutional investors, 133–134, 136, 138,
    275–276
Intel, 51, 110–112
Intelligent Investor, The (Graham), 199, 254
Interest rates, 42, 201, 294–295
Inverse funds, 223
Invesco PowerShares, 164, 165
Investing
  advantages/benefits, 12–14
  big discount, 23
  customized. See Customized investing
  expectation of price increases, 86
  index, 119, 200–201
  individual activity, 23
  methods of analysis, 82–83
  problems, 23–24
  risk, 16
  value, 199–200
  words of caution, 120
Investment allocation spectrum, 187
Investment broker, 141–150
  account category, 145–146
  brokerage commissions, 142
  buy/sell recommendations, 148–150
  cash account, 145
  discount broker, 143–144
  full-service broker, 142–143
  independent broker, 142
  interest on unused cash, 146
  margin account, 145–146
  registered broker, 142
  research source, as, 144, 153–154
  settlement date, 146–147

Investor's Business Daily, 154–155, 249
IRA, 194. See also Tax-advantaged account
iShares, 160, 161, 165, 173, 174, 201, 203, 225,
    249, 297
IVV, 173

Johnson & Johnson, 171, 250
JPMorgan Chase, 170

Kaul, Gutam, 210
Kiplinger's, 155

Late GO phase, 281, 286
Late STOP phase, 282–283, 286
Learn to Earn (Lynch), 257
Lehman Brothers, 43, 123, 124
Line chart, 87–93
List of stocks, 121, 135–138
Long-term capital gains tax rate, 284
Low-volatility effect, 197–199
Low-Volatility Effect: A Comprehensive
  Look, The (Soe), 197
Low-volatility (low-beta) ETFs, 168
Lowe's Companies, 99
LVOL, 203
Lynch, Peter, 242, 256–257, 268

Magellan Fund, 256
Margin account, 145–146
Margin call, 145–146
Margin of safety, 254
Mark-down, 104
Mark-up, 103
Market cap, 50–51
Market cap weighted index, 50
Market conditions, 31–32
"Market perform" rating, 149
Market Vectors, 164, 165
MarketWatch, 152
Materials (XLB), 171–172, 175
MDY, 173
Merchants Exchange building, 45
Merck, 171
Merrill Lynch, 142
MetaStock, 65, 153
Microsoft, 50, 98, 99, 172, 278
Mid-cap value stocks, 263, 264
Middle GO phase, 280–281, 286
Middle STOP phase, 282, 286

Modern portfolio theory (MPT), 196
Money center banks, 142
Monsanto, 172
Monthly line chart, 91, 92
Morgan Stanley, 123
Morgan Stanley Smith Barney, 142
Morningstar, 165, 250, 264
Moving average, 59, 108–115
    calculation of, 108–109
    chart time period, 113
    decision-support tool, as, 112
    defined, 108
    50-day, 112
    terminology, 109
    12-month, 59–63
    200-day, 112
Mutual funds, 185, 189, 242, 274, 276, 277, 278–279

Nasdaq 100, 51
"Neutral" rating, 149
New York Curb Exchange, 45
Nison, Steve, 95

One Up on Wall Street (Lynch), 257
O'Neil, William, 155, 245–246
Online charting programs, 153
Online discount brokers, 9, 143–144
OptionsXpress, 143

P/B ratio, 259–260
P/E ratio, 126, 127, 136, 199, 258–259, 260
Panic-driven markets, 47
Payment date (dividends), 267
Personal gains, 5
    build on your strengths, 79–81
    commitment, 19–20
    delegating, 270–271
    emotions, 180–182, 206–207
    gratitude, 139–140
    grow beyond your comfort zone, 289–290
    personal beliefs, 54–55
    resiliency, 116–117
    routine tasks vs. high-priority decisions, 239–240
    self-image, 156–157
    single-purpose focus, 38–39
Personal investing profile, 29
Pfizer, 171

Philip Morris, 170
Post-9/11 NYSE opening, 207
Post-retirement, conservative allocation strategy, 203
PowerShares, 158, 165, 166, 167, 168
Price charts, 9, 84. See also Chart reading
Price-earnings ratio (P/E ratio), 126, 127, 136, 199, 258–259, 260
Price fluctuations, 87
Price-to-book (P/B) ratio, 259–260
Price-weighted index (Dow), 50
Procter & Gamble, 50, 170
Professional money managers, 208
Prolonged range-bound market, 24
Protective stop, 44, 46, 52, 207. See also Stop order

Quantitative easing, 29, 137
Quarterly earnings reports, 125–126
Quarterly line chart, 91, 92

Rackspace Hosting Incorporated, 128, 129
Raging bull market, 241
Rath, Tom, 80
Reading the market's mood, 56–81
    GO sign, 58, 73–77
    review/points to remember, 78–79
    simultaneous movement of all indicators, 72
    steps in process, 77
    STOP sign, 58, 73–77
    tracking analogy, 63–64
    12-month moving average, 59–63
    utility stocks, 69–72
    volatility, 63–69
Recessions, 11, 43
Research sources
    broker's website, 144, 153–154
    financial newspapers, 154–155
    magazines, 155
    online information, 152–154
Return on equity (ROE), 247–248
Rising volatility, 64
Risk, 16, 196
Risk management
    GainsMaster approach, 32–33
    growth stocks, 252–253
    small but consistent gains, 224–226, 228
    value stocks, 267
Risk tolerance, 16, 35, 36, 187–189, 205

Roth IRA, 194. *See also* Tax-advantaged
    account
Russell 300 Growth Index Fund, 250
Russell 1000 Growth Index Fund, 250
Russell 1000 Value Index Fund, 264
Russell 2000 Growth Index Fund, 250
Russell 2000 Value Index Fund, 264
Russell 3000 Value Index Fund, 264
Russell Mid-Cap Growth Index Fund, 250
Russell Mid-Cap Value Index Fund, 264
Russell Top 200 Growth Index Fund, 250
Russell Top 200 Value Index Fund, 264
Rydex S&P Equal Weight ETF, 167

Safe Strategies for Financial Freedom (Tharp
    et al.), 23
Schlumberger Ltd., 166, 170
Schwager, Jack D., 183
Scott, Gordon, 2, 21, 56, 118, 183, 208, 272,
    291
Scottrade, 143
Search filter criteria, 135–138, 232
Seasonal line chart, 91, 92
Sector funds, 159, 169–173
Sector rotation, 273, 279–286
Securities and Exchange Commission
    (SEC), 141, 142
Securities Investor Protection Corporation
    (SIPC), 142
Security Analysis (Graham/Dodd), 11,
    254
Select Sector SPDRs, 169–173, 175–179

"Sell" rating, 150
*Short-Term Trading in the New Stock Mar-
    ket* (Turner), 17
SIPC, 142
Sjuggerud, Steve, 23
Small-cap value stocks, 263, 264
Smart ETFs, 167
Smart Money, 155, 165
Soe, Aye M., 197
Southern Co., 173
Sowell, Thomas, 42
S&P 400 Midcap ETF (MDY), 173
S&P 500, 50
    chart of closing prices, 60
    12-month moving average, 60
S&P 500 Growth Index Fund, 250
S&P 500 SPDR (SPY), 158, 173–175, 203

S&P 500 Value Index Fund, 264
S&P 600 Small-Cap Growth ETF, 250
S&P Mid-Cap 400, 52
S&P Mid-Cap 400 Growth Index Fund,
    250
S&P Mid-Cap 400 Value Index Fund,
    264
S&P Small-Cap 600 Growth Index Fund,
    250
S&P Small-Cap 600 Value Index Fund
    (IJS), 173, 201, 203, 264
SPDRs, 158, 249, 250, 262, 264
SPY, 158, 173–175, 203
Staples fund, 170, 176, 177
State Street Global Advisors SPDRS, 164,
    165
Stock-index mutual funds, 187
Stock market
    capital appreciation/returns, 12–13
    forward-looking vehicle, 41, 86
    future upward trend, 297–298
    growth and opportunity, 184
    market drivers, 47
    optimistic mood (GO sign), 58
    pessimistic mood (STOP sign), 58
    repeating patterns, 68–69, 297–298
    speed of the market, 124
    stock price movement, 42
    upward bias, 12, 43
    watching market on a daily basis,
        206–207
Stock market/bond market, simultaneous
    decline, 201
Stock market indexes
    Dow Jones Industrial Average, 49–50
    Nasdaq 100, 51
    Nasdaq Composite, 51
    smaller specific indexes, 52, 70
    S&P 500, 50
    utility index, 70
Stock split, 14
Stockbroker, 143. *See also* Investment broker
StockCharts.com, 153
Stocks. *See also* Stock market
    growth. *See* Growth stocks
    growth plus value, 267–268
    healthy/weak, 116
    list of, 121, 135–138
    price, 86
    settlement date, 146–147

Stop order, 233. *See also* Protective stop
  buy-stop order, 221
  GTC order, 252
  trailing stop, 233–234, 252–253
  when not used, 211–213
STOP screen, 137, 138
STOP sign, 58, 73–77, 137, 204, 281–283
STOP-sign ETFs, 222, 223, 293
Strategies for investing to win, 183–207
  diversification, 194
  low-maintenance strategy, 186, 195
  low-volatility effect, 197–199
  risk equals more opportunity, 196
  risk tolerance, 187–189
  switching between bond and stock mar-
    ket, 184–185
  tax-advantaged account, 194
  tax-deferred savings account, 185
  value-weighted investing, 199–201
StrengthsFinder 2.0 (Rath), 80
"Strong buy" rating, 149
Subprime mortgage crisis, 62
Supply and demand, 47–49

Tactical allocation, 174
Targeted annual investment performance,
  37, 38
Tax-advantaged account, 194, 209
Tax-deferred savings account, 185, 189, 191,
  205
Taxes
  ETFs, 162, 177
  matching donation to a retirement fund,
    274
  sector rotation, 284–285
TD Ameritrade, 142, 143
Technical analysis, 83. *See also* Chart
  reading
Technology (XLK), 172, 176–177, 178
Technology advances, 8, 65, 274
Technology stocks, 51
Tharp, Van K., 23, 184
TLT, 160, 203
Top-line growth, 122
Top reversal, 103–104

Trade Your Way to Financial Freedom
  (Tharp), 184
Traders, 83, 84
TradeStation, 153
Trailing stop, 233–234, , 252–253, 269
Treasury bond ETFs, 160, 201
Trend recognition, 102
Turner, Toni, 2, 7, 40, 82, 141, 158, 241, 291.
  See also Personal gains
24 Essential Lessons for Investment Success
  (O'Neill), 246

United Technologies, 171
UPS, 171
Uptrend, 68, 103
Upward bias, 12, 43
U.S. dollar, 292–293
Utilities (XLU), 172–173, 178, 179
Utility stocks, 69–72

Value-focused equity ETFs, 264
Value Line Technical Ranking System, 265
Value stocks, 253–268
  dividends, 265–267
  Dow stocks, 260–262
  ETFs, 263, 264
  legendary value investors, 254–257
  P/B ratio, 259–260
  P/E ratio, 258–259, 260
  primary goal of investing in, 253
  risk management, 267
  size matters, 263, 264
  value trap, 262
Value-weighted index investing, 200–201
Volatility, 63–69, 104

Wall Street financial district, 45
Wall Street Journal, 154, 261
Walmart, 278
Walt Disney Co., 89, 90, 92, 170, 241, 278
Weekly line chart, 88, 90
Wells Fargo, 50, 142, 170
Winning, 2ll, 214, 215

Yahoo! Finance, 152, 165

About the Authors

Toni Turner is the President of TrendStar Group, Inc., and the best-selling author of *A Beginner's Guide to Day Trading Online*, *A Beginner's Guide to Short-Term Trading*, and *Short-Term Trading in the New Stock Market*.

Gordon Scott, CMT, is a Chartered Market Technician (CMT) who has coached hundreds of students on methods designed to improve their trading and investing activities.

∎

Stay up-to-date with our

latest investing information!

Visit the "Invest to Win" website:

www.InvestToWinBook.com

We'll see you there!

Toni and Gordon

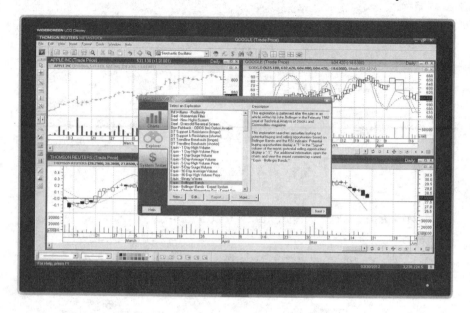
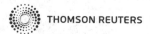